W9-CHK-679

Frantz Fanon

A CRITICAL STUDY

FRANTZ FANON

A Critical Study

IRENE L. GENDZIER

Vintage Books

A DIVISION OF RANDOM HOUSE NEW YORK

FIRST VINTAGE BOOKS EDITION, January 1974

Copyright © 1973 by Irene L. Gendzier

All rights reserved under International and Pan-American
Copyright Conventions. Published in the United States by
Random House, Inc., New York, and simultaneously in
Canada by Random House of Canada Limited, Toronto.
Originally published by Pantheon Books, a division of
Random House, Inc., in 1973.

Library of Congress Cataloging in Publication Data

Gendzier, Irene L
    Frantz Fanon.

    Bibliography: p.
    1. Fanon, Frantz, 1925–1961.
CT2628.F35G46   1973b   322.4'2'0924 [B]   73–5699
ISBN 0–394–71969–7

Manufactured in the United States of America

Preface and Acknowledgments

When I began research for this book, I intended to write a psychohistory of the subject. In time, the objective and the method changed. The questions of why a man acts as he does, what inner forces combine to propel him in one direction and not another, what private accounts are publicly resolved, all remain fundamental and, I believe, of interest to anyone whether he considers himself a historian, a political scientist, or a psychologist. But as I became more involved in the Fanon story, in the French, Martiniquean, and Algerian aspects of Fanon's life, I chose to concentrate more on the social and political dimensions of the man's world and less on the individual roots of his response to it. In practice, there was an attempt to remain sensitive to both, to integrate both in an effort to arrive at an explanation that might approximate the causes of the man's actions. But to concentrate exclusively on Fanon's case history seemed to me, as it still does, to produce a distorted version of what it was he was trying to say. The outcry against injustice, the demand that men recognize each other, and the "realistic" claims of self-determination and independence (in this instance, the claims of Algerians against Frenchmen) had roots in Fanon's private past. They serve to explain the particular nature of his reactions. But these roots were grounded in society, their form was molded by a world initially outside the private domain of the man's psyche. Still, the barrier between the outside world and the circumscribed terrain of a man's inner self is impermanent. The language Fanon used, the form his words took, reflect all that he became thanks to his private talents and the public education which channeled them. But what he chose to say was not merely a function of his psychological condition, the excesses of a certain personality type. Fanon wrote in the midst of political battles, impelled by a will to resist the dehumanization that he saw around him. The battle of Algeria became for him the battle for man. To do justice to Fanon, it became necessary to do justice to the situation in which he struggled, to turn away from him as a unique personality in order to see the world in which he lived, where the polarization of sentiments, the options for survival, the merciless wars of men against each other and against the accumulated privileges of the past acquired an extraordinary intensity.

There is another dimension of the subject that deserves comment, though it is of a different nature. And again this is by way of retrospective reflection. Algerians today are fond of reminding Fanon's readers that he was not really Algerian, by which they mean a good deal more than what this means from a common-sense view, although that too is implied. It is the common-sense view I am thinking of now, and not the political reasons that I believe account for the frequent repetition of the statement in Algeria. When Fanon began his psychiatric work in Algeria, he realized that to be effective he needed to understand the society his patients came from. The same could be said of his political work. This requirement would have been even greater had he survived Algeria's independence. I cite this to underline the importance of the man's relation to the world in which he acted and to indicate a consciousness of this same prerequisite of self-understanding as I consider my own relation to the multiple subjects involved in this text. Since I share the reaction against those historians who write with ease of worlds they believe they have definitively grasped but that have often eluded them, I hope to have at least guarded against that sin of arrogance. As to the problem of communication and the possibilities of communication between men of different colors and cultures, I share Fanon's optimism on that score. But this understanding must begin with a sense of one's own self, which means more than a description of the biological or even the psychological person. Only then it is possible to reach out to others without making them "Other."

Turning to the matter of acknowledgments, I would like to indicate first that many who have been of help in the thinking that appears in these pages are not personally named in the list that follows. I hope that they will recognize my debt to them and that they will understand that these words are also meant as a homage.

The research for this study was carried out in the United States, France, and Algeria, and it is based largely on works written by and about Fanon, on interviews held with members of his family and with friends and political associates, and on a part of the massive literature devoted to the Algerian Revolution. Without the help of numerous Algerians, both friends and officials, and I include residents of Algeria among them, there is little doubt that I would have learned considerably less and seen less of the people and places that were important to this study. There was a good deal left undone, though, notably a meeting with Mrs. Josie Fanon, who, in spite of attempts to meet, made it clear that she had had a surfeit of Fanon followers. More accessible were Mr. and Mrs. Joby Fanon, Dr. and Mrs. François Tosquelles, Maître Marcel Manville, and the journalists, writers, and friends who made these and other interviews possible and who were often themselves valuable sources of information. There were a number of people who read through all or parts of the manuscript, and whom I would like to thank for their criticism: Drs. Martin and Phyllis Albert, Dr. Paul Adams, Dr. A. Poussaint, Professor S. Schwarzschild, Professor A. Hourani, Professor D. Gordon, Mr. W. Sands, Ms. D. Meckle, and Ms. M. Kraar. There were less personal but no less helpful signs of support from Boston University in the form of summer grants and a one-year research grant from the National Endowment for the Humanities.

As I send this manuscript away, I realize how incomplete the effort remains and to what extent person and politics, community, and self-realization have played a part in its composition. Nevertheless, unfinished as it may be, I dedicate it to those friends who have shared in this experience and who have been companions in this odyssey.

Irene L. Gendzier
Cambridge, Massachusetts
July 1972

Contents

Introduction

Eleven years ago, in December 1961, Frantz Fanon, the Martiniquean psychiatrist who had become an Algerian militant through the Algerian Revolution of 1954–1962, died in the United States. His presence here was a consequence of his illness, although since his death his works have acquired an importance in this country which far surpasses his expectations. Fanon, however, was formed politically, primarily by the Algerian Revolution. It was in Algeria that he experienced his political awakening, and it was through the Revolution that he came to understand the meaning of the struggle for liberation. It was a concept which for Algerians, and for Fanon, meant more than political independence. It was the regeneration of men and societies. It was the process of self-liberation and rebirth. It was the travail of people undoing the effects of colonization and restructuring their relations with one another and with the former colonizing power on the basis of their new situation. Such was the dream. The reality has been harsher. For Fanon, the Algerian experience in its totality—his work as psychiatrist at Blida and Tunis and his subsequent commitment to the cause of Algerian independence from French rule—marked him deeply. On a private level, but one that has universal application, Fanon understood that the struggle for self-liberation was related to if not identical with the struggle for a people's liberation. As he made no effort to tie the two together, it would be a falsification of his recognition of this to present his political work in such a light. But readers of his brief works will be impressed by the coincidence of the two movements. They reflect an aspect of the man, and they reflect, in different forms, an aspect of his interpretation of the subject.

Fanon wrote four books. Insofar as they are a landmark in the analysis of colonialism and in the labor of decolonization they seek to define colonialism in terms of the human impact or more accurately, the distortion of human relations which colonialism engendered. Combined with the political sophistication and subtlety which characterize his writing, this psychological dimension focused on the human element in a political equation that had long been explored. Fanon had developed a sensitivity to minority-majority relations early in life. He wrote, from the outset, on the basis of his own experience, indeed as a result of a self-analysis which is evident in *Black Skin, White Masks*. But he was not satisfied to concentrate on the individual situation for he understood that it could not be studied without an examination of society. It is this transition from the individual to community and society that marks the first cycle of themes in Fanon's work.

The same sensitivity to the relations between the individual and the community appeared in Fanon's psychiatric work, of which relatively little is known. Fanon practiced in France and later in Algeria and Tunisia. His articles are presented here largely in summarized form and primarily to illustrate the progression of his ideas and the maturation of his experience. But readers familiar with current debates in psychiatric circles will recognize attitudes and criticisms in Fanon's writings that deserve a place in a professional milieu that has generally ignored and excluded him.

After 1953, Algeria came to replace France and Martinique as the focal point of Fanon's life. In Algeria, the organization of the National Liberation Front (FLN), on the eve of the Revolution, in the fall of 1954, was the culmination of political action that had begun earlier and that has deep roots in Algerian history. The identification of Fanon with the FLN which has come about as a result of the popularization of Fanon's works has led to considerable confusion concerning his relationship to the Algerian Revolution. It is a subject which has considerably exercised the Algerian government. In 1956, Fanon formally joined the FLN. From that time until his death, he devoted himself with the intensity and the enormous talents at his disposal to the many tasks he performed for the FLN and Algeria. The material collected in *Toward the African Revolution,* the essays of *A Dying Colonialism,* and the majestic and difficult analyses of *The Wretched*

of the Earth are the fruits of Fanon's Algerian experience. That
these books have been so widely taken up suggests that the
problems Fanon dealt with are not unique to Algeria. Fanon's
last book, his political testament, is evidence of the relevance of
Fanon's study to the political life of newly independent nations
and to people struggling to achieve their liberation.

While Fanon's political writing is indispensable to an understanding of the third world and specifically to the politics of
decolonization, this alone does not explain his wide appeal.
Fanon has not been read merely as another polemicist, and
certainly not as a politically oriented psychiatrist. The attraction
derives in part, certainly, from the universality of his themes.
The plight of the oppressed knows no boundaries and it is a
measure of Fanon's critical internationalism that he rejected the
signs of an exclusive nationalism which he saw in Algeria and in
Africa. The search for identity, in personal and in political
terms, transcends time and place. The politics of justice, which
consumed Fanon to the end of his life, is as eternal as it is
elusive. And yet in the hands of a man who was not a poet, even
those themes would have met with less response. There was in
Fanon a sensitivity to language and a terrifying love for the
Word that sometimes seemed to eclipse the action these words
were designed to provoke. There was in Fanon, to borrow the
phrase of another poet, a man who knew the "probing, unsettling, maddening and finally hopefully healing effect of words."
Whether or not Fanon experienced the healing effect of his own
words is doubtful. But that he derived a sensual joy from their
manipulation is an open secret. It is questionable whether the
American translations of Fanon's writings reflect this.

There have been three formal biographies of Fanon published to date.[1] One by an Englishman, one by a German, and
a third by an American. The works of David Caute, Renate
Zahar, and Peter Geismar represent the lengthier studies that
have appeared on Fanon. There are countless articles and more
can be expected. What is remarkable in all of this material is the
relative absence of repetitiveness and the emergence of distinct
interpretations of the man and his work. David Caute has written
a brief and informative political biography; Renate Zahar has
presented a Marxist critique of the concept of alienation in Fa-

non's work, and Peter Geismar produced a highly favorable biography replete with details not to be found elsewhere.

The present essay is offered as an interpretative study of Fanon's writings although it seeks to go beyond Fanon to an investigation of selected themes raised in his work. Originally conceived as a psychological study, this approach was replaced by the present organization which involves a three-part division beginning with an examination of the intellectual and familial roots of Fanon's life in Martinique and France; going on to an analysis of Fanon's psychiatric work; and finally, presenting an exposition of his political writings and the context out of which they emerged.

Unlike that of Caute or Geismar, each of whom emphasized the linear development of the man from the time he wrote *Black Skin, White Masks* to his Wagnerian finale in *The Wretched of the Earth,* my own position is that Fanon's works reveal a masterful orchestration of themes which are to be found in all of his writings, although his dominant concerns became clearer and more intense as he progressed from one phase of his life and work to another. There was the progression from self-analysis to an analysis of society, first metropolitan then colonial society. There was the progression from the Sartrean analysis of anti-Semite and Jew, which Fanon then transposed to black men in white society, and finally, to colonized and colonizer. And there was an understanding that was apparent in *Black Skin, White Masks* but that reached fruition in the Algerian phase of his life, that ultimately consciousness must be translated into action. The limits of individual freedom and choice became sharper as Fanon turned to a dissection of the colonial system. The option of authenticity, be it for the Jew, the black man, or the colonized, was not a matter of consciousness alone. Political mobilization must succeed the awakening conscience and the formed consciousness. It was in the Algerian Revolution that Fanon became a militant, but his militancy was not limited to the Algerian struggle for liberation. Nor was his comprehension of the goals of liberation limited to the political independence of the nation. Although he was not exclusively concerned with the rights of the individual, he understood that the criterion for the Revolution he engaged in was its liberation of man—the reconstitution of his integrity and the restoration of his right to his past as well as his future.

In contrast to other studies of Fanon, there is also an attempt made here to consider Fanon's thinking, in contrast to the official position of the FLN as expressed in the party organ, *el Moudjahid*. There is an emphasis on certain questions that emerged in the course of the Algerian Revolution that have relevance to developments in other states of the Maghreb and the Middle East. The role and position of the French left on the Algerian problem, the situation of the French and Jewish minorities, the treatment of the national question and the socialist orientation of the nation and the state, are matters that are touched on with varying degrees of depth in accordance with the attention paid them in the texts studied. While the first and second parts of this essay deal with the material that was eventually presented in *Black Skin, White Masks* and in *A Dying Colonialism*, the third section of the book is concerned with Fanon's political thinking. The essays written for *el Moudjahid* were collected in *Toward the African Revolution*, while *The Wretched of the Earth* is a political testament written against the background of Fanon's Algerian and African experience. It is in *The Wretched of the Earth* that Fanon developed his critique of the nation in formation, the nature of the colonial bourgeoisie, and the danger of spontaneity during and after the struggle for liberation. It is there also that Fanon developed his much publicized concept of the cathartic effect of violence, a subject which is frequently distorted out of proportion to the import assigned to it by Fanon himself.

Finally, in the last brief section of this analysis, there is an attempt to speculate on the meaning and the uses of Fanon outside of Algeria. While Fanon believed that the oppressed of all nations are brothers, he was not uncritical in his exposition of this view. He was, in fact, far more critical in his assessment of the identity of the oppressed than some of those who claim to speak in his name.

In the end, it is only by a critical and comprehensive examination of Fanon's works that one can judge to what extent his experiences and his formulations fit the experience of others. If there is anything which a reading of Fanon's work deserves, it is precisely this kind of thorough contemplation. In practice, this means accepting the limitations, contradictions, and incompleteness which his works sometime reveal. It means resisting the attempt to take that which is most easily understood—such as the concept of violence—and ignoring the complexity of the rest. It means learning the measure of the man and demanding of oneself what Fanon wrote at the end of *Black Skin, White Masks:* "Make of me always a man who questions."

-I-

IN THE BEGINNING: THE SEARCH FOR ROOTS, 1925–1952

I, who have been so many men in vain, want to be one man: myself.

J. L. Borges, *Dreamtigers*

A man hates his enemy because he hates his own hate. He says to himself: this fellow, my enemy, has made me capable of hate. I hate him not because he's my enemy, not because he hates me, but because he rouses me to hate.

Elie Wiesel, *Dawn*

-1-

Biographical Notes to 1952

It all began with a question. It ought perhaps always to begin with a question, the same one. Some would say it ought always to be present—an eternal doubt that would prohibit the emergence of arrogance and pride. The question was asked—not out of virtue or habit, but out of a doubt that was risking sanity. Who am I? In 1952 Fanon wrote that it is the duty of every man to pose that question, and to refine it further by asking, Have I been all that I am capable of being? Am I who I am?

The question was posed in the first place, when the age of innocence had passed and been replaced with fear and dread. It came out of conflict and it was to be answered only by a relentless scrutiny of that conflict. From a mood of affirmation and unsolicited love for the world, came a realization that affirmation was misplaced and love inappropriate. The desire to affirm and the knowledge of its denial were to remain as two poles—ever present, mutually exclusive, and yet bound up with one another in a fixed way.

The statement that Fanon was a humanist of violence and an optimist has often appeared to be excessive, illusory, or simply dishonest. After all it was attributed to a man who made violence a critical feature of his world policy, a man who described the world as divided, in manichean fashion, between the forces of good and evil. And yet, the intentions of the various commentators aside, what was described as paradoxical was true. There existed in Fanon an acute sense of what it is to be wronged, of what it is to be misunderstood, misinterpreted, rejected. And compounding the pain that comes from rejection was the added pain that came from the knowledge that this rejection was based on a willful confusion. It was a rejection of a man's attempt, as judged by another, to be what he was not. If this sensitivity to injustice gave him a permanent empathy with the sufferings of men, it also served to mark him in an indelible fashion with a sign that would never leave him. The memory of a primal pain, a primal injustice was there. With it, alongside of it, denying its monopoly, there existed an equally strong optimism, the affirmation of the world and of man's place in it. The dream of a just world, of recognition, of order, stood parallel to the realizations of injustice, the lack of recognition, and disorder.

Skeptics who claim to be free of such excesses may choose to see Fanon's dilemma as a personal one which ought not to have been inflicted on the world. Unquestionably, Fanon's vision of the world had roots in his private situation, roots that were even then not unrelated to the world, but which had a familial pattern and a unique base. But just as it would be erroneous to ignore the "I" that looms so large in Fanon's thinking, so it would be foolish to reduce his political and psychological preoccupations to the attempt to resolve a personal drama. The genius of the man lay in his ability to transcend the personal dimensions of that drama and to understand where it touched on a human condition.

Very early in his life and in his writing, Fanon arrived at the conclusion that he needed to understand himself as he was, as he believed himself to be, and as the world saw him. For this, he chose to write. Not as a way of describing the world or himself, but as a way of understanding it, its absurdities, and the possibilities of its rationalization. To write was a form of action; it was in its origins self-centered and reflexive. But by its very nature it was also a method of communicating, a reaching out to tell and to teach others. It was moreover, in its conception, a process that engaged the conscience and the consciousness of its author. It assumed not only the possibility of communicating with all men, but the possibility of communicating all experience to all men. Hence, even as he realized the particular nature of his own situation, a Martiniquean whitened by colonization but black in the eyes of the colonizer, Fanon insisted on the possibility of sharing his experience with others. When, in *The Wretched of the Earth,* he declared that he wrote not for Europe but for the third world, the implication was not that the West was incapable of comprehending, but that it chose to remain unyielding in its attitudes and it was therefore pointless to address oneself to it. Nine years earlier, at the time of the publication of *Black Skin, White Masks,* the disillusionment with the regenerative power of the world was not as acute.

Black Skin, White Masks was published in 1952, when Fanon was twenty-seven. He had, by then, embarked on his studies as a psychiatrist, but he knew that his vision of the world had been stretched beyond the relationship of one man to another. By 1952, or earlier, since this book was a compilation of essays written over a period of time, Fanon had fallen from that state of innocence which comes with the first experience of the world. *Black Skin, White Masks* was a first attempt at a systematic exposé of Fanon's past and the more general conclusions to which a review of that past led him. It was not only an investigation of the relationship between black skin and white masks, but a probing of the question as to whether or not normal relations between blacks and whites, skins and masks aside, were possible. The implicit assumption in this period was a loud if pained Yes. On the basis of this initial affirmation, it was imperative that the political and psychological deception practiced by blacks and whites, and other groups who shared something with the dynamic of black-white relations, be analyzed and exposed, the better to be transformed. Hence, the discussion of language and perception, of sexual relations, of philosophical conceptions of consciousness, all described against the background of experience, disillusionment, and hope. Out of this questioning and analysis there emerged an understanding of minority-majority relations that was to take shape as a sketch for a psychology of colonization. It was to involve what Fanon would elaborate in his succeeding books, a total review of the self-image of the minority man and of his partner, the colonized. Not only did it posit a solidarity of sentiment and reflex among the oppressed, it analyzed the falsified roots of their identity, and it underlined the nature of this deprivation. Out of the obsession with being and recognition, an obsession deepened by a study of its philosophical roots as presented by Hegel and Sartre, two men whose influence on Fanon was considerable, there followed a still uneven discussion which removed the relations he described from the realm of political accident to one of fixed if not entirely determined behavior. The individual existed in a social nexus, an enormous web which neither Marx nor Freud had described completely. They had not concerned themselves with black men, or with the colonized, in any adequate fashion. Out of the analysis of their failing came a more profound understanding of the requirements of a new synthesis.

Unlike Albert Memmi, whose understanding of the colonial situation has received less recognition than it deserves, Fanon understood the relations of blacks and whites, or colonizer and colonized, as part of a rigid system.[1] To unlock the system was to be the challenge he set himself in France and eventually in Algeria. It involved, on an individual basis, a constant struggle for recognition based on the achievement of consciousness and purpose. It involved, collectively, a process of rediscovery, a reevaluation of one's past, and ultimately a confrontation with a system that would have to be destroyed to make way for the birth of the new man who had assumed his true identity. If there was an excess of abstraction in this first attempt at drawing out the process, it gradually gave way to very concrete recommendations and examples in *A Dying Colonialism* and in *The Wretched of the Earth.*

Fanon's first experience with colonization was in Martinique, where he was born. Martinique and Guadeloupe had been integrated into France in 1946, when they became departments as opposed to dependencies. It does not seem to have substantially altered their status, particularly insofar as Franco-Martiniquean relations were concerned. In place of a rigid color consciousness and division such as characterizes black-white relations in the United States, the island possessed a graduated hierarchy of color in which the extremes of black or white were the least common. Historically, the ruling white minority had dominated black slaves and eventually proceeded to free an increasing number known as the "free colored" group.[2] In time this group outnumbered whites and formed a separate caste, distinct from both the free blacks and the black slaves. Although the vast majority of the island's population was non-white, even in the

. midst of that majority, distinctions based on proximity of white ancestry and physical resemblance to whites were prominent.

> . . . class grievances are mainly expressed in terms of race and color. The degree of significance varies with class. The elite take their ascription as whites for granted; color is an overt issue among them only in gross transgressions of the social code. Nor is color per se overwhelmingly important in lower-class communities; the interest in identifying ancestral strains focuses on line of descent, not degrees of whiteness. But in the middle class color is the crucial determinant of status, and status is the main goal in life.[3]

David Lowenthal, the author of these remarks, concentrated on the question of color and the more general matter of racism and its expression in the Antilles. Fanon, writing on the same questions, made the distinction between the West Indies before and after 1939. The great dividing line was the Second World War, not because it brought certain moral and political issues to the fore in the islands, but because it brought large numbers of French troops whose four-year residence resulted in a confrontation between Frenchmen and Martiniqueans. Among the former, racism was not an uncommon trait, and it was aggravated by the general hardships which the forced residence exposed. Before 1939, the West Indian lived in a state of relative innocence. After that date, when "the West Indian was obliged, under the pressure of European racists, to abandon positions which were essentially fragile, because they were absurd, because they were incorrect, because they were alienating, a new generation came into being. The West Indian of 1945 is a Negro."

Looking back on the pre-war days, Fanon continued:

> . . . before 1939, there was not on one side the Negro and on the other side the white man, but a scale of colors the intervals of which could readily be passed over. One needed only to have children by someone less black than oneself. There was no racial barrier, no discrimination. There was that ironic spice, so characteristic of the Martinique mentality.[4]

When he wrote the essay from which this passage comes, Fanon was bent on showing that "questions of race are but a superstructure, a mantle, an obscure ideological emanation concealing an economic reality." "West Indians and Africans" appeared in *Esprit* in 1955. It coincided with Fanon's continuing attempt to deal with the changing attitudes of West Indians and Africans toward one another, and toward the question of negritude which was preoccupying him in this period. "In Martinique it is rare to find hardened racial positions," he wrote. But the war changed that. Not only did it polarize relations between Frenchmen and Martiniqueans, it provoked a change in the relations of West Indians and Africans. It is difficult to read *Black Skin, White Masks* without feeling that even before 1939, in the generation of Fanon's parents, for instance, "greater or lesser amounts of melanin" did in fact make a difference. But what Fanon perhaps wished to emphasize was that this was not a consciously accepted basis for differentiation among Martiniqueans themselves. Nor were these attitudes put to so rude a test as that offered by the wartime presence of French forces. The occupation, however, produced an awakening, at least among the intellectuals. Hence, the decision by the government in Paris to introduce "departmentalization" in 1946, that is to say, to integrate the region into metropolitan France, fell on somewhat skeptical ears. But the degree of deception was not yet clear.

Aimé Césaire, a prominent political figure in the 1946 period, continues to be criticized by those who rejected his earlier acceptance of the French plan. Césaire explains that in fact his hopes had been trampled upon, and that he had been appalled at the way in which France had discouraged direct investment in the island in order to prohibit the emergence of independent economic life.[5] The result was to keep the Martiniquean economy tied to that of France and the European market. The result was predictable. Industrial growth was retarded and planning, when it took place, was done with an eye to the French rather than the local situation.

Césaire was not the only one to be aware of what was going on. Earlier, Albert Belleville, a militant theoretician and poet, had produced an analysis of conditions on the island and what ought to be done.[6] Recently, the *Le Monde* correspondent, Jean Lacouture, explored Martinique in a series of articles entitled, "Comment peut-on être antillais." Aside from his repeated confirmations of Fanon's diagnosis of cultural alienation, Lacouture recognized that the island population had all of the characteristics common to underdeveloped economies.[7] Reform projects exist now as they did earlier, but the needs of the island and the wishes of its population are changing. With the frustration of living as dependent subjects, Martiniqueans seem much less ready to accept today what may have been tolerable in the post-war period. The agitation to stem the tide of disintegration has changed, and what began as sporadic and culturally oriented complaints have now fused into a political movement with broader aims.

The question is often asked, If Fanon had lived, would he have taken a more active role in Martiniquean politics? Would he have worked with Manville and Césaire, and his brother Joby, in trying to change the status of the island? The accusation that Fanon lost all interest in his homeland seems exaggerated. In *Black Skin, White Masks* and in *Toward the African Revolution,* it is clear that Fanon continued to think about Martinique and that his attitudes towards its future were undergoing change. In 1960, Fanon wrote an article in *el Moudjahid* entitled, "Blood Flows in the Antilles under French Domination." It concerned an incident which had provoked strong French reaction giving rise to a discussion of national demands. Fanon welcomed the challenge. "The old politicians," he wrote, ". . . are also discovering the existence of a rebellious spirit, of a national spirit." He drew attention to events in the Caribbean, such as the Cuban Revolution, which were having an impact on the West Indies. Even Algeria was brought into the picture.

> We know now that there are links between the Algerian war and the recent events that have caused blood to be shed in Martinique. It is former French civil servants of North Africa, those who were expelled from Morocco, from Tunisia, and those who were too compromised in Algeria, who have provoked the retaliation of the Martiniquean masses. The violent reaction of the people of Martinique simply indicates that the time has come to clarify problems and to dissipate misunderstandings.[8]

Eleven years later, Josie Fanon, Fanon's wife, who remained in Algeria and assumed Algerian citizenship, was writing on developments in Martinique for *Révolution Africaine.* In the special supplement of the periodical issued in July 1971 to cover the mounting political action taking place on the island, Josie Fanon surveyed the work of the GAP (Proletarian Action Group), a militant group that is little known outside of Martinique, and that has undertaken to continue the challenge to the French presence.[9]

To go back in time from 1971 to 1946 or 1947, is to reenter another world. The political climate was not as acute and political action had not yet crystallized to the degree described above. The option of working for an independent Martinique, outside of the French system, does not seem to have been a real one for Fanon, or for his friends who today constitute the veteran core of the Martiniquean militants. If the disadvantages of life on the island were clear, the solution was not sought in bringing about change but, on the contrary, in escaping its confinement. This was the choice that a middle-class family offered its children, and it was this choice which Fanon was to make. That Fanon's family belonged to the upper middle class was one of those fortunate accidents which may justify later ironies. But the economic good fortune of the family was combined with other conditions characteristic of the mélanges common to the island which were to prove more difficult to adapt to, and less ironic in retrospect.

Joby Fanon, Frantz's brother, has explained how as the material situation of the family improved, they moved closer to the heart of the capital, Fort-de-France. Having reached the center, they considered themselves to have achieved status and success. The family lineage was another matter, and typically complicated in the Martiniquean manner. It is curious that Geismar, who compiled such a detailed mass of information on Fanon's life, was so silent on these matters.[10] According to Joby, who with Marcel Manville, a childhood friend, is doubtless the most authoritative source of information on the family background, Fanon's father was of mixed Indian-Martiniquean origin.[11] His mother was of Alsatian origin, herself the illegitimate daughter of parents of mixed blood. In the context of the islands, the factor of illegitimacy was of less importance than the ethnic quotient. Frantz's name reflected the Alsatian past. His grandparents on his mother's side had disapproved of their daughter's marriage to a man of a darker color, and one may assume that the questions of class and color entered the picture. Frantz, the fourth and youngest of four boys, and the middle child in a total of eight, was the darkest of the family.

The senior Mrs. Fanon appears to have been of rather difficult temperament, described as not overly affectionate and with a tendency to be domineering. In the years of their young adulthood, she seems to have favored her daughters. That Geismar and Joby Fanon testify to her current pride in Frantz is not surprising nor does it alter the earlier picture. In contrast to the mother, Fanon's father was less rigid in his attitudes; in religious matters, for instance, he was a freemason. Working as a government official, he does not seem to have spent much time with the family. But family and a sense of family existed nonetheless, with other relatives not far from the scene. Knowing that skin color was not an irrelevant subject, that Fanon's mother had apparently had a surfeit of boys by the time Frantz was born, and that she came to consider Frantz as a junior troublemaker, one may conclude that in the best of all worlds, Fanon's mother would have been a formidable challenge. In *Black Skin, White Masks*, Fanon noted that in the Antilles, "there is nothing surprising, within a family, in hearing a mother remark that 'X is the blackest of my children'—it means that X is the least white."[12] To know the meaning of whiteness in the Antilles among nonwhites is to understand the full range of identity-confusion that was in store for Fanon and for others like him.

From the accounts offered by his brother Joby, and corroborated by others, it seems clear that Frantz was a highly sensitive child and a difficult man. Incidents of playmates attacking and being met with unexpectedly harsh rejoinders are frequent, as are the stories that reflect his extreme self-consciousness and his defensiveness at an early age. Without adequate information as to the nature of family life and Frantz's emotional development it is hardly possible to do more than present these facts and to suggest some obvious lines of speculation.

It is in this spirit that it is tempting to ask whether there might not be a connection between color and rank in the family line and Frantz's obsession with the matter of recognition. The phenomena of perception and recognition were not merely personal traumas in the Antilles. In Fanon's case it is not difficult to sense the ways in which a certain social consciousness, based on values peculiar to Martiniquean society, came to permeate the most intimate aspect of family life. The congruence between social consciousness and self-image, as Fanon learned to see it, combined to intensify a sensitivity to self and society which never left him. Was Frantz's eagerness to prove himself, academically and later professionally—a characteristic remarked on by both his brother Joby and his mentor, Dr. Tosquelles—a result of this desire to combat self-doubts and to answer those like his mother and his society who had put him on the defensive?[13] Both of the men cited above, Joby and Tosquelles, independently of one another, have spoken about the combination of defensiveness and aggressiveness which they recognized in Fanon's make-up. The portrait of the man they have painted is one who was in a hurry, a man bent on doing as much as possible, absorbing as much as possible in as little time as possible. Peter Geismar inadvertently supports the view of Fanon as a man impatient with weakness, his own and that of others. This comes out very well in the citation Geismar used to introduce his biography, which Fanon had written into a copy of his thesis presented to his brother Felix:

> The greatness of a man is to be found not in his acts but in his style. Existence does not resemble a steadily rising curve, but a slow, and sometimes sad, series of ups and downs.
> I have a horror of weaknesses—I understand them, but I do not like them.
> I do not agree with those who think it is possible to live life at an easy pace. I don't want this. I don't think you do either. . . .[14]

I very much doubt that Fanon in fact understood the roots of his own impatience, or that he had the temperament that would understand the weaknesses of others. He does not seem to have been introverted enough to seek those answers in himself and what he did discover he chose to see against the background of the society that had formed him. If there is someone who was close to Fanon and who had the capacity to accept himself and to overcome the anxieties that accounted for his insatiable appetite for the world, it was his brother Joby. The relationship with Joby was an important element in Frantz's life. From his own account, it seems certain that Joby and Frantz were very close to one another. Two years older than Fanon, Joby was a support at home and at school; later, Frantz would consult him when he began to write. Their relationship included a deep friendship and a political accord that did not mean an identity of views. But the relationship survived these differences and Joby remained a close witness of his brother's life until his death.

Manville, Joby, and Geismar have all cited Fanon's admiration for Nietzsche, which fits well into the personality we have been describing. Geismar, whose personal penchant for activism led him to emphasize this aspect of Fanon's life, proposed the following liaison:

> Fanon was strongly influenced by Nietzsche. In *Thus Spake Zarathustra* he saw the superman as one who is not crippled by an excess of reasons for *not* acting. One who still knows passion, but is able to control it. One who stands above the masses by his ability to throw off the shackles of conventional morality and religion. One who has ideas and the will to carry them out.[15]

In the same text which Geismar referred to, there was a passage that underlined, not the final triumph of action, but the constancy of struggle and the quest for freedom. "There is much that is difficult for the spirit," wrote Nietzsche, "the strong reverent spirit that would bear much, but the difficult and the most difficult are what its strength demands." The triumph of the will without the triumph of human values was an arid and dangerous goal. In Fanon's life, from the period of *Black Skin, White Masks* to *The Wretched of the Earth*, it was the creation of new values that moved him. Had he found sympathetic chords in Zarathustra's speech on the three metamorphoses?

> My brothers, why is there a need in the spirit for the lion? Why is not the beast of burden, which renounces and is reverent, enough?
>
> To create new values—that even the lion cannot do; but the creation of freedom for oneself for new creation—that is within the power of the lion. The creation of freedom for oneself and a sacred 'No' even to duty—for that, my brothers, the lion is needed. To assume the right to new values—that is the most terrifying assumption for a reverent spirit that would bear much. . . .[16]

In relative terms, the Fanon family was well off and the eight brothers and sisters did not suffer unduly from material depriva-

tion. Of this sizable family, six children survive, and of these all
but one are in Martinique. In his early years, Frantz went to
school, like his brothers and sisters, in Fort-de-France. Between
1939 and 1943 he was sent to the local private lycée, the same
as that attended by his friend Marcel Manville, the son of another successful upper-middle-class Martiniquean family. In
1940 the representative of the Pétainist regime, Admiral Robert,
landed in Martinique and there followed an occupation lasting
until 1943. Frantz was in the capital at the time of the landing
of the Pétainist troops and he quickly learned the meaning of
what this paradoxical occupation-liberation was about. From
every point of view these were years rich in experience. Aimé
Césaire, the man who, according to Manville, Frantz, and Joby,
taught Martiniqueans to be proud of their blackness, was teaching at the lycée. The nucleus of young writers around Césaire
and his friends were beginning to publish their works and students followed their activities with interest.

But the preoccupation among Martiniquean youth was the
occupation and the war in Europe. In April 1943 Frantz went to
Dominica in order to join with the Free French Movement operating in the Caribbean. He was to return with the forces that
liberated Martinique shortly after Admiral Robert's capitula-
tion. By the end of 1943, Fanon had had a brief experience with
the military and the issues of the Second World War, and he had
completed his examinations, thus ending his lycée career. In
1944 Frantz decided to join the Free French army and to proceed to the European front. In relating this, Joby indicated that
there had been discussions between them as to the merits of
such a decision. Frantz was not convinced by the argument that
this was mainly a white man's war and that Martiniqueans had
no part in it. On the contrary, as in the Algerian case some time
later, humanitarian instincts prevailed. But this did not mean
that he lost sight of who he was or how he differed from those
alongside of whom he fought. Manville claims that Fanon
thought that the group of friends, including Manville and
Mosole, who went to war in 1944 should have fought under a
black flag.

A flag was hardly necessary to distinguish the Martiniquean
partisans from their other French colleagues. From Guercif in
Morocco, to Bougie in Algeria, to the moving front in France,
Frantz and his friends learned that the democratic French army

was no freer of color consciousness than the Pétainist army had been at home. They became aware of various attitudes associated with degrees of blackness. When he was writing *Black Skin, White Masks,* Frantz recalled some of the Algerian experiences that belonged to this period of his life.

> Some ten years ago I was astonished to learn that the North Africans despised men of color. It was absolutely impossible for me to make any contact with the local population. I left Africa and went back to France without having fathomed the reason for this hostility. Meanwhile, certain facts had made me think. The Frenchman does not like the Jew, who does not like the Arab, who does not like the Negro. . . .[17]

For a time at least, continued collaboration against the enemy was possible. It is one of the ironies of Fanon's life that in the winter of 1945, after having been wounded in battle, he was decorated with the Croix de guerre for his brilliant conduct in the operations in the valley of Doubs, near Besançon. The award was made by Colonel Raoul Salan, Commander of the Sixth Regiment of the "Tirailleurs sénégalais," and eventually a prime mover against an independent Algeria.

Fanon returned to Martinique, a veteran of two years of military service. He had been promoted to corporal and his participation in the service enabled him to obtain support from the French government to continue his education in France. The years of war had marked Fanon in other ways. Joby recalls that Frantz returned from the front a different man, haunted by what he had seen and reluctant to discuss it. He never shed this reluctance and his brother interpreted this as a sign of the despair generated by the sight of war.

In 1946, both brothers worked for the election campaign of Aimé Césaire, a subject of consuming interest.[18] In the same year Frantz decided to continue his studies in France. His father's death in 1947 impelled him to think in more practical terms, and his friend Mosole convinced him to consider dentistry as a profession. It was to be a short-lived decision. The plans for departure were complicated by the lack of money and by the number of those anxious to go to France to study. Joby Fanon recalled that he, his sister, and Frantz all wanted to go to France for the same reasons. Frantz's situation was better than that of the others because his military service guaranteed him some support. But it was not enough, and Frantz's request for additional funds from his mother brought out strong feelings on both sides. Frantz asked for some small things, including handkerchiefs. His mother—who provided her daughter with the desired objects—refused her son. Frantz was bitter about women needing to study, and about his mother's behavior towards him. Handkerchiefs and favored sisters were beside the point but ambivalent feelings towards mothers were not. The memory of the incident lingered with Fanon long after it had occurred. Joby remembers their discussing it in Tunis, two months before Fanon died.

The conversation between Joby and Frantz occurred at a time when both men reminisced about their home, education, and family. It was at the same time that Frantz talked about his having wanted to be named Ambassador to Cuba by the Algerian government, after independence. He looked forward to returning home, to Martinique, triumphant as Ambassador, and he described how he imagined being met by the diplomatic corps, with his mother watching the proceedings. As the story was told, it was clear that it had evoked all the mixed feelings in Frantz that the image of a triumphant return of this kind could inspire. In some way perhaps, Fanon thought that it would have evened the score, forcing mother and officials to recognize him as they had failed to do in the past. It would have freed the son to love that from which he came, with a freedom attained through recognition and achievement. Fanon died before he could have carried out his mission. The Algerian government, however, had already rejected his request, indicating its refusal to name him Ambassador to Cuba.

In 1947 Fanon went to France, moving from Paris to Lyon, to avoid "too many blacks," as Manville says.[19] He abandoned the idea of dentistry for medicine, and soon transferred from surgery to psychiatry. In the course of this period, Fanon mingled with leftist students and, according to Bouvier, in Trotskyist circles.[20] In Lyon, Fanon was politically active and an eager participant in debates and meetings. Unlike Paris, in the Lyon Faculty of Medicine there were less than twenty blacks—all male —out of a total of four hundred students. The Lyon period was marked also by an affair which ended with the birth of a daughter. It was a difficult situation in which Fanon sought out his friends for advice. Having decided not to marry the mother of the child, Fanon nonetheless wanted to have the infant brought up by his own mother in Martinique. This attempt failed and after the first year, Fanon saw less of both mother and child. After his death, other members of the family kept in touch with the daughter.[21]

In 1951, Frantz resumed a former relationship with Josie Dublé of Lyon, the woman who was to become his wife in the following year.[22] They had met some years earlier and the friendship matured. Those who have known Josie Fanon describe her as an intelligent and sensitive woman, an important intellectual influence on her husband, and a loyal companion. During his psychiatric training at Saint Alban, and later in Blida-Joinville and Tunis, Josie impressed those who met her. But she was more than her husband's companion, as her own work reveals. Politically involved, she wrote for Algerian newspapers after independence. At the present time, Josie Fanon has given up her French citizenship and lives in Algiers with her two sons.

While at medical school, Frantz helped to organize the Union of Students from Overseas France, and he edited their mimeographed newspaper, *Tam-Tam*. By the end of 1951, he had completed and defended his medical thesis and was engaged in the practice of psychotherapy, under guidance, at a hospital located outside of Lyon, the Hospital of Saint Ylie.[23] Before proceeding to Saint Alban, where he was to work with Professor François Tosquelles, Fanon returned to Martinique. There had been some thought of returning to work there permanently, but the consensus of opinion is that he found the situation politically and professionally stifling. It has been stated, in rather sharp tones, that Fanon was never again to set foot in Martinique: "that, except in one or two articles, he practically never again touched upon the problems of his own country."[24] The implication is that Fanon chose to forget his homeland and his past. But as the author of this observation, Albert Memmi, knows, "one doesn't leave one's own self behind as easily as all that." It is important, however, to consider why it was that at this stage and later, when he had found himself politically, Fanon did not apply his energies to Martinique. At an earlier period in his life, when he was educating himself and eager to practice, Martinique offered few incentives. The decision to stay away later is perhaps less easily understandable. But Memmi is in error if he thinks that Fanon succeeded in forgetting either his own past or that of his country.

This was not a problem peculiar to Fanon. On the contrary, it was then, as it remains now, a problem of the West Indian nation as a whole. The question was taken up in a symposium held in the fall of 1967 at Sir George Williams University, in Montreal. On that occasion, the cases of three prominent exiles were discussed. One of them was Fanon. "Garvey, Padmore, Fanon, all left the cramping conditions of the West Indies because they felt that to make the *first* leap to their free and full development, they had to go abroad." The authors of this statement asked the essential question: Why did these men feel that they had to leave?

> This much is certain. They left largely because they had no organic link with anything at home. Large scale agriculture, industry, small or large, commercial enterprise of any significance, were all rigorously kept out of their hands. They were within closed walls with no room to move. Either stay or get out.

> It is the constant social bruises and wounds inflicted upon a population that must live in such a situation, that is for the most part responsible for the heavy migration of West Indians from their native land.[25]

In Fanon's case, the question was discussed by his brother Joby some months before Frantz's death. It may have been that Frantz felt psychically unable and therefore reluctant to return to Martinique and implement those changes he knew to be essential. Between an atmosphere of conformism and social constraint, such as that of Fort-de-France, and the attractions of the French capital, where so many other Martiniquean and other foreign patriots continue to reside, it is not difficult to see where the temptation lay. In addition, he may have experienced greater satisfaction in fighting racism and colonialism in France, the mother country itself. Later in Algeria, where the elements allowing identification as a non-white non-westerner were more obvious, what ambivalent sentiments there may have been about not returning to Martinique would have been more than assuaged by the difficulty of the struggle. In the second volume of her memoirs Simone de Beauvoir reminisced about Fanon and had something to say about this. Paraphrasing Fanon's troubled feelings she noted that "his origins aggravated his conflicts: Martinique was not ripe for an uprising: what one gained in

Africa would serve in the Antilles; all the same one felt his awkwardness at not struggling in his native land, and even more so, at not being a native Algerian."[26]

Yet the connection between his own early experience and what he witnessed in Algeria was repeatedly made, strengthening the impression that Fanon was not only conscious on his part but that he felt it to be confirmed in his Algerian commitment. Thus, in a polemical review which appeared in *el Moudjahid* on November 15, 1957, of *Pour Djamila Bouhired* by Georges Arnaud and Jacques Vergès, Fanon ended his article with the question, "Is it so far from Réunion to Algiers?"

In the summer of 1952 Fanon entered the hospital at Saint Alban in order to begin work as a resident under the direction of Professor François Tosquelles. To say that this marked an important step in his life is an understatement. Tosquelles had a great influence on Fanon's psychiatric work both in terms of method and in the nature of the problems on which Fanon chose to concentrate. Whether Fanon's disdain for psychoanalysis, and for being psychoanalyzed himself, is related to the environment at Saint Alban is an open question. That probably had as much to do with the general ambiance in France which did not require that potential psychiatrists be analyzed, as with Fanon's reluctance to engage himself in that process. In any case, Tosquelles came to know Fanon well and he continues to exhibit an evident sympathy, shared by his wife, for both Fanon and Josie in the Saint Alban period.

Fanon worked with enthusiasm and he learned his lessons well. Tosquelles, impressed by his student's agility, expressed the wish that he slow down in order to absorb his discoveries with greater care. But Fanon was no more responsive to this request than he was to later invitations to take a more reflective pose. While he was at Saint Alban, Fanon and the young doctors who worked as a team listened to the organic conceptions of psychiatry and medicine that Tosquelles espoused. The conception of sociotherapy, with its emphasis on the importance of the social role and the social context of patients in hospitals, was part of a more extensive critique of existing psychiatric methods and hospital care. When he moved to Blida-Joinville and later to Tunis as a psychiatrist, Fanon transposed the ideas of Tosquelles with amazing fidelity. All the more surprising was the way in which these ideas, grounded as they were in a certain conception of man and society, supported Fanon's political thinking. The evolution of Fanon's activity, from psychiatric orientation to political action, was based on certain assumptions about men's relations to one another and on a way of perceiving these relations. It was not accidental that Tosquelles contributed, by his own example, to the concerned approach to the human element which figured so prominently in Fanon's thinking.

Tosquelles' ideas, and Fanon's psychiatric work are discussed in detail in the second part of this book. Suffice it to state here that in the period between 1947 and 1952, Fanon was enjoying a period of intellectual activity and professional experimentation that were to stand him in good stead for the rest of his life. Tosquelles and the whole atmosphere of Saint Alban were not the only important ventures of this period. The same years coincided with remarkable developments on the political level and Fanon was not immune to them. Tosquelles himself was an exile from the Spanish civil war, a man who was not reticent about discussing politics, and for whom life was not compartmentalized. But the civil war had been overshadowed by other events, notably the Second World War, and after 1945, the intellectual and political turmoil of post-war France and Europe.

Marcel Manville and Joby Fanon have both indicated that Fanon was deeply influenced by the wave of existentialist literature and philosophy that was current in post-war France. It was in this period that Fanon turned to Sartre, Heidegger, Jaspers, Kierkegaard, and Merleau-Ponty.[27] His political education had already begun and he was pursuing his acquaintance with Lenin, Marx, and Trotsky at the same time that he was reading Freud. Marcel Manville recalls that Fanon developed a great interest in Trotsky and asked Manville to bring him the proceedings of the Fourth International, which he did. Manville had become a member of the French Communist Party, which separated the two friends, but their personal friendship and their general political commitments remained very similar. Aside from his voracious reading, encouraged by Josie, Fanon was aware of the intellectual agitation taking place in the French capital. *Les Temps Modernes*, the literary-political journal of the Sartrean school, began to appear in 1945. It carried articles on the subjects that Fanon was to concern himself with as time went on: communism and terror, the politics of the oppressed, black-white relations, the third world and the European left. *Présence Africaine,* the important journal inaugurated by Alioune Diop with a host of France's most eminent literary leftists to support it, came out in 1947. It dealt with the cultural heritage of Africa and negritude. It had had a long history before emerging in its present form, but Fanon became familiar with it only at this stage of its development.

Les Temps Modernes and *Présence Africaine* symbolized two spheres of influence that were important in Fanon's life. On the one hand Sartre's political orientation was to exercise a considerable influence on Fanon; on the other, *Présence Africaine,* with its quest for a definition of African uniqueness, exerted a pull in another direction. The confrontation of the two became a critical turning point in Fanon's life. But out of the amalgam of men and ideas that affected Fanon, there were other historic figures, notably Marx, Freud and Hegel, whose presence is to be discerned in his works. It was through the inner debate he engaged in with these men, a debate molded by events in which he found himself, that Fanon eventually evolved an intellectual and political position of his own.

Conscience and Consciousness: The Relevance of Hegel and Sartre

The background of Hegel's thought is the remarkable human phenomenon of the subordination of one self to another which we have in all forms of servitude— whether slavery, serfdom, or voluntary service.
Notes by J.B. Baillie to G.W.F. Hegel, "Independence and Dependence of Self-Consciousness: Lordship and Bondage,"

The Phenomenology of Mind.

Although he devoted a mere five pages to Hegel in *Black Skin, White Masks,* it is impossible to read Fanon without realizing to what extent *The Phenomenology of Mind* is present. And if he was not philosophically inclined, it was nonetheless evident that Fanon, like Hegel, experienced the "long journey of consciousness looking for itself."[28] In the days when he was trying to make some sense out of the shocking contrast between his own self-image and how he discovered that others, especially white Frenchmen, looked at him, Fanon was understandably preoccupied with questions of identity and self-definition. Unlike Geismar, who relegates this kind of questioning to a period of adolescent self-doubt, I believe that what may have begun as a result of self-doubt generated an interest that became something more lasting and important. It was not a passing *tristesse* associated with youth that Fanon experienced when he read

Hegel. It is more probable that he began to understand that the situation he himself was in was common to other men. It is striking that both Fanon and Memmi, as well as Sartre in his analysis of *Anti-Semite and Jew* and in *Being and Nothingness*, made full use of the master-servant paradigm in their respective discussions of relations, political and otherwise. Fanon and Memmi, who incidentally does not mention Hegel in *The Colonizer and the Colonized*, nevertheless confirmed through their experience that the master-servant relationship was borne out in the colonial situation. When Fanon and Memmi and other political essayists such as Mohammed Sahli, Anouar Abdel-Malek, and Abdallah Laroui, to mention but a few of the contemporary partisans of decolonization, emphasize the Other-directed nature of the reactions of the colonized and his need to struggle to free himself of this externally determined definition of Self, they are using a language that is reminiscent of Sartre, and certainly of Hegel.[29]

Fanon was undoubtedly aware of the Hegel revival which occurred in France after the war. He read Jean Hyppolite's translations of Hegel and came full force into the center of the circle of intellectuals who were themselves influenced by the master: Sartre, Merleau-Ponty, and Hyppolite. Three elements dominated Fanon's discussion of Hegel, which was limited to an analysis of the section in *Phenomenology* on "Lordship and Bondage": recognition, reciprocity, and struggle.[30] That man *is* to the extent that he is recognized, that he can be for himself only when and as he is for another, raised the double question of the nature of this dependence and the relevance of the nature of the Other. Identity, or rather the consciousness of Self, was intimately linked with recognition. The relationship that existed between the two selves facing each other and dependent on each other was the reciprocal process that was recognition. But reciprocity, while it described the mutual character of the process, was not necessarily equal. It was the tension between an awareness of the mutuality of dependence and the expression of recognition with the implication of equality, that described the course of the struggle which eventually differentiated the person as object, from man as subject.

Accepting the impossibility of achieving self-consciousness in isolation and accepting the necessity of the existence of an Other as a prerequisite for being, the discreet Self experienced desire and simultaneously the resistance of the Other to this expression of desire. It is as though sensing the movement of the emerging Self, the Other moved to block its passage, to retain it in the fixed pattern of an immobilized dialectic. But as each Self attempted to ascertain its certainty of its self and as each realized that this could be done only with the recognition of the Other, the frozen dialectic began to dissolve into open conflict. The will to struggle was thus the expression of the will to live, if to live as other than mere object was understood to mean the achievement of recognition as separated, though not isolated, individuality.

> . . . it is solely by risking life that freedom is obtained; only thus is it tried and proved that the essential nature of self-concious-ness is not bare existence, is not the merely immediate form in which it at first makes its appearance, is not its mere absorption in the expanse of life.[31]

As he groped to understand who he was, when he confronted the image of himself which he discovered facing white Frenchmen, an image which in no sense corresponded to his own inner self-portrait, Fanon began to understand that he was either doomed to struggle, or to exist, not as he was, but as he appeared in the eyes of others. If the objective of struggle was clear, if it was the only way of attaining "recognition as an independent self-consciousness," the process seemed to unravel unexpected layers of imposed otherness. The more he was to fight his way to the surface of this recognition, the more he realized that he fought as others locked in the bond of servitude peculiar to the historical relationship of blacks and whites, colonizers and colonized, oppressors and oppressed.

Not only was his existence contested, separate from the mirror image of the Other, but his willingness to risk his life was doubted. How could a nonexistent self be prepared to die? For what? In a footnote addition to his commentary on Hegel, Fanon noted that he had originally intended to write something on the subject of the Negro and death. It seems, he observed, that some people wonder whether or not Negroes commit suicide, in much the same way as Durkheim wondered about the prevalence of suicide among Jews.[32]

Although his debt to Hegel appears to be great, Fanon insisted that the situation of blacks differed from that described by

Hegel in his portrait of the master and the servant. He claimed that in the black-white relationship, the master never exhibited an interest in the consciousness of the servant. The role which labor performed for the servant in the Hegelian instance did not apply to the historical experience of the blacks. "I hope I have shown," wrote Fanon, "that here the master differs basically from the master described by Hegel."

> For Hegel there is reciprocity; here, the master laughs at the consciousness of the slave. What he wants from the slave is not recognition but work.
>
> In the same way, the slave here is in no way identifiable with the slave who loses himself in the object and finds in his work the source of his liberation.
>
> The Negro wants to be like the master.
>
> Therefore he is less independent than the Hegelian slave.
>
> In Hegel the slave turns away from the master and turns toward the object.
>
> Here the slave turns toward the master and abandons the object.[33]

In his discussion of the difference between liberation which is granted and struggle which forces the granting of recognition, Fanon touched on what he felt to be the critical factor responsible for the liberated but not independent nature of the French black vis-à-vis his master. In saying that "the Negro wants to be like the master," that he is "less independent than the Hegelian slave," Fanon expressed not only the untouched analysis of the particular situation of a black slave as opposed to a white slave facing a white master, he also expressed his pained awareness of how successfully the white French world had imprinted its own image on the consciousness of its black populations. Had he not, though, exaggerated a point rather than introduced a new one? Was not the wish to become like the master an inevitable corollary of the servant-master relationship? Did not Fanon find the same situation in his reading of Sartre's *Anti-Semite and Jew*, when Sartre considered the inauthentic Jew? Did it not figure in Albert Memmi's portrait of the colonized, one of whose wishes was to successfully emulate the colonizer? Had not others discovered that the disinherited were sometimes more eager to become the minority that possessed the earth than to remain loyal to those wretched who would one day inherit it?

When Fanon said that Hegel's master differed from the master of the Negro slave, he claimed that the former "laughs at the consciousness of his slave. What he wants from the slave is not recognition but work." But was it not Hegel's argument that at some point the master realized that "it is not an independent, but rather a dependent consciousness that he has achieved. He is thus *not* assured of self-existence as his truth; he finds that his truth is rather the unessential consciousness, and the fortuitous unessential action of that consciousness."[34] For this reason, in order to satisfy his own need, his own self-certainty, the master must take an interest in the consciousness of his bondsman. What did it matter, in the argument, whether the bondsman was of the same color or not, regardless of what color may have meant to him. Here, I think that Fanon was in error; certain as he was of the importance of underlining the radically different character which the black-white relationship imposed on the Hegelian paradigm, he did not see where it remained valid.

In making his comments Fanon was thinking primarily of the economic exploitation of the servant. He may have been reflecting on the utter disdain in which the white master held the black servant, a disdain so totally destructive that it seemed to obviate any consideration of the servant, save as a labor-producing machine. The confusion may lie in the common-sense meaning of Fanon's distinction, as expressed in his sentence, between recognition and labor. It is clear what Fanon had in mind when he used both terms, and they appear to have been used in an ordinary, non-philosophic sense. But when Hegel wrote of labor, it was not in the restricted and exclusively economic sense of the word at all. He thought in terms of its function in the process of the servant coming to a consciousness of self, and in related fashion, as this applied to the master.

In a curious way, Fanon's remarks bore out Hegel's long-range view, though he seemed unaware of it. For his anger at seeing the exploitation of the servants was not simply his reaction to their abominable treatment in the fields or factories. It was the realization that what was at stake in this process of depersonalization was precisely the withholding of recognition of the consciousness, the Self, of the servant. It was the attempt to push servants beyond the pale where they would no longer even qualify for thinghood. Yet to have done this successfully would have destroyed the servant whom the master needed alive.

The question of being liberated vs. struggling to liberate one-self was another issue about which Fanon had a good deal to say. In the pages he devoted to Hegel in *Black Skin,* Fanon dwelled on this at some length. He understood that the external libera-tion of the black slave had in no sense really led to his liberation, and consequently that it was imperative to reconsider both the method and the requirements of a genuine liberation. The most obvious error of the black slave was that he had not, at least under French control, taken the struggle for liberation into his own hands. He had not struggled to liberate himself. He had benefited from the eventual action of his white master, and as a result he had simply gone superficially from one style of life to another. But in reality, nothing in him had changed and time alone would not alter it. His struggle had to take place on two levels, vis-à-vis the colonizer, and in himself.

There were times when the black man had fought for his liberation, but even on these occasions, he had fought for the values of his master's world, he had fought for white freedom and white justice. But what were his values, where was the self for which he ought to have fought? Fanon wrote of the slave who has no memory of the struggle for liberty, or the anguish of liberty, in Kierkegaard's terms. Such a man was not capable of taking up the challenge offered him by white society. He pas-sively accepted what was done to him and for him. He remained as much a victim in the second case as in the first. This pessimis-tic portrait of the man unknown to himself and therefore incapa-ble of mobilizing himself in the face of battle was not, however, the only portrait of the black man which Fanon drew.

There was another kind of black man, who was not at all internally passive, who knew himself to be different from his white counterpart, and yet, who had not the courage to shout this out, surrounded as he was by the signs of a presumed equality. He longed for the declaration of war that would justify his doing battle. Then at least, the lines would be clear, and the struggle would provide an opportunity to work out externally what had built up internally in the form of this private knowl-edge. This man sought confrontations, for he saw them as pro-viding him with the means of becoming who he was. The terms struggle and confrontation are never meant as exclusively physi-cal acts, and they do not imply an exclusive reliance on violence. In *The Wretched of the Earth,* the attitude towards the use of violence changed, and the experience of the Algerian Revolution was largely responsible for it. But in this period, it was clear that what was involved was primarily a philosophical and psychological struggle rather than a political one.

Fanon was under the impression that for the black man, the situation in the United States, because of its polarization, was preferable to that which existed in France. But this was true only in a partial sense. What Fanon was reacting to was the ambiguity that existed in France because of the hypocritical pose of freedom and equality, a freedom that was legally in existence but in no sense part of the social fabric of the country. In the United States, according to Fanon, the American black was faced with struggling for constitutional rights. Little by little he saw that thanks to his efforts discriminatory regulations were wiped off the statute books; he could therefore be certain of his place and of what he had accomplished. But this was overly optimistic since legislation, even when achieved by these means, did not mean a transformation in the mores of the citizens. There were battles, and some were decisive, but it is debatable which was "better" or "easier," the situation in France or that in the United States. Fanon romanticized the existential aspect of the struggle in the sense that he assumed that the perfect coincidence of an internal struggle accompanied by a political fight would invariably lead to a total regeneration of the social order. Fanon felt that the black man's situation in France was intolerable. He never knew as a black man, when whites considered him as he was, as a man in full possession of his self, or merely as an object. It was this persistent doubt that led him to consistently test and provoke those around him. While he offered this as a generalized description of the behavior of black men in France, it seems to have conformed strongly to his own feelings on the subject. Jeanson, in his Postface to the 1965 edition of *Black Skin,* described an exchange he had had with Fanon that confirmed this condition. Jeanson had been asked to read *Black Skin* in manuscript.

> In 1952, we almost broke off our relations, he and I, the very day of our first meeting. Having found his manuscript exceptionally interesting, I committed the error of telling him so, which made him suspect me of having thought, "for a Negro, that wasn't so bad." As a result of which, I showed him the door and expressed my own reaction in the liveliest terms—which he had the good sense to take well.[35]

Remarks such as these won Jeanson a number of unfriendly comments,[36] but it is difficult to imagine that they were made in bad faith. Sartre, for whom Fanon felt nothing but admiration —even when he felt that he was not doing enough at the time of the Algerian Revolution—was quoted by Josie Fanon, in *el Moudjahid,* as having said that Fanon was the only black man before whom he, Sartre, could forget the fact of his blackness.[37] Not only was Fanon extremely sensitive to blackness, but most whites were also conscious of blackness, regardless of how much they intellectually rejected a sense of difference based on color. It was this that obsessed Fanon and that made him wonder whether it would ever be possible for whites and blacks to have normal relations with one another. It was the realization of how deep the confused meaning of blackness had gone, even into the consciences of those men with whom he had the closest affinity and to whom he turned for friendship and intellectual leadership, that led Fanon to undertake an analysis of the fact of blackness as a prelude to reestablishing a just order between white and black.

The question whether it would be possible for men of different color to behave normally with one another, without the imposition of the consciousness of value-laden differences which they had been brought up to accept unquestioningly, this question of communication—of an authenticity of communication—was to preoccupy Fanon all his life. The man with whom he is sometimes compared, the Tunisian novelist Albert Memmi, anguished over the same question, only he experienced it not as black vs. white, but as Tunisian vs. Frenchman, as non-westerner vs. westerner, and finally as a Jew in a non-Jewish environment. The exclusiveness of each category, the falsification of these situations created in both men a passionate desire to unmask the hidden and false assumptions that most men live by. If their paths diverged, the two had nevertheless, independently of one another but with amazing congruity, articulated the existential condition for the man who is molded by an Other; an Other who is, historically, the Master.

It was not an accident that it was Jean-Paul Sartre who wrote the introductions to the major works of both Memmi and Fanon. And it was not an accident that both men recognized him as an intellectual guide of impressive proportions. In his reading of Sartre, Fanon was preoccupied with two questions: communication between men, and specifically communication between men of different color. Neither Hegel nor Sartre, according to Fanon, had given adequate consideration to this second matter. "Jean-Paul Sartre has forgotten that the Negro suffers in his skin differently than the White man," he wrote.[38] That observation was made after the painful deliberations provoked by Sartre's introduction to Léopold Senghor's anthology of poetry. The appearance of this anthology was a literary event that was doubly controversial as a result of Sartre's essay. In Fanon's life, the Sartre essay was to be a turning point. It forced him to focus on the matter of negritude and to work out a position which was to have serious consequences in the development of his political thinking. I shall return to this question in connection with the *Présence Africaine* group and Fanon's relations with it. But it is clear that Fanon was sensitive to Sartre's remarks about negritude not only because they were critical and made a political point which Fanon discovered he could not dismiss, but because they were written by a man for whom Fanon had the highest regard, a man who had helped Fanon to understand the perverted dimensions of human relations where racism and anti-Semitism were concerned.

It was in *Anti-Semite and Jew* that Fanon felt the overwhelming sense of comprehension and empathy which he shared with the man who wrote this book and with the men about whom this book was written. But three years before it had appeared, Sartre's *L'Être et le néant (Being and Nothingness)* had been published. Fanon refers to it in *Black Skin, White Masks*. Even a superficial reading of this difficult book would have had its rewards. For here again was the analysis of the problems of communication and being; being for others and for oneself, and the inextricable connection between the two. Here again was the challenge to authenticity, to understanding the existential postulates of the situation which determined the limits of man's freedom, his freedom to choose to be himself as he chose himself to be, and not merely as others allowed him to be. Here was Sartre writing about "concrete relations with others" and the significance of "the Look," unaware of how close to home his words would be for a man like Fanon, haunted by the look that was directed at him but that seemed to miss his very being and to impose another, alien body on his own. It is worth while quoting Sartre's text to appreciate his impact.

> If we start with the first revelation of the Other as a look, we must recognize that we experience our inapprehensible being-for-others in the form of a possession. I am possessed by the Other; the Other's look fashions my body in its nakedness, causes it to be born, sculptures it, produces it as it is, sees it as I shall never see it. The Other holds a secret—the secret of what I am. He makes me be and thereby he possesses me, and this possession is nothing other than the consciousness of possessing me. I in the recognition of my object-state have proof that he has this consciousness. By virtue of consciousness the Other is for me simultaneously the one who has stolen my being from me and the one who causes 'there to be' a being which is my being. Thus I have a comprehension of this ontological structure: I am responsible for my being-for-others, but I am not the foundation of it. It appears to me therefore in the form of a contingent given for which I am nevertheless responsible; the Other founds my being in so far as this being is in the form of the 'there is.' But he is not responsible for my being although he founds it in complete freedom—in and by means of his free transcendence. Thus to the extent that I am revealed to myself as responsible for my being, I lay claim to this being which I am; that is, I wish to recover it, or, more exactly, I am the project of the recovery of my being. I want to stretch out my hand and grab hold of this being which is presented to me as my being but at a distance—like the dinner of Tantalus. I want to found it by my very freedom. For if in one sense my being-as-object is an unbearable contingency and the pure 'possession' of myself by another, still in another sense this being stands as the indication of what I should be obliged to recover and found in order to be the foundation of myself. But this is conceivable only if I assimilate the Other's freedom. Thus my project of recovering myself is fundamentally a project of absorbing the Other. . . .
>
> In fact the problem for me is to make myself be by acquiring the possibility of taking the Other's point of view of myself.[39]

The phrase, "I am the project of the recovery of my being," may well have struck Fanon as his raison d'être in the days when he sought to understand who he was and how others saw him. If we translate Sartre's paragraph into concrete terms for a man like Fanon, the implications are devastating. Having acknowledged that his existence was predetermined—or over-determined—by the perception of him which others had, which the Other had, Fanon understood that this perception did not coincide with his own image of himself, and yet his self was not completely distinct from that reflection which came back to him in such a disturbing fashion. Sartre was to explore the distinctions between the philosophical and historical dimensions of the question in his essay *Anti-Semite and Jew.* It is not surprising that it struck responsive chords. It was in many respects a logical continuation of the reading of Hegel and of Sartre's *Being and Nothingness.* To specialized readers, whether philosophically or politically inclined, the question of freedom was given a different twist in the reflections on the Jewish question. Could it have been the experience of the war that made Sartre more vulnerable to the limits of human endurance, even on a philosophical level? Fanon understood the critique of anti-Semitism with a rapidity and an affirmation that thrilled him. Again and again he was to return to Sartre's essay to compare the situations of Jews and blacks.[40]

From the beginning there was a coincidence of thought and experience that was obvious. Sartre also returned to his own master, Hegel, and to the Master-Servant paradigm. He understood the peculiarly threatening situation of the French Jew living in France, in a society ostensibly free of legal discrimination but corrupted by the insidious presence of a sense of exclusiveness and exclusion that made a mockery of the Jews' rights. The social character of the Jew and the false conditions of his life are two of the qualities that seem identical with the conditions which Fanon repeatedly turned over in his mind as characteristic of the situation of the black Frenchman. They coincided perfectly with the problems of being and authenticity of being with which he was grappling. The Jew, wrote Sartre, "is the social man par excellence, because his torment is social."

> It is society, not the decree of God, that has made him a Jew and brought the Jewish problem into being. As he is forced to make his choices entirely within the perspective set by his problem, it is in and through the social that he chooses even his own existence. His constructive effort to integrate himself in the national community is social; social is the effort he makes to think of himself, that is, to situate himself, among other men; his joys and sorrows are social; but all this is because the curse that rests upon

him is social. If in consequence he is reproached for his meta-
physical inauthenticity, if attention is called to the fact that his
constant uneasiness is accompanied by a radical positivism, let us
not forget that these reproaches return upon those who make
them: the Jew is social because the anti-Semite has made him
so.[41]

I have raised the question elsewhere, as to the accuracy of
Sartre's exclusively social definition of the Jew.[42] But it would
be emphasizing a point which it was not the object of the author
to make, to ask Sartre what the Jew is for himself, as opposed
to the way in which others see him. When he wrote, in 1944, it
was not the autonomous conception of the Jew in his private
milieu that was at issue, but the rampant proportions of anti-
Semitism and the solidarity of little men who had the power
to implement their diseased hatred. Fanon understood that
the fear of the anti-Semite is no different than the fear of the
racist. He was to elaborate on the similarities as well as the differences between the anti-Semite and the racist in *Black Skin,
White Masks.*[43] Both types, often concealed within the same men,
succeeded in creating conditions in which neither the Jew nor
the black man were free to live as they chose.

To complete the project of recovering himself, and to do this
while not absorbing the view of himself which the Other imposed, which the Jew looking at the anti-Semite recognized as
false, was a herculean task. Was a man to be perpetually condemned to choose himself in false conditions? Or was the authenticity of his ultimate choice promoted by his ability to
understand, at the least, the falseness of the conditions under
which he must choose? "Authenticity, it is almost needless to
say, consists in having a true and lucid consciousness of the
situation, in assuming the responsibilities and risks that it involves, in accepting it in pride or humiliation, sometimes in
horror and hate."[44] A true and lucid consciousness of the situation decreed that the Jew was not choosing freely and that until
the world purged itself of the power and privilege of the anti-
Semites, their presence would be a perpetual source of difficulty. But a true and lucid consciousness, by virtue of what it
forced men to admit, allowed them to perform that surgery
which society resisted but which Sartre chose to see as the pre-
cious prerogative of every man. Internally, in his own psyche, in

his relations with men, the Jew who understood was on the path of authenticity. Not especially consoling when one considers where that authenticity led in 1944. But the point was made and understood. Was it a far cry from this to Fanon's excessively optimistic hope that for every man to be free to choose himself in freedom, one must create new conditions and new men?

At the end of his study, Sartre quoted Richard Wright as saying that " 'there is no Negro problem in the United States, there is only a White problem.' In the same way, we must say that anti-Semitism is not a Jewish problem; it is *our* problem."[45] Fanon was to repeat and to elaborate on the same theme, taking it one step further by formulating a conception of relations between oppressor and oppressed that included the relations of minority men and colored men within the larger context of a colonial situation. This was the logical extension of a vision of both a psychological and a historical situation which he was to experience and record.

Sartre's essay on anti-Semite and Jew contained ideas and implications not only for the Jewish question, and by analogy for the black question, but for the vexing national question. The contrast between the desired, freely chosen self-determination of the authentic Jew and the universalistic inclinations of the democrat who defended him constitutes one of the powerful paradoxes which Sartre seems to have considered under various guises at different times. It was a variation on this theme that was so troubling in his introductory essay to Senghor's anthology, and it was this theme offered in sharp contrast to negritude that caught Fanon by surprise. The option of a universalism as opposed to a particularism of any kind, be it religious, racial, or nationalist, strongly appealed to Fanon. Perhaps it was this which he had in mind when he spoke of the impact which a reading of Sartre's essay had on him. Certainly, insofar as it forced him to consider the limitations of negritude as a tool of analysis and reform as opposed to a cultural stance or consolation, Sartre's admonition was strong. But the lure of internationalism haunted Fanon in Algeria as well. Firmly committed to the Algerian Revolution as a nationalist revolution, he was to criticize those who believed they could bypass the nationalist phase of the independence struggle. Yet he himself was most sympathetic to those members of the Algerian resistance who recognized the long-range needs of Algeria in non-nationalist terms. The Algerian aspect of the problem arose after Fanon had moved to Algeria, and especially after 1956. The question of negritude and the nature of Sartre's opposition to it belong to an earlier period.

-3-

Présence Africaine and Negritude

Sartre's introduction to the *Anthologie de la nouvelle poésie nègre et malgache de langue française,* edited by Léopold Sédar-Senghor, was dramatically entitled "Orphée Noir," Black Orpheus.[46] It appeared in 1948, well after the movement which the anthology was meant to illustrate was under way. In a masterful study, in 1965, entitled *Les Ecrivains noirs de langue française: naissance d'une littérature,*[47] Lilyan Kesteloot was determined to expose the alleged error in Sartre's interpretation of negritude, thereby confirming the continuing impact which his essay had on critics of the movement. For all of his criticism of negritude, Sartre was no stranger to the milieu out of which it emerged. He was one of the editors of the prestigious journal launched by Alioune Diop in 1947, *Présence Africaine,* the most effective of a number of small periodicals that had been devoted to a revival of West Indian and African culture.

"Black Orpheus" is an oddly beautiful piece of writing. It betrays the degree to which Sartre was moved by his subject, and the extent to which he was involved in the questions he posed for his readers. Directed at whites and blacks, at potential enemies as well as advocates of negritude, Sartre presented each with an assessment of what he took to be the ambitions and the limitations of the movement. Once again, but now in considerably amplified form, the question of universalism vs. particularism came to the fore. To his white readers, Sartre wrote as though anticipating their objections and their non-comprehension. He scolded them for expecting anything other than an exclusivist movement after the history that had preceded it. In a tone and with words reminiscent of what he wrote in the preface to *The Wretched of the Earth*, he reminded white men that for the first time they were being watched. They were the objects as well as the antagonists in those writings. The subjects who spoke for themselves were the black men who wrote in their own language and poetry. Sartre knew, as did any French intellectual who had followed the growing number of small movements and circles devoted to black African and West Indian activities in Paris, that this was not the first expression of black poetry. But he recognized that the publication of Senghor's volume was a landmark.

He wrote, as he was to do after reading Fanon's manuscript, that this work is not meant for "us," for white men. Those who read it, he said, will have the impression of reading over someone's shoulder. They will sense that these poems are not directed at white men. They constitute nothing less than "une prise de conscience."[48] In his defense to the white reader, Sartre pleaded in a convincing style. He wrote about the need that black men had to achieve a measure of their own self-consciousness, and how, in spite of the inherent particularism of their position, this poetry was the "only really revolutionary poetry."[49] While Sartre acknowledged that negritude was a necessary phase in the self-consciousness of black men, he proceeded to elaborate on his own conception of African civilization in a way that may not have been identical with the views held by the exponents of negritude. For Sartre, there was a highly romanticized version of black African civilization that he saw as opposed to the technological civilization of the West. It was an image that evoked the lost innocence and harmony of another world. From the text, it is difficult to determine if this was what Sartre believed a revival of African civilization involved, or if this was how he himself saw the African past. In his essay, the passages devoted to this were placed as a buffer between the remarks addressed to white readers and the sharp criticisms leveled at the advocates of negritude. It was this latter section that was to cause a stir and which Fanon was to find so profoundly disturbing.

Sartre was sympathetic to negritude, of that there is no doubt. But he was uncertain as to precisely what the movement was

about; he suggested that it may not have been clear to its followers either. Was it an expression of liberty or necessity? Was it
a form of pantheism appropriate to Africa, or was it a condition
applicable to all of mankind? Was it fact, or value, or both? Did
it create an anti-racist racism, or was it but a stage in the total
development of mankind, albeit mankind divided into black and
white, proletariat and capitalist? Sartre understood that there
were differences among the followers of negritude on this point;
some were Marxist and others were not. He did not hesitate to
indicate where his preference lay, and it was not merely a matter
of taste. The goal of negritude must be to eventually transcend
it; its objective, paradoxically, is to create a consciousness which
will render it ultimately únnecessary. It is, therefore, a means
and not an end. The end is a society without racist consciousness. Or did Sartre mean a society without racial consciousness,
which would put him in precisely the same position as the democrat vis-à-vis the anti-Semite, who felt mildly uncomfortable at
the thought that the Jew willed himself different. Sartre's view
was summed up in the phrase: "en fait, la Négritude apparait
comme le temps faible d'une progression dialectique. . . ."[50]
Negritude was but a moment in the dialectical progression
which would ultimately erase black and white racism to create
a new human synthesis. Sartre agreed that the black man was
caught between the nostalgia for a past into which he no longer
fit, and a future that had not yet come into being. His was a tragic
situation, and it was not surprising that it found its most satisfactory expression in poetic form. Negritude was not to be confused with a political movement; it was a cultural expression of
the most eloquent kind.

With his characteristic lucidity, Sartre had managed to touch
on the central issue of the movement, and his criticisms were not
lightly taken. Some felt that he did not adequately comprehend
the need for an African cultural awakening, and that he mistook
a moment in a dialectic for what, in fact, was the revival of
African civilization. Others felt that he overlooked the revolutionary character of this specifically African movement, insisting
that it merge with the struggle of the world proletariat.

Léon Damas, one of the founders of the negritude movement
along with Aimé Césaire and Léopold Senghor, was recently
interviewed on the matter. He made it clear, defending himself
against the more militant, no longer non-violent exponents of

Black Power, that in their day, Césaire, Senghor, and he had struggled to prevent the total absorption which the "grand-children of the Gauls" wished to impose.[51] This was the first step, he claimed, and it had been conceived as a preventive measure in a colonial situation. He referred to Sartre's view acknowledging that whatever the future of negritude might be, it had indeed been, in Sartre's terms, a moment in human consciousness. But for Damas that moment had also changed human history.

When Damas spoke, it was as a veteran of the negritude movement. And when he confidently answered queries about the relationship between negritude and the Black Power movement in the United States, it was as a man who had personally taken part in the historic past out of which Black Power arose. When Senghor's anthology appeared, and when *Présence Africaine* was first published, the movement known as negritude was no longer a novelty. Its roots lay in the political and literary experiments that had involved men of different continents and political orientations. What had brought them together was a common reaction to the predicament of the black man's history. Léon Gontran Damas had been active in one of the very first expressions of this evolving consciousness. In 1932 a periodical called *Légitime Défense* was published in Paris with Damas as one of its collaborators.[52] In the preceding year, another short-lived but similar review had been published, again in Paris, this time in French and English, with the collaboration of students from the West Indies and other centers. This was *La Revue du monde noir*.[53] The degree of activity among West Indians, Africans, and black Americans in Paris in the years between 1929 and 1940 was intense. The roots of the negritude movement in this period lay not only in a revival of the indigenous cultures of Africa and the Antilles, but in the tremendous influence wielded by a group of black American poets and writers, who had already formulated the ingredients of what was to become negritude. It was men such as Claude McKay, Jean Toomer, Langston Hughes, and Countee Cullen who transmitted the American experience to the black poets and writers in Paris. They in turn imbibed this powerful example, along with the literary and political ferment that accompanied the surrealist movement in France in the same period. The mood of exultation and defiance, the energetic rejection of assimilation found expression in *Légitime Défense*. In the pages of this journal, the process of questioning the values that had been taken for granted for too long began in earnest. Not surprisingly, *Légitime Defénse* was subject to pressure and the journal folded after its first number. Less than two years later, in 1934, it was replaced by *L'Etudiant Noir*.

Etienne Léro, the editor of *Légitime Défense,* had concentrated on the cultural deformations produced in the West Indies by the process of literary assimilation. He urged a return to authentic values and a renaissance of a West Indian literature. In *L'Etudiant Noir,* the goal was no longer the West Indies alone, but the entire world of black culture as it was represented in Paris. Instead of a revival of West Indian culture, it was African culture that was emphasized. The experimentation with communism and surrealism which Léro had urged was considered unacceptable since they too had European origins. The search for authentic sources began in this fashion, and with it came a rejection of the uncritical imitation and acceptance of western values and culture. Eventually the political differences among the editors and authors was to result in splits, but for the time being, the break had been made and it forged a new mood. The men responsible for the leadership of this movement were the same men to be found some years later in the team around *Présence Africaine:* Aimé Césaire from Martinique, Léon Damas from Guyana, and Léopold Senghor from Senegal.

Concern with the common roots of black men led to a concentrated effort to study the routes that had led from Africa outward to the old and new worlds. This process, in turn, generated an interest in the work of historians, anthropologists, and ethnologists, men whose labor was to be an important building block for the black renaissance. It was not an accident that the advisers to the *Présence Africaine* editors were taken from such circles, men whose scholarship was not tainted by racist prejudices or tones of cultural superiority: Monod, Rivet, Leiris, and Balandier.

Between 1933 and 1935, Senghor and Césaire began to use the term negritude. "Negritude is the cultural heritage, the values and particularly the spirit of Negro-African civilization," according to Senghor.[54] Born out of a time of search and conflict, it was designed to be a tool and not a final goal. The objective was to be the integration of a revived "Negro-African culture into the realities of the twentieth century."[55] Senghor and Césaire emphasized different aspects of negritude, in accord with their own experience and with the immediate history with which they identified. The results were necessarily different and the differences have entered into the history of the negritude movement itself. Senghor's negritude was Africa-centered, and carried an implicit eulogy of pre-colonial days, pointing to the essential African characteristics which the colonial world would effectively destroy. For Césaire, negritude was more a mode of being, a consciousness of color, race, psychology as well as history.[56] The definition of negritude remained controversial but there seemed to be consensus that it was not a racial distinction but the definition of a total cultural heritage.

The three founders of negritude, Damas, Césaire, and Senghor, were not the only ones to find inspiration in the work at hand. Fanon was certainly influenced by the movement and the works of these three men. He talked and wrote about them, and he was consciously or unconsciously driven to imitate some of the majestic words and tones of Aimé Césaire, perhaps the greatest of the poets produced by the movement. More important than the influence of a particular work or poem, however, was the influence generated by the group as a whole, and the ambiance it created for sympathetic students who found a haven and a sense of mission among its members. The work of the triumvirate and those who gathered around *L'Etudiant Noir* remained mostly literary although as the years progressed and the situation in Europe worsened, the tendency was to take a more direct political position. This remained an individual affair, however, until well after the war.

After the start of the Second World War Césaire, Damas, and Senghor went their separate ways. Césaire returned to Martinique where his activities attracted the attention of the young Fanon and Manville, as well as other future writers such as Edouard Glissant and Joseph Zobel. In 1941 Césaire and his wife, Suzanne, a writer and critic, published the journal *Tropiques* whose influence was felt in Martinique and the Caribbean. In addition to exposing the cultural weaknesses of Martiniquean life—an inevitable product of the imposition of a foreign culture —it introduced the idea of a return to African sources as well as the appreciation of indigenous folklore. To this was added a sizable dose of surrealism, a way of looking at the world that not only implied revolutionary change in society, but an internal transformation that would bring about a new consciousness.

With the end of the war, the negritude movement underwent further changes. Césaire, Damas, and Senghor returned to their former positions in Paris, only now all three were elected deputies from their respective territories to the French Assembly. Senghor had encouraged other Senegalese writers to join him in Paris, and the number of intellectuals and students coming from Madagascar, Dahomey, and the West Indies increased. It was between 1942 and 1943, in the midst of the war and the terrible chaos and self-questioning which it produced, that the circle of students from France's colonial possessions began to question themselves on their own identities and values vis-à-vis the society around them. Alioune Diop, the Senegalese writer who was to become the guiding force behind *Présence Africaine* and eventually the publishing house of the same name, explained the motivations of the group in the first issue of his magazine. *Présence Africaine* appeared in October-November, 1947, with a preface by André Gide, and a committee of "patronage" that included such prominent figures as Gide, Mounier, Sartre, Camus, Richard Wright, Maydieu, Rivet, Monod, and of course Césaire, Senghor, and the Dahomean Paul Hazoumé.

It was an auspicious beginning. Alioune Diop presented the raison d'être of the journal in its first issue.

> This review [he wrote] does not fall within the range of any political or philosophical ideology. It seeks the collaboration of all men of good will (white, yellow or black) who are capable of helping us to define the nature of the African essence, and hastening its integration into the modern world.[57]

The review was to be scholarly and cultural in orientation, encouraging the publication of studies by specialists pertaining to African civilization and society, and soliciting novels, poems, plays, and other literary forms. The October-November issue was an extraordinary feat. Diop's essay set the tone, but others such as Monod, Mounier, and Sartre intensified the effect by their respective analyses of the relations between the blacks and whites, and the just goals of men dedicated to reviving an African presence. Sartre discussed the role of language in a colonial situation. He warned against the false pride which Frenchmen might feel at reading this new literature in their own language. He reminded them that it was merely the result of historical accident, the accident of colonialism, that Senegalese writers spoke in French and not in English. The real problem was how colonized people were to restore their own identities while forced to use the language of the colonizer.[58]

In succeeding issues it was clear that the cultural orientation of the journal would be given the broadest interpretation. Sartre's works were often the subject of explication, particularly those essays that lent themselves to the black situation.[59] More overtly political articles were not missing, although the editors of *Présence Africaine* made it a point not to take any one political position, save in the most general sense of being for the liberation of black populations from colonial domination. It was clear that the principle of adopting a political stand irked many of the contributors and some of the editors. Generally speaking, however, the journal retained its emphasis on cultural matters; although on occasion the rule was waived. In one instance, a special issue entitled *Le Monde noir,* edited by Th. Monod, carried an article by Senghor entitled "Subir ou choisir," a frank call to create a French commonwealth. Another, opposite view was conveyed in an essay by Maghemout Diop in a special issue devoted to black students, *Les Etudiants noirs parlent.*[60] Diop's article was the most devastating exposé of colonialism to appear in the pages of *Présence Africaine.*

The issue of a political vs. a literary periodical was not to be lightly dismissed. But it would be an error to overlook the important work accomplished by *Présence Africaine* within the limitations it chose to impose on itself. Within a five-year period, the editors had brought together men with a commitment to cultural authenticity and to exposing the cultural alienation characteristic of colonial situations. In 1956 and 1959, *Présence Africaine* held international congresses to discuss problems of common interest to black writers and intellectuals. The barrier was no longer culture vs. politics, and the gamut of opinions expressed reflected the growing impatience and self-confidence. *Présence Africaine* was carrying out the mission of *Tropiques* in its invocation of the double aim of social and psychological revolution.

While this double aim ought to have coincided with Fanon's interest, in fact he was not in harmony with the *Présence* circle. As he became more politicized, it is doubtful that he would have accepted the restrictions imposed by the journal. But more important than this was the question of negritude and Fanon's attitude towards it. For Césaire, Damas, and Senghor, no matter how they differed on their interpretations of the negritude movement, they were in accord as to its function and its potential. Fanon recognized the historic importance of negritude and admitted its powerful personal effect, but he eventually took a strong position against it. From *Black Skin,* to the essays collected in *Toward the African Revolution*[61] and *The Wretched of the Earth,*[62] Fanon's thinking on the subject of negritude was open and changing. The clash provoked by Sartre's essay had begun a process in Fanon's thinking that led far away from negritude as anything more than a moment, a vital moment that changed history. Fanon's hostility to the movement may account for the coolness which his name evokes in the offices of *Présence Africaine* today. There is certainly no illusion about where Fanon stood on this matter, although there is great respect for his books. There was even talk, in the spring of 1970, of publishing a study of Fanon.[63] Reda Malek, who knew Fanon well and who worked closely with him on *el Moudjahid* in Tunisia, has expressed surprise at the American admirers of Fanon who seem to ignore his feelings on negritude.[64] Malek was thinking of Black Power advocates who considered Fanon an ally if not a model.

On a personal level, no matter how much he may have disagreed with them, Fanon appears to have remained close to some of the people in the *Présence* group, particularly Alioune Diop. Diop was one of the people at Fanon's bedside when he was critically ill in Washington, D.C., in the winter of 1961.[65]

- 4 -

Black Skin, White Masks:
A Synthesis

"Je crois en toi, Homme."

_____

By 1952 the pieces of the puzzle had begun to fit together and the different strands that were essential to a comprehension of the whole were placed side by side. In this manner, *Black Skin, White Masks* came into being. Like other introspective reflections that are often disguised autobiographies, this essay spoke to the experiences of the author but it was never merely anecdotal, nor was it written as a confessional exercise. Fanon was both poet and polemicist, and perhaps in no other one of his books is this combination so striking. Possessed with the poet's intoxication with language, Fanon seemed sometimes to yield to the magic of his own words, at least as much as he hoped his readers would. Peter Geismar has written of this early period of Fanon's life as one which was formative and which was to be superseded by a clarity of purpose still missing. But to read *Black Skin, White Masks* in this fashion is misleading. The great themes that haunted Fanon are to be found here and to reduce them to temporary signs of depression, existential torment, or poetic introspection as though these were deviations from some central purpose, is to miss the essence of the man.[66] But by refusing to rest content with a subjective solution to these conditions, Fanon transcended the limitations of the excessive individualism Geismar suggested.

In *Black Skin, White Masks,* the poet reached out and in so doing made his agony a bond of fraternity, while the militant resisted the inner counsels of despair and turned anguish into a call to consciousness. The desire to communicate and extend himself to others as an expression of his desire to understand, to share, and to love, was so near the surface of this first book that it made Fanon's vulnerability palpable. But the fragility of the man was an expression of the fragility of all men, and the sense of solidarity transformed this into a bond of common strength. It was the persistent innocent in the man who could dare to write, "I believe in you, humanity." It was the same man who sustained the tension between his own being as a black man and the conviction he never abandoned that the subjective experience of one can be understood by all.[67] This was no sentimental testament to humanism. Fanon vowed to understand why it was that black men wore white masks. In the process he came to learn that the dynamic of minority-majority relations was universal. He acknowledged that colonial racism did not differ from other kinds of racisms, and that anti-Semitism left him robbed of a sense of humanity. He quoted at length from Karl Jaspers' *La Culpabilité allemande,* citing the philosophical justifications for collective responsibility.[68] But it was his own commitment to individual responsibility that emerged clearly; the wish not to draw a line around himself and his own kind, and not to plead indifference to the sufferings of others.

And yet, the material that made up Fanon's first book, for all of its universal implications, was drawn in the main from Martiniquean experiences. It was organized around two principal themes: the fact of blackness and the education to "whiteness" as expressed in language, education, and the distorted relations of blacks and whites in the West Indies and in France; secondly, the analysis of the same phenomena, using the psychoanalytic tools he had begun to work with in Lyon and Saint Alban, in conjunction with what he had learned of the theoretical writings of psychoanalysis. He became convinced that only a psychoanalytic interpretation was suitable to an understanding of the human relations he described.[69] But he did not ignore the fact that these relations were themselves the product of a peculiar system which was more than the manifestation of psychological realities.

Black Skin, White Masks tends towards a psychoanalytic interpretation of racism. Its opening chapter is about the black man and language. It might as well be about any man whose native language is not the language of the country in which he lives, and who carries his own tongue as a cultural mark of Cain. Not only does Fanon explode the myth of the neutrality of language, he offers an astute elaboration of what it means to speak the language of the dominant class. Simultaneously a tool of integration into society, language is also the cultural vehicle of an elite whose values are accepted as normative. Hence, Fanon can write that for the Martiniquean to speak the Frenchman's French is to speak the language of the master, the language that opens doors to French culture and society. The French spoken in Martinique is not only shaded by the accents of the islands, it translates the intonations of the islander's status, it reflects the extent to which he is black, white, or a mixture of the two. The Martiniquean, to the degree that he wishes to progress in society, will learn the correct, Parisian French. If he is fortunate enough to afford a trip to the mother country, he will perfect his language there. In the interval, at home, he will train his children to speak correctly and thereby to assume the privileges of the culture that language offers. In the process he may also instill a sense of shame of the colloquial language, a part of the general denigration of native as opposed to metropolitan values.

The ambiguity inherent in the position of the Martiniquean is obvious and Fanon is, ironically, a perfect example of the lengths to which successful assimilation—linguistically—may lead. The Martiniquean knows that his destiny is French and white, hence he is impelled to progress in this direction; but the dimensions of his success will also determine the extent of his alienation.

The use of language as a tool of assimilation and the subsequent rebellion against linguistic integration and alienation have become familiar aspects of colonial life. What Fanon described in Martinique, symbolized by the choice between Creole and French, could be reproduced elsewhere in North Africa and the Middle East, wherever a colonial situation introduced a colonizer whose language differed from that of the colonized. Albert Memmi described the situation in Tunisia, Kateb Yacine and Malek Haddad wrote about their experiences in Algeria. An entire literature devoted to North African writers of French expression emerged in the years after the consolidation of French control.[70] But it was only as the reaction to that control and the resistance to its continuation became acute, that the revolution against the linguistic monopoly exercised by the colonizing power, took place. In Martinique as in the other territories under foreign control, it was the nature of the choice offered that prejudiced the situation in the interests of the colonizer. In the case of North Africa, the bulk of the population was illiterate to begin with, but the native intellectual elite that was educated—necessarily in the language of the colonizer and sometimes, though less frequently, also in its own language—invariably understood the nature of the choice offered. French was the key to admission to another world, the world of the West, of progress, and of power. But Arabic was the mother tongue and the language of the people. To choose both, as some tried to do, was perhaps the solution to the problem, but it was a difficult choice and it was made successfully by relatively few people. Fanon himself pursued this problem in his studies on Algeria and the depersonalization wrought by colonization, but his studies were not the only ones to touch on it. It has been poignantly described by writers who suffer a permanent nostalgia as a result of their inability to address their brothers in their own language. And it remains one of the most visible signs in Algeria today of the cultural and psychic damage brought about by colonization.[71]

In *Black Skin, White Masks* Fanon understood that the language question was symptomatic of the problem of assimilation. From his observations on the gamut of reactions provoked by the use of Creole, and the wide range of French spoken by Martiniqueans on the island and in France, he proceeded to an analysis of education and the process of acculturation. He did not pursue this in connection with his interest in language. It was, rather, in the section of his book devoted to "The Negro and Psychopathology," that he discussed the roots of pathology for the child brought up in a Martiniquean home and sent out into a white world. While contact with this different world was traumatic, the elements constituting the trauma had been set into motion before any kind of personal contact had ever been established between the child and the foreign adult world.

The beginning lay in the education a child received; an education which not only derived from an environment totally different from his own, but one in which he was taught to identify with the society from which he was excluded. And yet, as Fanon pointed out, until the Martiniquean child realized that his identity choice was based on the model of French whites, he did not begin to comprehend the dimensions of the drama being played out. Nor was it merely the contradiction between the temptations of assimilation and the reality of rejection, which would have been enough to produce shock. In the cultural matrix of white society, and in this instance the reference is to French and Martiniquean society, the educational process included, as was the norm, the ordering of aggression into socially acceptable channels. It was the purpose of some children's games, psychodramas, some folktales, to provide the catharsis which society needed to expel its collective anxieties. In many stories written in the main for white children, these characters who symbolized fear and evil were often represented by Indians or blacks.[72] The black child identifying with the hero found himself identifying with the white figure against the black one, i.e. against himself although he did not perceive this as such. Until the Antilles-West Indian child learns otherwise, and this occurs only when there is sufficient contact with white European society, he will be growing up in the image of the white models he reads about and will not be aware of any conflict. He is aware of himself simply as being. Fanon emphasized this with great effect in his reply to Mannoni's analysis of the Malagasy reaction to white men.

> It is of course obvious that the Malagasy can perfectly well tolerate the fact of not being a white man. A Malagasy is a Malagasy; or, rather, no, not he *is* a Malagasy but, rather, in an absolute sense he "lives" his Malagasyhood. If he is a Malagasy, it is because the white man has come, and if at a certain stage he has been led to ask himself whether he is indeed a man, it is because his reality as a man has been challenged. In other words, I begin to suffer from not being a white man to the degree that the white man imposes discrimination on me, makes me a colonized native, robs me of all worth, all individuality, tells me that I am a parasite on the world, that I must bring myself as quickly as possible into step with the white world. . . .[73]

Fanon realized that what he had described was applicable to any colonial situation where the colonizing power had established a strong base and had begun to penetrate the population. Where colonization remained superficial, indigenous culture could survive. But wherever colonization was more ambitious, where the educational processes were transformed, where the values of the dominant majority became the accepted values of society to the denigration of the local values of the minority, the same process was at work producing the same results.

Fanon was concerned with the dynamics of acculturation as well as with the effect which this process had on the individual and the community. He recognized that both sides were affected, the dominant and the dominated. It was this mutuality which was inherent in the discussion of human relations and communications in Hegel's master-servant paradigm. It was the same formula which Sartre applied to his anti-Semitic Christian and Jew which led him to affirm that it is the anti-Semite who creates the Jew. Fanon discovered that the alienated Martiniquean existed only where there was a dominant society that had reduced him to an inferior status. What concerned Fanon with respect to the Martiniquean, was the gradual process of alienation from his culture and tradition, and the fact that this was accompanied by self-hatred or at the least, a profoundly disturbed ambivalence. The rejection of self came as a result of identification with the Other and as a result of the acceptance of the Other's image of one's "inferior" caste.

So profoundly did this affect individuals that Fanon was led to wonder about the possibility of normal relations existing between the peoples concerned. It was this which led him to question whether sexual relations between blacks and whites were possible; that is, without the self-consciousness about each instilled in the other by a racist society. The question was not gratuitous and Fanon's examples could be multiplied in different places and times. Anyone familiar with human relations in a mixed society in which such mixture is superficially condoned but essentially condemned will readily agree with Fanon's discussion. Albert Memmi's novel *Agar* dealt with the same theme in a particularly moving way. *Agar* concentrates on the story of a mixed marriage, but it was not a mixed marriage that was Memmi's main interest.[74] What concerned him was the underlying question: Could two people of different cultures and traditions live with one another, and ultimately could people overcome the limitations and obstacles posed by exclusivist pretensions within society?[75]

In *Black Skin, White Masks,* Fanon analyzed the situation of a "Woman of Color and the White Man," in the case of Mayotte Capecia, a Martiniquean woman who had published her mildly scandalous memoirs under the title *Je suis martiniquaise* in Paris in 1948.[76] With the evidence he had gathered among other West Indians and Martiniqueans in France, and based on his own experience, Fanon concluded that sexual relations between women of color and white men contained all the diseased elements which French-Martiniquean society generated. Mayotte Capecia was an ideal case. A woman of mediocre talents who was completely unaware of the origins of her own prejudices and the roots of her self-hatred, she wrote freely about her attachments to various white men. What emerged was that Mayotte Capecia had been taught from a young age that whiteness was good; that given the choice between a man of color and a white man, there was no doubt as to whom she would choose. And yet in spite of her apparent naiveté she was not immune to being hurt by her favored Frenchman, André. Having spent a blissful time together, André left with the Admiralty for Guadeloupe and it was clear that Mayotte Capecia was not destined to follow. What was permissible within the context of the island, far from the society of white men and women, was not tolerable in other circumstances. Mayotte accepted her fate—which is what gives her book the bittersweet taste of self-hatred. So much does she share in the attitudes of the white French society that excludes her that she is shocked by the discovery that her Canadian grandmother had loved a Martiniquean. "How could a Canadian woman love a Martiniquean?" she asked. "I decided that I could never love anyone but a white man, a blond with blue eyes, a Frenchman."[77]

If the woman of color, in this case, hoped to be whitened l virtue of her proximity to the white lover, so the couple consisting of a black man and white woman—to the extent that they had not freed themselves of the conditioning imposed by their society—would be acting out more than a casual encounter in their own relationship. In his discussion of the black man vs. white woman, Fanon wrote about a character out of a novel by the Martiniquean writer René Maran. In *Un Homme pareil aux autres,* the hero, Jean Veneuse, is deeply in love with Andrée Marielle, a white woman. But to say this without adding more information about the man himself would distort the picture which Fanon intended to bring out. For Jean Veneuse is a sick man. Not only had he been abandoned as a child and therefore permanently afflicted with an abandonment neurosis, but he was brought up in a white environment that had further dislocated him. If the implicit theme of this novel was man's search for his identity, and for the legitimacy of his being, the combination of familial and societal abandonment could hardly have been matched. Jean is cursed by the extent of his successful assimilation. Constantly told that he is in spirit just like the other Frenchmen, and that his color is barely noticeable, he develops an intense desire to be accepted on his own terms. Fanon was careful to point out that Jean Veneuse did not represent an instance of black-white relations, but rather the case of a man who is neurotic and who happens to be black.[78] But for Veneuse himself the neurotic situation produced by abandonment only heightened an awareness of the conflict at issue. The question was not whether Jean Veneuse could be "cured," but whether it was possible, given the nature of the society he lived in, to have normal relations between men and women of different color.

The response to the situation he described in the case of Jean Veneuse and Mayotte Capecia was, for Fanon, the beginning of a long exploration into the historial and psychosexual origins of relations between men and women of different colors. It led him to explore the ideals of negritude and the psychic benefits of such a movement. It led him to consider the impact of the confrontation between blacks and whites and the group myths which seemed to operate in such circumstances. Working simultaneously as a psychiatrist, Fanon was faced with patients who daily acted out the situations he pondered. Eventually, he came to believe that it was not an individual neurosis that was at stake, but that relations were poisoned by a system that was at the core of the society itself. He concluded that a racist society contaminates all of its subjects, and that the individual resolution of the problem was not possible within a social context that perpetuated the condition. Past myths and present policies were opened for examination. The conclusions that followed led Fanon far from the practice of psychiatry or the contemplation of negritude. There are times, he quoted Pierre Naville as writing, when the social nexus is more important than the individual.[79]

> I came into the world imbued with the will to find a meaning in things, my spirit filled with the desire to attain to the source of the world, and then I found that I was an object in the midst of other objects.

> Sealed into that crushing objecthood, I turned beseechingly to others. Their attention was a liberation, running over my body suddenly abraded into nonbeing, endowing me once more with an agility that I had thought lost, and by taking me out of the world, restoring me to it. But just as I reached the other side, I stumbled, and the movements, the attitudes, the glances of the other fixed me there, in the sense in which a chemical solution is fixed by a dye. I was indignant; I demanded an explanation. Nothing happened. I burst apart. Now the fragments have been put together again by another self.[80]

The new self that put the fragments together had traveled a long path from the time of incoherent mute suffering and non-understanding, to the time of consciousness. It was a path that had led through a maze in which the guidance of thinkers like Hegel and Sartre had been critical. But they too belonged to the other world, the world that did not comprehend the being of the non-white man, and so they too would be guilty of either indifference or objectification. Sartre's analysis of the Jewish question touched Fanon precisely because the Jew among Christians was over-determined from within. He was judged irrespective of what and who he was and the judgment was imposed on him so that it became virtually impossible for him, in a predominantly Christian and anti-Semitic environment (and the two were not always identical) to free himself of the unstated views of his associates. The syndrome of ensuing self-hatred and shame were equally familiar. For both black man and Jew, contact with racism provoked similar reactions and derived from similar roots. The anti-Semite and racist were often one and the same man, and if they did not recognize their own compatibility, circumstances offered opportunities to cement their alliance. Sartre's description of the anti-Semite is close to Fanon's image of the racist.

He is a man who is afraid. Not of the Jews, to be sure, but of himself, of his own consciousness, of his liberty, of his instincts, of his responsibilities, of solitariness, of change, of society, and of the world—of everything except the Jews. He is a coward who does not want to admit his cowardice to himself; a murderer who represses and censures his tendency to murder without being able to hold it back, yet who dares to kill only in effigy or protected by the anonymity of the mob; a malcontent who dares not revolt from fear of the consequences of his rebellion. In espousing anti-Semitism, he does not simply adopt an opinion, he chooses himself as a person. He chooses the permanence and impenetrability of stone, the total irresponsibility of the warrior who obeys his leaders—and he has no leader. He chooses to acquire nothing, to deserve nothing; he assumes that everything is given him as his birthright—and he is not noble. He chooses finally a Good that is fixed once and for all, beyond question, out of reach; he dares not examine it for fear of being led to challenge it and having to see it in another form. The Jew only serves him as a pretext; elsewhere his counterpart will make use of the Negro or the man of yellow skin. The existence of the Jew merely permits the anti-Semite to stifle his anxieties at their inception by persuading himself that his place in the world has been marked out in advance, that it awaits him, and that tradition gives him the right to occupy it. Anti-Semitism, in short, is fear of the human condition. The anti-Semite is a man who wishes to be pitiless stone, a furious torrent, a devastating thunderbolt—anything except a man.[81]

To the anti-Semite, the Jew represents evil, an evil condoned by a mischievous interpretation of the history of Christianity, by a malicious deformation of the economic ambitions of Jews in restricted societies, and by an envy-ridden conception of the Jew as an omnipotent intellect. Irresponsible, in his own mind, for any of these conditions which he regards as self-evident, the anti-Semite feels justified in being afraid and finds no confusion in the bizarre combination of this alleged conspiratorial image fraught with sexual overtones which he has himself created. Fanon and others, such as Winthrop Jordan and Joel Kovel, for example, have paid close attention to the sexual connotations implicit in racist and anti-Semitic situations.[82] Sartre discussed the implications in his own essay with respect to the Jew and the Jewess, a word which he said seemed to carry the very odor of rape and violent seduction.[83] Eventually Fanon transferred the sexual analysis to the colonizer-colonized situation, as witness his discussion of the veil in *A Dying Colonialism.*

In *Black Skin, White Masks* Fanon wrote about the assumptions which the white man held about the black man; about his alleged sexual superiority; about his inordinate sexual appetite; about his "primitive" character. All of these images suggested the portrait of the black man as an inferior in the hierarchy of human development, but the characteristics could be applied to any other group of people in a comparable relationship vis-à-vis the "master race." Was it the illegitimacy of the position of the oppressor, regardless of his color or nationality, which resulted in the creation of the myth of the inferior, the colonized, as frightening, unclean, and invariably sexually threatening? Studies on the association of blackness with fear extend into more profound mysteries.[84] Joel Kovel, who has treated this theme in abundant detail in his study, *White Racism: A Psychohistory,* writes that "a mountain of evidence has accumulated to document the basically sexualized nature of racist psychology."[85] And he suggests that "sexuality in racism is not an isolated phenomenon but is most intimately connected with issues of power and dominance."[86]

For the majority of whites, wrote Fanon, black men represent an uneducated, primitive sexual instinct. Blacks incarnate genital power over and above societal prohibitions and morals.[87] In *Black Skin, White Masks* Fanon tried to go further with this association of sexuality and the white man's image of the black man. In the explanation of the myth "A Negro Is Raping Me," Fanon attempted to show how it was possible to expand theories of feminine sexuality by introducing the prevalence of the fantasy-ridden myth about blacks and their sexual-aggressive potency, into the developmental process of women.

Roger Bastide, who has written extensively on racism, contends that Fanon wrote from the "psychopathological standpoint," and that what he said ought to be understood as applying primarily to certain categories of people; to the West Indian, on the one hand, and to intellectuals on the other. "Sex," wrote Bastide, "can be properly understood only in its social context."[88] But did this contradict Fanon? On the contrary, Fanon himself was becoming progressively more aware of the fact that sex was understandable only in the social context. It was the social context affected by a racist society that made normal sexual relations between people of different races virtually impossible. Bastide seemed to come to the same view when he wrote that "it is not so much that love breaks down barriers and unites human beings as that racial ideologies extend their conflicts even into love's embraces.[89]

The more he delved into the psychopathology of his Martiniquean brothers, the more Fanon was led to ask himself, What should be the reaction of a man who discovers that he is "living in error"? Was it enough to conclude that "the Negro lives an ambiguity that is extraordinarily neurotic"?[90] Having learned that he is black, the Antillean also learned that blackness was identified with sin and evil. "In other words, he is a Negro who is immoral. If I order my life like that of a moral man, I simply am not a Negro. . . ."[91] What then? "Either I ask others to pay no attention to my skin, or else I want them to be aware of it."[92] It was in the midst of the realization of what his own error had been that Fanon turned to negritude. It was a discovery that produced a euphoric state, but from the outset Fanon appeared ambivalent about its consequences. "Out of the necessities of my struggle I had chosen the method of regression, but the fact remained that it was an unfamiliar weapon; here I am at home; I am made of the irrational; I wade in the irrational."[93] Here was history to deny those who pretended that the black man had no past of his own. Like others who suffer dispersion and recognize the strength that a common past brings, Fanon understood that for the black man, negritude, for all of its shortcomings, was a source of self-respect.

Even before reading Sartre's "Black Orpheus" Fanon had begun to express his doubts on the subject. In 1955, in an essay on relations between Antilleans and Africans, he reverted to this theme. Referring to the West Indian's discovery of his African past, he wrote:

> He discovered himself to be a transplanted son of slaves; he felt the vibration of Africa in the very depth of his body and aspired only to one thing: to plunge into the great "black hole."
> It thus seems that the West Indian, after the great white error, is now living in the great black mirage.[94]

Yet the need for this absolute, this mirage, was also clear. So much so that Fanon could describe Sartre's definition of negritude as a form of betrayal. "In any case I needed not to know," he wrote with shattering honesty.[95] He accused Sartre of having robbed him of his last chance; of having deprived him of the solution he had found—not to an intellectual dilemma but to his very being.[96] The hint of disdain in Fanon's restatement of what Sartre's position meant to him was an added sign of his own anguish. By the time he wrote *The Wretched of the Earth,* though even in the earlier essays collected in *Toward the African Revolution,* the tone was sharper and the feeling, less vulnerable. But in the earlier period, when he was composing *Black Skin,* Fanon appeared to continue the debate within himself, arguing for and against negritude, hiding his pain and then exposing it, to prove the difficulty with which he had accepted the necessity of rejecting this concept. His conclusion offered him this consolation:

> Still, in terms of consciousness, black consciousness is immanent in its own eyes. I am not a potentiality of something. I am wholly what I am. I do not have to look for the universal. No probability has any place inside me. My Negro consciousness does not hold itself out as a lack. It *is.*[97]

Sympathetic to negritude as a historical force and as a movement that had affected him in his own rediscovery of himself, Fanon nevertheless rejected it as an analytic tool capable of exposing racism and eliminating it. He turned, for a time, to what a psychological explanation could offer of men and relations in the context in which he studied them. He was to conclude after what appears to have been a hasty and incomplete study of the literature of psychoanalysis, that Freud and some of his successors were unaware of the existence of a black question and that their hypotheses were not applicable to non-white, non-western cultures. Given the importance of this too brief challenge, it is regrettable that Fanon never pursued the point. In his writing on Martiniqueans, he merely demonstrated that the concept of the family was so different in the Martiniquean as opposed to the French milieu that to borrow assumptions from the latter and apply them to Martiniqueans was guaranteed to produce errors. It was not only the process of socialization that was at work in the growing up of the Martiniquean child, but the necessity of making the transition from what he had come to accept as the norm in his family and community, to a society in which these elements were substantially different. What were the consequences for a European child who sensed the continuity between family, community, and nation, and the Martiniquean child who was aware of the discontinuity between family, community, and nation? The Martiniquean adolescent confronted with the French-European world discovered that he must make a choice between the values represented by his society and those offered by the French-European society. If he wished to transcend his family circle to the extent that he reached into the other world, he would have accepted the challenge of assimilation. What would be the results for him as an individual and for his society?

In reviewing the psychoanalytic studies he was familiar with, Fanon concluded that there was not enough sensitivity to these issues because of the Europocentric nature of the analysts. The most dramatic case that came to Fanon's attention and that was particularly relevant because of its treatment of colonialism, was the study by O. Mannoni, *Prospero and Caliban*.[98] Mannoni, a French psychoanalyst who has written on Freud, produced what might charitably be called an ambivalent analysis of the colonization enterprise. In the period in which he wrote *Prospero*, Mannoni recognized the need to prepare young men for a colonial career by giving them a "really modern psychology," the better to understand the natives and their relations to them.[99] That he had no doubts as to the nature of colonialism itself was obvious from his writing. But if he was a partisan of the process, it was precisely because he believed it corresponded to the psychic needs of those who were colonized—and in a different fashion, to the needs of the colonizers.

> To my mind there is no doubting the fact that colonization has always required the existence of the need for dependence. Not all peoples can be colonized: only those who experience this need. Neither are all peoples equally likely to become colonizers, for, as I shall show later, certain other equally definite predispositions are required for that role.[100]

To emphasize the point further, he added:

> Wherever Europeans have founded colonies of the type we are considering, it can safely be said that their coming was unconsciously expected—even desired—by the future subject peoples.[101]

According to Mannoni, colonization was made possible by an inherent dependency complex in the subject populations, a complex that was positively balanced by the high degree of individualism and self-dependency characteristic of Europeans. Hence, the peculiarly psychological combination satisfied by colonialism. The absence of any historical discussion that would explain the initial contact between allegedly inferior and superior populations, or how this balance was maintained, did nothing to improve Mannoni's credibility. Avoiding anything that could be construed as a political statement, Mannoni emphasized the predilection that certain peoples had for colonization, or more accurately, their predilection to be led. He was not averse to self-government or even to the benefits of democracy, but in the context he constructed, these appeared to be long-range possibilities that were perhaps irrelevant given the nature of the peoples concerned. To Fanon, the suggestion that colonization might be justified in this fashion was anti-historical and a distortion of psychoanalytic objectives. He not only contested the notion of a "dependency complex,"[102] but he challenged Mannoni's notion that inferiority is related to numbers. It is not because a man is a member of a numerical minority that he behaves like a member of a minority, according to Fanon, but because of the relationship in terms of power between the group that is the "minority" group and the other dominant group— which may not be at all in the majority. In Martinique, Fanon pointed out that roughly two hundred whites considered themselves superior to three hundred thousand members of the colonized population.

Mannoni's book deserves a careful reading and the selections cited here are perhaps the most flagrant. To a man like Fanon it was not only the abuse of the method that was distressing, but the underlying assumptions, the values of the man offering the conclusions. In addition, he must have been impatient with the non-political turn which Mannoni strove so intensely to project. As he progressed in his own work as a psychiatrist, he became increasingly concerned with the larger dimensions of the problems with which he dealt. He began to speculate on the function of the psychiatrist and on the limitations of the psychoanalytic approach. Both roads were to lead him away from psychiatry into politics, but not before Fanon had urged a more interventionist role for the psychiatrist—one that would put him in closer touch with the world of his patients. To a large extent he was encouraged by the example of his mentor, Professor Tosquelles, who conceived of the analyst as a man who lived in and was responsible for the same world that his patients knew in a different guise. There was no all-pervasive identity of doctor and patient here, only a breaking down of the more rigid and artificial walls that some assumed to separate them. For Fanon, there was no other way to proceed. It was in this frame of mind that he conducted his work in France, and it was with this attitude that he was to set out for Algeria in 1953.

-II-

TOWARD A PSYCHOLOGY OF COLONIAL RELATIONSHIPS, 1953–1959

Car enfin qu'est-ce qu'être des hommes neutres sinon
des hommes justes?

Aimé Césaire, *Une Saison au Congo.*

-1-

A View of Psychiatry and the Nature of Therapy

_____

By the time Fanon received his appointment to the psychiatric hospital in Blida-Joinville, in the fall of 1953, he had arrived at some general notions on the function of psychiatry and he had absorbed the methods of his professor, Dr. François Tosquelles. He intended to put some of the ideas he had seen implemented at Saint Alban into practice, and he was looking for a place that was more challenging to work in than Pontorson, Normandy. There are indications that he had wanted to work in Africa, and that he had contacted Léopold Sédar-Senghor to this effect, without a satisfactory response.[1] When Fanon arrived in Blida he was prepared to work as the director of a major psychiatric hospital, and to concentrate on those psychiatric problems that interested him. It was in the process of attempting to do this that he became aware of the futility of applying, in mechanical fashion, theories and methods based on European models. This was the first and the most critical break for Fanon in Blida. It made him aware of the necessity of studying local conditions, which was to prove a disconcerting matter.

When he arrived in Algeria, Fanon came to work with patients whose identity he did not know. Some were Frenchmen and some were Algerians; he treated both. It was first the failure of a mechanistic application of foreign techniques that forced him to take a longer look at Algerians vis-à-vis the medicine he offered them. It was only after this that he realized that he must broaden his consideration to include external realities that impinged on his patients' psyches. He was eventually to condemn the system he studied because he believed it to be destructive of human life. But he went further. He argued that psychiatrists and the entire medical profession were part of the society and hence no more objective than its other participants. He rejected the notion of neutral men and he emphasized the active role which psychiatrists, for instance, played in disseminating and perpetuating the values of society. In Algeria, what Fanon asked from his colleagues was that they be conscious of the system within which they worked; that they recognize the human consequences of the colonial system. In time, this realization was not enough.

As he came to believe in the illegitimacy of colonialism, Fanon was unsatisfied with a static consciousness of the situation. He left his medical practice in order to transform, in a more direct manner, what he considered to be an impossible system. That is, he abandoned psychiatry for politics. But long before he decided to do this, he was aware of the relationship between psychiatry and politics. He was critical of the implicit tolerance which he sensed among some of his colleagues and he interpreted it as a form of collaboration with the French administration against Algerians. The relation of psychiatry to politics is hardly a novel discovery and Fanon's position is in accord with the views of the anti-establishment psychiatrists active in the United States and in Europe.[2] What he shared with them is the realization that theirs is a profession that is not value-free; that it has the power to define normality and madness, and that these are politically potent terms. But more important is the consciousness that the world of the patient is not always exclusively the function of his illness, that the line that divides his perspective from that of the physician may be accounted for by more than the label of his disease.[3]

While Fanon was ultimately responsible for the nature of his commitments, that is, for his decision to translate his beliefs into political action, he was deeply influenced as a psychiatrist by the atmosphere prevalent at Saint Alban and by the views and personality of its director, Professor François Tosquelles. Tosquelles was also to be Fanon's thesis director and a close collaborator in years to come. When Fanon was granted admission to the hospital, Tosquelles and Saint Alban already had a considerable reputation. Geismar notes that "at the time, this doctor and his hospital were the model for numerous psychiatric reform projects within all of France."[4] Tosquelles had, and continues to have, definite views on the nature of psychiatry, and he was not reticent about expressing them. In 1953, on the occasion of a Congress at Pau, at which he and Fanon gave some joint papers, Tosquelles had the opportunity to discuss his views at some length.[5] He took the position that the compartmentalization of medicine that marked specialization had weakened it. The psychiatrist was aware of this atomization, and it was part of his function to combat it. His was an integrative role. Unlike other specialists, his concern was with the total behavior of his patients. He was concerned with the "physiology of expression," with the physiological and the psychic, the individual and the social dimensions of life. Tosquelles thought in terms of a unitary vision, a community of medicine, in which the results of each would be shared by all, to the common benefit of the man of science as well as the patient.

As for the individual patient, Tosquelles approached him with the utmost respect. There are times, he recognized, when one must accept the inability of the patient to cope with his situation. There are times when one must recognize that "illness is . . . a compromise or an armistice," and nothing less than the genius of the doctor is sufficient to reach the patient. Under all circumstances, he counseled his colleagues, and especially young psychiatrists, to pay utmost attention to the concrete life history of the patient, aside from the history of his psychic development. The doctor was to create a climate in which the patient would be led to situate his condition in a broader context. The process by which this occurred, the process of interviewing and questioning, was the first act in therapeutic treatment. Therapy was understood by Tosquelles, and later by Fanon, to operate within an institutional framework. This is the kind of situation in which both men worked. It coincided with their views on the role of medicine in the community, on the reponsibility of the doctor towards the entire community, and in a more general way, it reflected their reluctance to consider the individual in isolated treatment.

Tosquelles was deeply engaged in the promotion of sociotherapy, or what we know of as "milieu therapy," a form of treatment that places emphasis on "socio-environmental and interpersonal factors." He was eager to point out the differences between this and other kinds of therapy that took place in hospitals: work therapy, group therapy, and institutional therapy. While he was interested in all kinds of therapeutic treatment, his objective was to maximize the effectiveness of the institutional setting from the point of view of doctor and patient. In existing circumstances, he pointed out in the paper he wrote jointly with Fanon, the patient often receives considerably less treatment than he could or should. What Tosquelles wanted was to raise the consciousness of doctors and assistants in hospital settings so that they would not restrict therapy to certain hours of the day, or in the case of group therapy, to a particular limited formula. He speculated on the entire range of activities that occurred within the hospital setting and recommended that institutional therapy might be more meaningful if certain changes were made. What he urged was a transformation in the physical plant, and a transformation in the relationships of the hospital staff.

In 1953 and again in 1956, writing with a number of colleagues from Saint Alban, Tosquelles recommended a reevaluation of the organization of hospitals from a therapeutic viewpoint. In 1953 he insisted on the importance of the layout and the need to group patients according to new methods. He maintained that the physical plant was instrumental in effecting treatment.[6] In 1956 he and his colleagues raised the issue of centralization and urged the reversal of the trend.[7] They spoke of decentralization on the ground that this was beneficial for some patients, and more efficient for all concerned. Tosquelles and his colleagues did not hesitate to express their concern with the condition of hospitals as they saw them. They indicated that for the most part, the patient was the least important element in the hospital situation; that depersonalization and bureaucratization were destroying the purposes for which hospitals had been created. The criticism is similar to that heard in England and in the United States today, where psychoanalysts and sociologists—not to speak of patients—seem increasingly preoccupied with the paradox of the negative potential of hospitals in treatment.[8]

Tosquelles argued that small units composed of from ten to twelve patients were immeasurably superior to larger groups, which encouraged a sense of anomie. To create small communities linked together in "quarters" which would be loosely coordinated at the central level in a hospital of roughly six hundred persons, was an imaginative reconstruction of the human community within the confines of an institution.[9] It offered the opportunity for interaction and support that combined elements of spontaneity with direction. The patient was not isolated, nor was he totally at the mercy of his peers. Each community, the nuclear group, was to provide patients with the means of self-expression and with the means of taking advantage of existing psychiatric treatment. This was to include work therapy within the larger perspective of group and institutional therapy.

Tosquelles was conscious of the value of having teams of doctors and nurses instead of relying on a single individual, even if that was materially possible."A single doctor does not allow for the rapid resolution of most oedipal or pre-oedipal conflicts which patients project or 'incarnate' during the course of their illness."[10] There was a conscious effort to avoid this situation by working with several doctors and by making greater use of the nursing staff. For Tosquelles, nurses were an essential part of therapy. They were the link between the doctor and patient, and often knew more of the patient's situation than the doctor who saw patients infrequently. This increased responsibility placed on nurses was the key to intensifying the special care which only private clinics could offer. It was a felicitous arrangement which fitted the requirements of large public institutions without sacrificing the patient or the staff.

Close attention was also paid to the question of admissions policy for fear that a too rapid or random admission threatened the orderly procedure of the hospital. Turning to the organization of patients Tosquelles recommended a relaxation of the rigid formula whereby patients were divided according to age, culture, and nature of illness. In 1953 at Pau, he indicated that this fixed organization was not necessarily constructive and that it might be positively harmful if it served to identify patients with certain pathological phases of their development. The question of reforming hospitals was motivated by the desire to transform institutions so that they would end the patient's sense of alienation and not increase it. It was an uphill battle.

Sensitivity to form and function within the hospital context was demonstrated in a short piece written by the Saint Alban group for the Bordeaux Congress of 1956.[11] It dealt with the role of the court in the hospital, and the uses to which it might be put. Tosquelles and his collaborators, Gentis, Paillot, Bidault, and Enkin, questioned the purpose of the court and recommended that it be incorporated into the hospital instead of serving as an external decoration for a limited number of staff. It was not a misguided sense of democracy that inspired them, but their desire to undo the static conception of the hospital and to diminish the difference between the hospital as a community and the world outside. It pointed again to their belief that the hospital ought to be something more than a bureaucratic center to which sick people were assigned. "We do not ignore the fact," they wrote, "that to present the problem as we do suggests a 'global' conception of hospitals. The court can only disappear, in a functional sense, if the entire hospital becomes, so to speak, a court. This means that the 'gardens' are no longer administrative buildings, but that they become part of the patients' community."[12]

This global conception of the hospital involved a permanent flexibility—not only in the sense of reconsidering their practices, but with respect to patients in the implementation of a transferal system touched on earlier. This was illustrated in a paper written by Tosquelles and Fanon, entitled "Sur un essai de réadaptation chez une malade avec épilepsie morphéique et troubles de caractère graves"[13] (On an attempt at readaptation in the case of a patient suffering from narcolepsy and serious character disorders). It was a case study of sociotherapeutic methods applied to a twenty-eight-year-old woman who had been described as "inaccessible to all psychotherapy."[14]

The young woman had been transferred to Saint Alban on the request of a Dr. Despinoy, who was at the hospital and who had formerly been a student of the doctor in charge of the patient's treatment at the Vinatier hospital, where she had previously been. Described as a young woman who had been admitted to Vinatier in 1944, the patient had been found at the railroad station of Perrache, "disoriented or confused," after having seen her mother and father killed near her in the course of a bombardment at Saint Lo. The descriptions of her condition at Vinatier left little reason to hope that a new environment would prove more beneficial. Given to melancholy and attempts at suicide, she had also had numerous and increasingly regular epileptic fits.[15] Dr. Christy, who had treated her, recommended that she be transferred to a psychiatric hospital and confined. He indicated that he believed her to be virtually immune to successful therapy.

In writing their observations on this case, Fanon and Tosquelles endorsed Dr. Christy's pessimism, indicating that the patient had indeed demonstrated grievous symptoms, but they also indicated that she had been kept in a cell for almost eight years—or as they put it, "during eight years, she had to be kept almost constantly in a cell, in a strait jacket. She had become the privileged object and the most enterprising subject of the free play of sado-masochistic myths so often incarnated in our psychiatric institutions."[16] Despinoy's decision to remove her from Vinatier and to take her into Saint Alban was recognized as a test and a challenge.

The admission of the patient was full of difficulties of adjustment for her as well as for the other patients in the quarter to which she was assigned. Fanon and Tosquelles discussed the medication she was given and the tests performed to have an indication of her condition. They repeated her own very revealing statement at the beginning of a turning point in her stay at Saint Alban, when she admitted the difficulty in transferring from a large institutional setting to an almost familial atmosphere where no one was in uniform and there was even a certain gaiety in the air.[17] The medical and psychiatric observations were carried out in different ways. The medical tests posed no difficulty and were performed directly. Psychiatric treatment was offered in the form of work therapy in which the entire quarter worked at some project, such as the newspaper (primitive to be sure) which every quarter possessed, and in which this particular patient had become interested. There was collective or group therapy which provided another occasion for the kind of observation desired. In the second phase of this patient's history, she had improved to the extent of playing a role within the quarter which allowed her to leave freely for various purposes. Fanon and Tosquelles pointed out the fears created by this venture, from the point of view of other patients.

At Saint Alban, the conclusions drawn from the case of the woman from Vinatier were these. In the first place, the doctors endorsed the idea of transferring patients from one hospital to another, for the same reason that they endorsed the idea of transferring patients from one quarter to another within the same hospital. Certain conditions were associated with particular environments and the transfer could operate to provide external support to another phase of development. Maintaining patients within the same environment, irrespective of their own changed situations, and ignoring their sensitivity to the surroundings in which they found themselves might mean perpetuating a condition that could otherwise have been altered.[18] The second conclusion concerned the use of hypnotic agents against certain depressed states, and argued for a reevaluation of the use of barbiturates for the same purpose. This was a theme which Fanon and Tosquelles returned to often in their writing.[19]

The second case which is of interest is that entitled, "Sur quelques cas traités par la méthode de Bini"[20] (On several cases treated by the Bini method). There are two issues to be pointed out here. The first has to do with the continued illustration of institutional therapy, the second has to do with the use of shock treatment which Tosquelles and Fanon recommended with moderation and care. Because the emphasis in this text is on the therapeutic innovations and particularly on Tosquelles' conception of sociotherapy, little attention is paid to the important and justly controversial matter of shock treatment. For a complete evaluation of Tosquelles' and Fanon's methods as reported in these cases, a more comprehensive review of all of their practices would have to be made.

The case of the forty-five-year-old nun who comes to Saint Alban reproduces some of the characteristics already seen in the case of the twenty-eight-year-old woman from Vinatier. The patient, as described by the doctor who had had her transferred to Saint Alban, was seen as suffering serious mental troubles, characterized by delusions of persecution, and serious behavioral deformations.[21] Fanon and Tosquelles phrased their diagnosis as a paranoia with symptoms of conversion hysteria. They proceeded to offer treatment which combined therapy and medication. At first, the patient was subjected to an intense, active interventionist therapy designed to show her the nature and extent of her condition and to force her to confront herself as a patient. This was followed by a transfer of location and by a reproduction of the hospital environment, in the traditional sense. The patient, having recognized her condition, was comforted by finding herself in an institution with appropriate sources of care. From this stage on, there was an attempt to allow the patient to relive her life from the earliest time to the present, with an almost theatrical shifting of environments relevant to each stage. What is significant for the quarter-sociotherapy treatment is the constant reference to the environment and the supportive role which the other patients and members of the same quarter play, offering an opportunity for interaction with the patient, in keeping with her particular stage of development. In summing up, Fanon and Tosquelles recorded that their patient had been hospitalized for three months; during a five-day period of extreme depression she received 17 electro-shock treatments; she was subjected to 40 sessions of insulin therapy; and a total of 40 days of directed institutional therapy.

Bearing in mind the import of each element in the total treatment of the case, its outcome appears to have been a relative success.

- 2 -

Blida-Joinville and the
Experiment That Failed

The papers presented by Tosquelles and Fanon at the Pau
Congress in 1953 had been offered in July.[22] In the same month,
Fanon satisfactorily passed the examinations in pathology,
neurology, forensic medicine, and other areas, including the
oral examination of patients in the presence of a team of physicians. This allowed him to qualify for the prestigious title of
Chef de service, which in turn meant that he was eligible to
become the director of one of France's psychiatric hospitals,
either within metropolitan France or in the territories. Fanon
originally went to Pontorson, in Normandy. It was an experience
that convinced him that this was not the place for him. There is
some disagreement as to how he managed to get to Blida-Joinville. Renate Zahar states that it was on the invitation of Robert
Lacoste, whom she erroneously claims was in Algeria in 1953 at
the time Fanon applied.[23] This seems unlikely, not only for
political reasons, but because the procedure for application to
such service would not have gone through the Governor General's hands at this stage. Furthermore it would be an error to
project Fanon's ideas backward in time. Fanon may not have
anticipated becoming as involved as he did in Algeria; and Lacoste, in turn, may not have heard about Fanon until 1956, when
he arrived in Algeria himself. Still, the explanation that Peter
Geismar offers seems to be the most reasonable one. That is,
that while at Pontorson, Fanon read an advertisement for an

opening for a position at his level in a professional journal. The location of the position was Blida-Joinville, and Fanon applied.[24]

In November 1953, then, Fanon arrived in Algeria on his way to Blida-Joinville as Chef de service of the largest psychiatric hospital in Algeria. The conditions which he found on his arrival, not only in Blida, but in all of Algeria, with respect to medical and particularly to psychiatric care, were not encouraging. In 1954 and in 1955, Fanon published, with other doctors, two very important articles on this matter. The study which appeared in *L'Information psychiatrique* is what I refer to as "the experiment that failed." I believe it represents a critical turning point in Fanon's understanding of certain political and psychiatric problems in the Algerian context. The 1955 study was a comprehensive survey of psychiatric care in Algeria, written by a group of doctors who practiced at Blida-Joinville.[25]

"Aspects actuels de l'assistance mentale en Algérie," published in *L'Information psychiatrique*, by Doctors Fanon, D'Equequer, Lacaton, Micucci, and Ramée, portrayed Algerian medicine in 1955, or at least the psychiatric branch of it, as in grave need of aid.[26] The doctors pointed out that between the increasing number of patients applying for admission to mental hospitals and the numbers of Algerians in France who were being repatriated and who were in need of assistance, existing facilities were severely limited. They provided a brief survey of the origins of psychiatric care in Algeria, in institutional form, from 1932 to 1955. It was in 1932, under the French doctors Lasnet and Professor Porot, the latter a man whose name is well known and a persistent source of controversy, that psychiatric assistance was first introduced into the country.[27] By a decree of the following year, psychiatrists were actively recruited, primarily from metropolitan France. In time this preference was to deprive Algerians of a cadre of physicians and psychiatrists for which, even after independence, they are still seeking to compensate. In 1934 the lines had been set, and psychiatric institutions were in operation in Algiers, Oran, Constantine, and Blida. Porot was responsible for urging the administration—with little success—to allocate additional funds to expand medical-psychiatric care.

In 1954 the situation was roughly as follows: for a population of 10 million, including 8.5 million Muslims and 1.5 million Europeans, there were 8 psychiatrists and 2,500 beds.[28] Under such circumstances psychiatric care was necessarily limited.

In September 1954 the authors noted that the waiting list for admission to Blida-Joinville contained no less than 850 names. Among these 850 people, the largest category was that described as "native-males," which numbered 583, with "native-females" accounting for the second highest number of 141. The rest were Europeans. Most likely, more Europeans were able to afford private care than Algerians, so that the comparative figures may not be an accurate measure of the condition of the population. Fanon and his collaborators were sensitive to the problems of delays in admission, not only for the patients who sometimes waited as much as one year, but for their families who suffered with them and sometimes against them, aggravating their conditions in a serious manner. The question of payment for treatment was another source of difficulty, since those patients who applied for free admission were subjected to a lengthy examination designed to make certain of their destitute nature. There is no point belaboring this issue since it can be repeated in any country that lacks adequate medical care, and that has to exercise a selective process of admission in which financial considerations play a part.

Crowded conditions were accepted as a matter of course and this, in turn, seriously affected the kind of treatment that could be offered. A hospital built with a capacity for 971 patients was housing more than 2,000 people, and areas planned for specific use, even rooms originally constructed for bathing, were transformed into dormitories. Therapy was necessarily limited where there was barely room for anything other than minimal care. This was in marked contrast with the provisions for medical equipment, which appear to have been favored over and above the allotment made for psychiatric care. Nevertheless, at Blida-Joinville, Fanon and the group of doctors with whom he worked managed to accomplish far more than one might have imagined possible. The effort to introduce something like the Saint Alban model was attempted with considerable success. I leave aside for the moment the famous failure described earlier. In 1955, one year after the learning experience which he wrote up with Dr. Azoulay, Fanon and the other doctors at Blida-Joinville who sympathetized with his thinking managed to introduce the sociotherapeutic environment that Fanon had seen in operation in France. Given the circumstances it was remarkable that they had

a newspaper functioning, that the "cafés-maure" were in operation, that entertainment was offered and organized by doctors,
nurses, and patients, and that religious holidays were celebrated
in some meaningful if modest fashion.

Not only was there concern lest circumstances prohibit adequate treatment, there was a recognition of the psychological
problems that arise in the post-hospital phase. These varied
from one individual to another, and they also depended on the
family, community, and cultural environment into which a patient was reintegrating. The Muslim woman who might have
been divorced on her admission into a hospital would be returning to her family. They might be difficult to locate, and when
located, other prejudices against divorce and the implications of
psychiatric hospitalization might also come into play. Entering
a foreign world, such as that of the European capital, however,
was regarded as too difficult and definitely discouraged.

If psychiatric care was limited, so were the services involving
partial care. In many instances they were nonexistent. In other
cases, cooperation by the family was essential to carry out a
transition process, and given distance or material difficulties,
such care would not be available. Under such circumstances,
one might well ask what real possibilities of treatment existed.
The situation generally worsened the further away from the
capital one moved. The solution proposed by the medical-psychiatric team of Blida-Joinville involved the creation of post-
hospitalization centers and the training of select people in the
rudiments of mental health. Some years later, while in Tunis,
Fanon worked out an alternative solution to the problems of
overcrowded facilities in the form of daytime hospitalization,
and variations of the "open-door" policy he had learned about
from English experience.[29]

In 1954, one year after he had arrived, Fanon and a colleague
published an article on their experience at the Blida-Joinville
hospital. "La Socialthérapie dans un service d'hommes musulmans" (Sociotherapy in a ward of Muslim males) discussed the
methodological difficulties they had encountered as a result of
trying to apply techniques and conceptions derived from one
culture and environment to another.[30] It was an important experience for the doctors at Blida, and for Fanon, it was the beginning of an awakening to the cultural and political background
essential to an understanding of what Blida and Algeria were

about. Little by little, Fanon and Azoulay noted they had learned to approach the men of this culture in an attentive manner; and gradually the bits and pieces of the puzzle of their failure began to fit together.[31] The account of sociotherapy in the Muslim male ward is really an account of Fanon's attempt to apply Tosquelles' methods to Blida. To a large extent, he was successful and even his failure contributed to his long-range success, in the sense of his comprehension and reform of hospital practices. To judge by the people who remember Fanon's stay at the hospital, this was not marked by a tentative approach.

Fanon and his wife Josie were given a special house designated for the Chef de service.[32] It is a modest but comfortable house surrounded by greenery and altogether peaceful, as is the atmosphere of the Blida complex. This atmosphere must have been nothing more than a superficial impression to those who were present when Fanon arrived. Within one week after his appearance Fanon was carrying out what are still regarded as feats. He had interviewed as many doctors and nurses as he could when he first arrived. He asked them what their ideas of mental illness were, and he made it clear that unlike his predecessor he did not regard his role as a passive one. He meant to be a working doctor and teacher, for Blida was not only a hospital but a teaching institution. And in effect, Fanon's influence was felt in his dealings with patients, colleagues, and students. As in other mental hospitals of the day, at Blida patients considered seriously ill or dangerous were confined to their beds by being tied to the springs. When Fanon saw this he wasted little time in changing the situation. He walked through the hospital wards unchaining men and women, informing them that henceforward they would be free to walk and talk, to consult with him and with other doctors and nurses. The effect was electric. Those who were witnesses to the event recall it as a historic day for Blida.

Today, in the house which is under the protective eye of Mr. Longo, the remarkable man in charge of the Jauberty Pavilion to which epileptic cases are assigned, the evidence of Fanon's influence is eagerly pointed out. Not only do patients walk around freely, they are encouraged to paint and engage in crafts which were initially introduced by Fanon. According to Longo, it was Fanon who promoted a sense of pride in the place in which these men lived, and the rooms—once cells—were shown off as

proof of the new look. While it would be unfair to suggest that
no one other than Fanon was sensitive to the needs and the
restrictions of his patients, there seems to be a general consensus among men of his generation, that he introduced something
which others had not dared try. The same vitality and irrever-
ence for tradition that was to cause so much unhappiness among
traditional members of the staff, was the condition that allowed
that hasty and profound transformation of the hospital from a
prison ward to a quarter inhabited by patients.

Fanon arrived and promptly set to work. He found that there
were some five to six doctors to care for roughly two thousand
patients.[33] Tosquelles' insistence on the need for team work was
impossible. The group was near exhaustion and to work consistently together would have brought it to a point of collapse.
Because of this, though still under the guidance of Tosquelles,
whose ideas had become so much a part of his thinking, Fanon
made greater use of the male nurses. It is in fact many of these
highly competent people who remain at Blida today. Under the
colonial regime, they had been deprived of the opportunity to
become physicians and psychiatrists. For Fanon they were important because of the shortage of personnel and because they
were closer to the patients in time and in feeling than the European staff. Nurses were useful in communicating with patients,
in translating Arabic and Kabyle into French, which few of the
European staff could do. This was a problem which troubled
Fanon greatly and he sought to remedy it by learning Arabic.
The effort was stillborn, but he did not fail to recognize the
effect of language on the therapeutic situation.[34]

Shortly after his arrival in Blida-Joinville, Fanon and the staff
assigned to work with him proceeded to a reorganization of the
hospital. That this was the cause of some stir, particularly among
the older traditional members of the staff who regarded Fanon
as a young foreign meddler in their affairs, is not surprising.
Nevertheless, at least while he was present at Blida, the work
which Fanon sought to do in the Tosquelles tradition was accomplished. The effort was greater and the difficulties were
other than those anticipated. In the division of the hospital
complex in which he worked there were 165 European women
and 220 Muslim men.[35] They were segregated, which permitted
Fanon and Azoulay to realize the different impact their operations had on both groups. What they initially planned to in-

troduce were bi-weekly meetings of the pavilion, meetings of the staff, meetings of the newspaper, and bi-monthly holidays. The results were quickly apparent in the women's division. Christmas was celebrated in the new fashion with the participation of the staff. Special committees in charge of movies, records, and the newspaper were set up. Fanon and Azoulay wrote that the editorial policy of the paper sought to "promote the thought of the hospital in its entirety,"[36] which perhaps was more wishful thinking than fact.

> Fanon's new newspaper in the hospital, *Notre Journal*, never worked out the way he had envisaged it would. The Moslems couldn't read, nor did the European patients care much about writing for it: the paper was most successful in providing a new kind of work therapy to those who printed it. Reading through several years of the back issues re-enforces the concept of Fanon, quite often alone, continuing to work for a better hospital amidst the apathy and hostility of most of his peers, the European doctors. Each weekly issue had an editorial by Fanon; the rest of the paper was the work of the nurses; once in a great while there was an article by a patient. The only other doctor who ever contributed to *Notre Journal* was Lacaton. Fanon used the paper to defend his own reforms within the institution and as part of the new training program for nurses. Weekly, the doctor would describe details of new plans for extended work therapy as well as remind the staff of the benefits that had accrued from older projects. Each ward had its own section within the paper in which nurses would speak of the patients' gardens, the woodwork completed, plans for religious celebrations, the fabric being woven in the women's workshops, and so on. *Nortre Journal* continued to urge all of the staff and patients to think of new ways to make daily life within the institution more interesting and pleasant.[37]

In spite of the skepticism suggested by this interpretation, the success of the experiment was greater than might have been anticipated. The joint participation of staff and patients created that sense of community which Tosquelles had spoken about, and the net effect seemed beneficial. Work therapy operating on an individual level supplemented the committee activity. From the point of view of Fanon and Azoulay, there was so much of an improvement in the attitude and condition of the patients, that there was a marked acceleration in the dismissal proceedings.[38] It was in contrast with this experience that the total failure of the same techniques applied in the division of the Muslim men appeared so striking.

At the outset, the method used in this section was the same as that applied in the women's division. Regular meetings were called between patients and staff, doctors and nurses included. The first problem encountered was that of the language barrier, but here the nurses were used with good results. Attention was paid to these gatherings to impress patients with the importance attributed to them by the doctors. But the results were not encouraging. While the staff discussed the committees and plans for movies, holidays, and the newspaper, the patients seemed to linger in their own private worlds, talking to one another or more often to themselves. After a time, meetings were abandoned since it became clear that they were meaningless to the patients and difficult for the staff. Instead of giving up the entire process, another attempt was made. This time, smaller groups of patients were selected by the nurses, the assumption being that those with potential for cooperation would be singled out. Once again the efforts were unproductive. The games chosen to create the desired atmosphere were useless and at the end of the time allotted for the experiment, the nurses were pessimistic as to what could be done. The next step was to concentrate on a festival of sorts, with music and theatrical presentations. But this time the nurses assigned to organize this refused, and after a new group of nurses were selected who again refused, the plan was abandoned. Some of the patients in the male group participated in activities organized by the women's division that were open to them, such as movies and other recreational programs. But even there, the men did not sit out the entire performance and it was noted that their participation had something haphazard about it. The newspaper introduced into the male group was a total failure and when it did appear it was only read by the nurses. As for efforts at work therapy, some such efforts had existed before Fanon came to the hospital and they were continued. There were some doubts as to the therapeutic value of these activities, the feeling being that the patients were simply distracting themselves as best they could. Special attempts to introduce work therapy involving straw weaving were made, but the patients' interest was minimal. After three months, the staff was forced to admit that the atmosphere was tense and progress was nil. In describing their failure, Fanon and Azoulay made it clear that the staff assigned to them had been so burdened with routine activities, that their experiment was an added and unwanted responsibility.

To those members of the staff who were hostile to Fanon's innovations, the failure to change the character of the male ward was merely a confirmation of their views. Convinced that patients were unfit for the activities introduced by this European doctor unfamiliar with the Algerian scene, they were not perturbed by his failure to effect a change. But Fanon and Azoulay, and those nurses who were beginning to develop a sense of loyalty to the new doctor and his ideas, thought otherwise. They were impressed and encouraged by what had occurred among the women, where the innovations had taken hold and where a significant change was visible. Why had the same plan failed so totally among the men? Instead of resigning themselves to failure, Fanon and Azoulay concentrated on a study of their division and particularly, on the character of their patients.

This was the turning point. In their auto-critique the two doctors pointed out that they had committed a cardinal error in automatically assuming that they could impose the techniques of one milieu to another without paying attention to the nature of the group to which they were applying their methods.[39] The first rule was to conduct a stringent examination of the nature of the community, in this case, the nature of the Algerian male community within the hospital. In restrospect they asked themselves how it was possible to function on the basis of a theoretical analysis that was not grounded in the particular geographical, historical, cultural, and social milieu of the group in which they worked. Their answers had implications that could not be lost on their colleagues and that determined their own subsequent course of action. It was far beyond the gates of Blida-Joinville that Fanon and Azoulay went, as indeed, it was far beyond the hospital complex that they had to go in order to discover the roots of their difficulties.

In providing an account of their work, Fanon and Azoulay reviewed their operative assumptions, suggesting that these were automatically accepted by others in their position. Hence, it was taken for granted in this circle that North Africa was French and no special effort need be made to understand another culture. In addition, the psychiatrist "adopts an assimilationist policy," hence the burden of effort lies with the "native" who has to fit himself into the European mold which is expected of him. The psychiatrist is, therefore, not under any obligation to understand the "native" in his cultural uniqueness. "Assimilation in this instance does not assume any reciprocity in perspectives. There is an entire culture that must disappear to the advantage of another."[40] Referring to themselves, the authors noted that in their "Muslim service," aside from the need for an interpreter, no effort was made to adapt to or get to know the circumstances of the patients. Having admitted their error, the authors indicated that "a revolutionary attitude was indispensable, for it was essential to go from a position where the supremacy of western culture was evident, to a cultural relativism." They pursued their auto-critique in these terms.

> Finally, and above all it must be said that those who preceded us in the exposition of the North African psychiatric reality, limited themselves too much to motor phenomena and neuro-vegetative conditions, etc. The work of the Algerian school, if it has revealed certain peculiarities, has nevertheless not proceeded to a functional analysis that appears to be indispensable. It was necessary to alter perspectives, or at least to complete or carry out some elementary perspectives. It was necessary to attempt to seize the North African reality. It was necessary to require this "totality," in which Mauss sees the guaranty for an authentic sociological study. A leap had to be made, a transmutation of values had to be carried out. Let us admit it, it was necessary to go from the biological to the institutional, from natural existence to cultural existence.
>
> The biological, the psychological, the sociological, had only been separated by an aberration of the spirit. In practice they were undifferentiatedly linked. It was as a result of not having integrated the notion of Gestalt and contemporary anthropology in our daily practice that we suffered such rude failures.[41]

Describing the participation of a group of Muslim women in parties organized in the European pavilion, the authors were struck by the different nature of their response. This led them to ask how it was possible to ignore the "social morphology" and "forms of sociability" of a cultural group. The next step was to investigate the values of the other society, the society of the men that had failed to respond. "What are the biological, moral, aesthetic, cognitive, religious values of Muslim society?" Increasingly, the authors attempted to take stock of the cultural roots of the Algerian patient whose identity they had previously ignored. There is a reference in this work to a study of North African society being written by one of the authors. "In a work in preparation, one of us will show the complexity of North African society, which at the present time is undergoing profound structural changes."[42] Was this Fanon's *A Dying Colonialism*? There is no clue in the text, but the the nature of the description fits what Fanon later wrote.

In their investigation of Algeria and Muslim society, the authors produced a collection of facts and bits of historical data which honor their efforts more than the subsequent reputation of Fanon, at least, as an expert on Algeria. Fanon and Azoulay discovered, for instance, that an Islamic society is a theocratic society, and there is no room in it for secularism. Algeria, they went on to announce, is also a society in which the elders of the community play an important role. In fact they discovered that communal organization per se existed on several levels; from the role of the elders they proceeded to look into the *djemaa*, the community itself, and then the municipal council. They wrote that "at least until recent times, there did not exist a real national community, but more of a familial clan-community." The remark is of more than usual interest given Fanon's later involvement in the nationalist movement.

While they may have appeared naive in a political sense, Fanon and Azoulay recognized that there had been fundamental changes going on in the economic structure of society since the advent of the French. Thus they took note of the change in property ownership resulting from the French presence and colonization. They indicated that a movement of dislocation was taking place in Muslim society whereby former landowners found themselves tenants on their own land. Others, having become landless, were migrating towards big urban centers, vaguely hoping to find employment near the cities. Instead they were to form the lumpenproletariat that Fanon wrote about in *The Wretched of the Earth,* the revolutionary allies of the peasants. In 1954, Fanon and Azoulay noted that this segment of the population was being swollen by the integration of nomads who had come north and gradually abandoned their traditional life styles. Attracted by the cities, they were soon to find themselves unemployed and living in a fashion far removed from their imaginary conceptions of city life. This bidonville population was to be a political force during the revolutionary period, but at this time, Fanon and Azoulay wrote, it not only constituted a defiance to aesthetic considerations, it was a "grave danger from the point of view of sanitation and morale."[43]

In trying to define the Blida-Joinville hospital population the two doctors broke down the Muslim population into the following categories: of 220 patients, there were 35 *fellahin,* farmers who cultivated small strips of land; 76 workers, agricultural day laborers, or tenants; 78 workers such as bakers and painters; 5 intellectuals, and 26 men listed as being without profession. In interpreting these figures, Fanon and Azoulay warned against being unduly impressed by the proportion of workers. Of the 78 probably no more than 20 or so could vouch for some kind of specialization. As for the intellectuals, they were teachers with a minimum of training. The conclusions Fanon and Azoulay drew from these figures was that they constituted a form of evidence for that societal transformation which they sensed beneath the surface of Algerian society. While numbers were lacking and figures had to be interpreted with care, existing evidence suggested a measure of change that involved the disruption of traditional cadres of organization. These facts, the authors maintained, had to be taken into consideration in the application of sociotherapeutic techniques.

Reviewing their failure, the doctors asked themselves what errors they had committed in their earlier experiments and what could be done to correct them. The language question reappeared, but this time the analysis of the problem was interpreted differently. It was acknowledged that the inability of doctors to communicate directly with patients required the presence of Arabic- and Kabyle-speaking interpreters. This removed the doctor from the patient in that it placed someone between them, a man whose presence facilitated and also damaged that intimacy which was a prerequisite of therapy. But it was not only for medical reasons that this third party was a disturbing factor. The presence of the interpreter underlined the gap between those generally in charge and the mass of the population. The authority was French and French-speaking and the population was Algerian and, for the majority, Arabic-speaking. The staff of Blida-Joinville was representative of that authority, and the inability of the doctors to communicate with Algerians reproduced a situation that was all too familiar. "In normal periods, the patient has already found this image of the interpreter in his relations with the administration or with justice. In the hospital the same need for an interpreter spontaneously produces a mistrust that renders all 'communication' difficult."[44]

As they reviewed their attempts to introduce holidays, movies, newspapers and certain kinds of theatrical performances into the Algerian ward, these activities began to appear in a different light. On the basis of what they had learned about their patients' lives, the doctors realized that they had acted without a proper sense of the ambiance into which they had entered. Theater was not a familiar sport, nor was the production of a newspaper particularly profitable since the vast majority of Algerian patients were barely literate. Holidays that were not of Muslim origin had little meaning for Muslims, and the kind of socializing common to the European section was often foreign to the Algerians. Choral groups for example were unpopular and other forms of group activity were found to be more appropriate. It was a matter of discovering the relevant activities and introducing them in such a manner that they could provide the same supportive and therapeutic function which the activities introduced into the European ward had accomplished.

To make this transition and to understand its implications were a major task. It appeared to some of Fanon and Azoulay's colleagues that the enthusiasm of these two men was excessive. They were neither grieved at their failure, nor prepared to follow in their new footsteps. In their own terms, their positions were understandable. Fanon was coming to appreciate the fact that psychiatric innovations were worse than useless unless they were grounded in the particular human history to which they were to be applied. Abstract notions that were dignified by being called universal or neutral were merely the product of false reasoning, or worse. To have introduced work therapy and sociotherapy was perhaps controversial enough, or merely disruptive of traditional ways of doing things, but to attribute failure to the lack of political and cultural sensitivity on the part of the European staff was something else. Fanon and Azoulay did not stop at their admission of failure, nor were they satisfied to study the conditions from which their patients had come. They insisted on making it known that their conclusions had validity for others, and that what they were discovering was that response and perhaps indeed pathology were related to the environment

—to the political as well as the cultural environment.

To have gone this far in the midst of a society that was undergoing turmoil soon to explode into war made it unlikely that Fanon or his colleagues could turn back and close their eyes to what they had so painfully begun to discover. There is no evidence that they did, and Blida, as we shall see, was not isolated from the rest of Algeria. But Fanon continued to practice and his articles continued to reveal the hand of a man bent on looking beneath the surface.

Demystification was the objective of another important article to come out of Blida-Joinville, this time under the joint authorship of Fanon and Dr. Lacaton. Dr. Lacaton and the interns Azoulay and Sanchez, whose names often appear in articles written with Fanon, were Europeans at Blida-Joinville who sympathized with Fanon's psychiatric orientation and with his political beliefs.[45] They appear to have found a common language and to have traveled the same dangerous road from political indifference and conformism to collaboration and empathy with Algerians. In 1955, at a Congress in Nice, in southern France, Fanon and Lacaton presented a brief paper on "Confessions in North Africa."[46] The paper did little more than to suggest that the offering of a confession was an act that had to be studied in its social context and that this context was quite special in the Algerian case. A confession, for the man who chooses to make it, is a form of "ransom" for his readmission into the group from which he excluded himself, or was excluded, by his criminal act. But this assumes that in the mind of the man who confesses, there will be forgiveness by the group. There is implicit in this interaction a consciousness of mutual recognition, since without it confession is meaningless. To understand how the criminal feels about his action one must have a sense of how he relates to his community. Is he extraneous? How does he respond to punishment? One can always say, Lacaton and Fanon added, that North Africans are simply untrustworthy and that they have a tendency to lie. But this is an evasive response and it does nothing to solve the problem at issue.

In order to understand the nature of confession one needs to return to the relation of the individual to his community. If this has been a destructive relationship, or if there has been none, the results will affect the behavior of the man in question. "There cannot, in effect, be a reintegration if there was never any integration."[47] If one pursues this line of thinking, it is the whole society, and in Algeria this meant French and Algerian society, that one must reflect upon. Is it homogeneous or not? What is the place of subordinate groups in it? What is the nature of their relations? If there is no fundamental consensus in the population as a whole, then how is one to judge the crime or the confession of a member of one of the subordinate groups judged to be inferior and therefore outside the mainstream? What is the significance of the confession in this case, and what is the significance of the refusal to confess? In the case of the criminal who confesses but whose confession is regarded as unreliable, are we not faced with something other than an instance of continued criminality of a tendency to dishonest behavior? Is there not behind this a refusal to voluntarily accept a social contract which leaves the subject out of the community? Is there not a difference here between the confession that is the submission before a superior power and one that involves reintegration into a society that accepts the subject? Fanon and Lacaton concluded their article with the remark that the situation they had described was worth further study and that it was incumbent on the medical expert to be aware of it since it affected his work.

To suggest that criminality was perhaps affected by colonization was to go far in the direction of stirring up a consciousness dangerous to the maintenance of the status quo. There is little doubt that Fanon's predilections in this direction went unrecognized by his medical colleagues, particularly those who did not share his analyses. And it was all the more striking that Fanon and those who sympathized with him at Blida made it clear that they had arrived—or were arriving—at their political positions because of what they had discovered working as psychiatrists in a non-political milieu. To discover that the conception of normality and abnormality, that legality itself, were built on false assumptions about the nature of Algerians and on their relations with French society, undermined confidence. When they began their experimentation with the Muslim ward, the participating doctors did not anticipate the conclusions they reached. Nor is there any indication that in the article on confession, the objective was a political one. The decision to work to subvert the system was crystallizing. It had not come, however, as a result of an a priori decision made in conformity with a political stance.

1956 was the year in which Fanon was to submit his resignation in a dramatic letter that stands as a monument to the integrity of the man and his high evaluation of his own profession as psychiatrist. It was also the year in which he and another colleague at Blida-Joinville, François Sanchez, wrote an article on "The Attitude of the Maghreb Muslim Towards Madness."[48] There is no sociopolitical content here that would suggest as much as the article on the confession did. Instead there is the questioning of two different cultural approaches towards madness, and there is an attempt to undo the romantic notion that the North African Muslim has historically reacted to madness as a sign of the presence of genies and that the attitude towards men considered mad has been that of a blind veneration. Fanon and Sanchez began their study by pointing out that institutions for the mentally ill existed in the Muslim world before the Middle Ages, and before anything comparable was introduced in the West. They contrasted the attitude towards madness that they found in North Africa with what they knew of European attitudes. "The westerner generally believes that madness alienates man, that it is impossible to understand his behavior without taking his illness into account."[49] But this attitude is often belied in practice, when the man alleged to be ill is held responsible for his behavior, in spite of all such considerations. There is a tendency to assume that such a man indulges himself, and that he is some sense enjoying living like a parasite. He punishes others by making them accept his condition, which he, from this point of view, is not beyond savoring.

In comparison with this, the North African regards a man who is considered "mad" as totally irresponsible. He is considered a man possessed, and a distinction is made between the man, who retains his humanity and his sense of self, and that which is visited on him in this condition. Here too, although in theory the group does not exclude the sick man, there are times when rationalizations inspired by the desire to protect the community result in his exclusion. There is, however, no visible aggressiveness directed at him. This attitude which divorces the man from his sickness leads to the view that the sickness is itself an accident and that it can be removed or "cured," freeing the patient and allowing him to resume his former place in society. Given this combination of sentiments, it is not surprising to find a positive attitude towards "assistance mentale," elementary forms of social welfare for the mentally ill. Without exaggerating the medical value of these forms of aid, Fanon and Sanchez pointed out that the attitudes underlying the aid were useful in later supporting more extensive forms of help. They maintained a view of man as an integrated personality, in spite of his illness.

> It was not madness that inspired respect, patience, indulgence, it was man affected by madness, by genies; it was man as such. The attentive care that one lavishes on a tubercular patient, does it imply a particular sentiment vis-à-vis tuberculosis itself? Respect for the madman because he remains, in spite of everything, a man; aid to the madman because he is subject to enemy forces. It is never a question of respecting and even less a question of worshipping him.[50]

The authors qualify their remarks with the acknowledgment that there were instances where one did find a veneration of an individual believed to be possessed, and in such instances there was no end of superstition associated with his powers. In less dramatic fashion, the doctors at Blida today recalled how, when their hospital was enlarged, they tried to advertise for personnel in their own city and how poorly they were received. There appears to have been no such patience, tolerance, or respect as that which Fanon and Sanchez found. Relations between Blida-Joinville, the hospital, and the town are now quite different. But it is clear from the testimony of the present staff that there is much that needs to be done by way of educating the populace about what mental illness is.

- 3 -

Politics and Medicine:
From Algeria to Tunisia

Writing and working between 1953 and 1956, Fanon learned through his experiences at the hospital at Blida-Joinville what many of his European colleagues had apparently not thought it necessary to learn: that Algerians are not merely "natives" to be manipulated and educated, but a people with their own history and traditions. Whether in the confession, the review of the Maghreb attitudes towards madness, or the analysis of the failure at the hospital, the conclusions pointed in the same direction. There was an urgent need for Europeans in Algeria to turn towards Algeria and Algerians in a new way. For the doctors of the Algerian school, it had been sufficient to declare that "scientific evidence" demonstrated certain tendencies among Algerians which placed them in an inferior situation vis-à-vis Europeans. Fanon recognized that even on the restricted level of medical-psychiatric practice, an attitude such as this was destructive. But there was a certain logic in the critical attitude of his colleagues for they seemed to understand that a crack in the wall of non-communication would inevitably alter the nature of Algerian-French relations and the existing balance, or imbalance, would not survive. Fanon was guilty of understanding what Mouloud Feraoun wrote about in 1955 when he had begun his *Journal* of the war years. In his commentary, Feraoun, the Kabyle writer and teacher, spoke of those Algerians who had benefited from the French presence but now wanted a formal separation. People may be surprised, he wrote, that this segment of the population wishes so final a break. But they do not realize that for a divorce to occur, there has to have been a marriage. That had never occurred. "The French stayed apart. Disdainfully apart. The French remained strangers. They thought that they were Algeria." To have become something other than strangers, what would have been necessary?

> What would have been necessary in order to love one another? To know each other; but we do not know each other. . . . It is useless to look elsewhere. For a century, we passed each other by without curiosity. There is nothing left to do but to contemplate this conscious indifference which is the opposite of love.[51]

Fanon did not advocate love between peoples, but he understood, emotionally and intellectually, that the consequence of indifference was worse than indifference, that in this non-communication there lay the seeds of mutual destruction. It is perhaps a strange thing to compare Feraoun, who was an avowed pacifist and a man seemingly incapable of hate, especially of hating the French, and a man like Fanon, who did not consider non-violence as a tactic in struggle and who was not given to reflectiveness as was the Kabyle teacher. But at this moment in time their sentiments were in accord. As Fanon watched French troops coming in and out of the Blida-Joinville hospital to remove suspected nationalists, as he watched others carry in men who had been tortured and who lay dying under the hand of doctors who preferred not to risk themselves by doing anything, Fanon began to turn towards Algeria.

Feraoun, who was to remain as critical of the FLN as of the French extremists, could not remain silent before those who were the loudest exponents of an assimilated Algeria and who by their action, their indifference, their insensitivity, and their self-centeredness rendered the ideal of assimilation obsolete. Feraoun resisted participating in any active nationalist group, but his sympathies were not in doubt although his reticence angered some of his French and Algerian contemporaries. Fanon, in 1955, began to lean in the direction of a more active kind of participation, and within one year he resigned from his job at Blida, had himself expelled from Algeria, and went to work for the FLN in Tunisia. By the time he wrote the introduction to his study *A Dying Colonialism*, he was able to speak of "our cause" and "our Revolution."

It was through Pierre Chaulet, a second-generation Algerian of European origin, that Fanon made contact with the men working for the nationalists in the FLN.[52] Chaulet was at Blida, having completed his medical studies in the capital and having been sent to the smaller city in order "to set up a local unit of Les Amitiés Algériennes, supposedly a charitable organization, but one which was actually used by the FLN to channel funds towards the needy families of nationalist warriors." Geismar leaves no doubt that Chaulet's contact with Fanon was not random and that the two men understood each other quickly. "Somewhat later, Fanon himself began to contribute to the same periodicals (underground publications for which Chaulet wrote). The two remained friends throughout the revolution, working together for the FLN newspaper as well as in various nationalist health centers throughout Tunisia." Fanon's work became known and he was invited to lecture at the University of Algiers by Professor Mandouze, one of the earliest supporters of the nationalists and a contact for them.[53]

At Blida-Joinville, the tension increased as the situation in the country deteriorated. The hospital was not considered as neutral territory and both Algerian nationalists and French officials, and then troops, entered it virtually at will. Geismar relates Fanon's attempts to control this situation for the benefit of his patients—and for those nationalists he was protecting. But the efforts proved short-lived. Fanon, Lacaton, and Charles Geromini, another European doctor who supported the FLN and who was to remain in Algeria, were under mounting pressure. Chaulet had been sent to Blida to continue the underground work of the resistance. Geromini went to Blida in pursuit of his medical work, but not exclusively for this reason as his letter to Fanon made clear.

> I had left Algiers for the psychiatric hospital in Blida, which had the reputation of being a nest of fellagha. As an intern with a doctor known for his anti-colonialist views, I was soon classified, rejected by some and adopted by others. I remained for eight months in Blida, wholly absorbed in my work as an intern. My solidarity with the Revolution was limited to helping distribute tracts, and passing around copies of *El Moudjahid* that I had in my possession. I had agreed to do medical work, but the opportunity

to commit myself further never materialized. In late December 1956 I left Blida for Paris.[54]

Fanon remained in Blida until he was expelled in January 1957. He observed his colleagues and he wrote his impressions of the medical profession at war.

> We have seen military doctors, called to the bedside of an Algerian soldier wounded in combat, refuse to treat him. The official pretext was that there was no longer a chance to save the wounded man. After the soldier had died, the doctor would admit that this solution had appeared to him preferable to a stay in prison where it would have been necessary to feed him while awaiting execution. The Algerians of the region of Blida know a certain hospital director who would kick the bleeding chests of the war wounded while lying in the corridor of his establishment.[55]

There was more to say about doctors, who finding themselves in the midst of war were ordered to withhold vital medicine for Algerians suspected of participating in the resistance. It was not only Europeans who complied, though the orders came from the French administration. Was this form of compliance in conformity with the Hippocratic oath, or had these doctors too crossed the line and become political partisans who only incidentally practiced medicine?[56] With restraint in *A Dying Colonialism* and with greater detail in his last book, Fanon described the use of torture by police officials collaborating with doctors in an effort to obtain information or to punish those who refused. He contrasted the tradition followed in other wars, in 1944 for example, in Belfort, France, where the neutrality of the medical corps was respected. Looking around him in Algeria, Fanon found men who rose above the barbarism of this war, but they were few. Neutrality, in these circumstances, had been prohibited by the administration and alarming methods were being used to determine men's commitments. Though he continued to work with French as well as Algerian patients, Fanon was losing his own faith in the ability of a psychiatrist to function in Algeria. It was impossible for an honest man not to speak out and to denounce what was going on so as to retain some semblance of decency.

Long before he joined the FLN and even before leaving Blida, Fanon had correctly assessed the attitudes of physicians in France working with Algerian immigrants, particularly with the migrant worker population. In 1952, in an article that is reproduced in *Toward the African Revolution*, but that first appeared in the French journal *Esprit*, Fanon discussed some of these attitudes and the evidence produced by doctors in defense of their position. "The 'North African Syndrome' " foreshadowed what Fanon was to write in *The Wretched of the Earth*, in the passages devoted to Algerian criminality and the work of Professor Porot.[57] In the 1952 article, Fanon was concerned with the images and assumptions current among doctors working with Algerian patients. He questioned the manner in which these prejudicial positions were arrived at, as well as the way in which they affected patterns of treatment. He discovered that the resentment against foreign workers in general, and the racism which affected Algerian workers in particular, formed a consistent base against which other more specific practices had to be studied.

The situation Fanon confronted in 1952 has not changed and the reactions of both parties, the Algerian workers and the French, does not appear to have changed either.[58] The former arrive in France eager to find work with the hope of making enough money to live on and to send or bring back when they return home. In coming to France they are often ill-prepared for the conditions of life they find, and they are generally ignorant of French society, about which they may have heard, but with little accuracy. For those who arrive in search of work, and for those who search for cheap labor, the economic benefits are uppermost. But all are affected by the social tensions that have consistently accompanied the pattern of foreign worker settlement. The formation of ghettos inspired by the housing problem quickly produces reactions of hostility from those who view the formation of these secluded and poor housing developments as something for which they bear no responsibility. With exclusion comes resentment and bitterness. Before 1962 as well as after there persisted a heavy dose of suspicion, disdain, and a vague fear about this barely literate, "uncivilized" mass. Racial and sexual fears intertwined to produce a state of unease which was often self-perpetuating.

What Fanon had in mind when he wrote about the "North

African syndrome" was related to this spiraling tension. Physicians who were not particularly conscious of the situation, or who were frankly unsympathetic to foreign workers, raised little resistance to the prejudicial atmosphere that existed. That this affected treatment is a banal yet often contested observation. Doctors who were perplexed by the difficulty of communicating with foreign workers were often—to judge by Fanon's account —unpardonably indifferent to signs of malaise that did not require interpreters to be understood. Cultural differences doubtless played a role in the expression of discontent or ill-health, but it would seem that the hostile ambiance created by hostility or indifference also contributed to making diagnoses and treatment difficult. The kinds of rationalizations that were offered for this unsatisfactory situation startled Fanon by their poorly disguised intentions. While at Lyon, where he was pursuing his medical studies, Fanon came across a medical thesis that had been presented in 1951. Its author was Dr. Léon Mugniéry.

Mugniéry was convinced that North Africans had inordinate sexual appetites and that they "naturally," therefore, led lives of intense sexual activity that transcended the bounds of what was considered acceptable in French society. Prostitution, for instance, had "an important role in the North African colony," due to "the powerful sexual appetite that is characteristic of those hot-blooded southerners."[59] Mugniéry realized the social implications of his discovery immediately. In the absence of adequate numbers of Algerian women, who did not generally accompany the men to France, these hot-blooded Algerians had to resort to French womanhood, or for that matter to French manhood, since homosexual inclinations were also common. Public morals were in danger. Mugniéry was also concerned with public policies and with what he considered the danger of too liberal politics—when applied to the North African question. He drew conclusions that seemed entirely appropriate to him.

> The granting of French citizenship, conferring equality of rights, seems to have been too hasty and based on sentimental and political reasons, rather than on the fact of the social and intellectual evolution of a race having a civilization that is at times refined but still primitive in its social, family and sanitary behavior.[60]

Mugniéry's analysis of the Algerian patient led him to make political recommendations. Fanon's argument was that Mugniéry and others like him actually began with these political attitudes and looked for material which justified their position. This, in effect, was the syndrome phenomenon. It had an immediate impact on treatment of Algerians as patients. But it also reflected attitudes towards Algerians that fed political reaction which was perpetuated through certain popular myths. "The medical staff," wrote Fanon,

> discovers the existence of a North African syndrome. Not experimentally, but on the basis of an oral tradition. The North African takes his place in this asymptomatic syndrome and is automatically put down as undisciplined (cf. medical discipline), inconsequential (with reference to the law according to which every symptom implies a lesion), and insincere (he says he is suffering when we know there are no reasons for suffering).[61]

Fanon objected as much to the way in which these evaluations were arrived at, i.e. "not experimentally," as to what they implied. The conclusion was that the North African is not to be taken seriously. Mugniéry had linked the disadvantages of dealing with a refined but essentially "primitive" population with the dangers of granting it political equality. It was not far from primitive behavior with respect to sexuality, to the elaboration of a more general definition of the consequence of such behavior. The conclusions were the same. They involved a justification for retaining the protected status of North Africans on the basis of the evidence of their own serious limitations. The more scientific the rationalization, the more persuasive the case. Eventually, what had been presented as a hypothesis became the underlying assumption. Sexuality was as important a social question as was criminality. Fanon became interested in both, particularly as he discovered that scientific evidence was adduced in both areas to demonstrate that North Africans were primitive and undisciplined, and dangerous in these domains. In his study of the Algerian school of psychiatry, Fanon concluded that the leading psychiatrists of the school were in essential agreement with Mugniéry's thesis. Mugniéry had written in 1951. Professor Porot, the prominent leader of the Algerian psychiatric circle, had a far greater influence and according to Fanon, was responsible for greater damage as a result of his own writing in this field.

In the section on colonial war and mental disorder in *The*

Wretched of the Earth, Fanon discussed the concept of the latent criminality of the Algerian and North African, as he found it presented in the Algerian literature on the subject.[62] There, the portrait that emerged was of a distinctly unsettling personality with a pronounced inclination towards criminality.[63] The problem was recognized as one of the major problems of Algerian society. In the light of the material offered, the Algerian or North African was described as being lazy, undisciplined and aggressive toward himself and others. He has a primitively developed brain (poor cortical development) which helps to account for his condition. Little wonder that he is considered a political liability, not to speak of his potential as a citizen or neighbor. Prior to 1954, according to Fanon, these assumptions were generally accepted by professionals such as doctors, lawyers, judges, and others of comparable status working in Algeria. This unappealing deviant was said to demonstrate a marked calling for criminality and to be prone to kill in the most brutal manner possible, When caught, he often seemed incapable of expressing a reasonable motive for his actions.

In looking for the roots of these myths, Fanon came across the work of Professor Porot, professor of psychiatry at the Faculty of Algiers, who with the aid of other students and scholars put together material to provide the evidence for these views. Porot had no doubt about the "predatory instinct" of the Algerian, or his intense aggressiveness. That he was led to commit violence was a function of his inability to exercise control over his impulsive behavior. Porot's contribution was in the presentation of scientific evidence on which these conclusions were based. Porot's research, first written up in 1935 and continued in later years, rested on the view that North Africans suffer from the deprivation of certain critical activities of the cortex. The part of the cortex that does not function in the North African brain is precisely that part which distinguishes primitive man from his successors. In 1939, Porot and a student of his named Sutter collaborated on a paper in which they developed their theories. "Primitivism is not lack of maturity," they wrote,

> nor a marked stoppage in the development of the individual psychism. It is a social condition which has reached the limit of its evolution; it is logically adopted to a life different from ours. . . . This primitivism is not merely a way of living which is the

result of a special upbringing; it has much deeper roots. We even consider that it must have its substratum in a particular disposition of the architectonic structure, or at least in the dynamic hierarchisation of the nervous centres. We are in the presence of a coherent body of comportment and of a coherent life which can be explained scientifically. The Algerian has no cortex: or, more precisely, he is dominated like the inferior vertebrates, by the diencephalon. The cortical functions, if they exist at all, are very feeble, and are practically unintegrated into the dynamic of existence.[64]

If the Algerian was like other North Africans, biologically determined as an inferior personality, what were the standards of behavior one might expect from him, and what were the social and political prerogatives one might offer him? If one pursued the line of thinking expressed by Porot, the war that broke out in 1954 was not a war for national independence or a revolution, it was the result of masses of cortically deprived criminals on the loose. If Porot's thesis was wrong, criminality did not disappear, but the approach to dealing with it would have to change.

Fanon's work at Blida-Joinville and his experience outside the hospital convinced him that there was a direct relationship between the colonial system and the prevailing psychological condition of Algerians and Frenchmen. To Fanon, it was axiomatic that the colonial system tended to produce a unique psychological conditioning, and even a unique pathology. As he became more sensitive to this conditioning and as he became more aware of the damage done by the system, Fanon became less tolerant of the attitudes of those, like Porot, who rationalized the existence of a lopsided situation by pseudo-scientific means. One did not need the war of liberation to demonstrate that those supposedly cortically deprived men and women could organize themselves and carry on a resistance of impressive proportions. And if the use of violence and eventually terror posed critical questions for Algerians and Frenchmen, it was not latent criminality that provided an answer. As he considered the developments before him, Fanon concluded that his work as a psychiatrist in Algeria was worse than futile. Although he was to resign in 1956, it was only a short time later in Tunis, where he engaged in work of a political and a medical nature, that he resumed his psychiatric work. It was not psychiatry that Fanon abandoned in Algeria. It was the commitment to help men and women adjust to colonial society. It was this which Fanon had decided no longer to accept, as he made clear in his letter to Robert Lacoste, Resident Minister of Algeria.

> If psychiatry is the medical technique that aims to enable man no longer to be a stranger to his environment, I owe it to myself to affirm that the Arab, permanently an alien in his own country, lives in a state of absolute depersonalization. . . .
>
> Monsieur le Ministre, there comes a moment when tenacity becomes morbid perseverance. Hope is then no longer an open door to the future but the illogical maintenance of a subjective attitude in organized contradiction with reality. . . . The function of a social structure is to set up institutions to serve man's needs. A society that drives its members to desperate solutions is a non-viable society, a society to be replaced.
>
> It is the duty of the citizen to say this. No professional morality, no class solidarity, no desire to wash the family linen in private, can have a prior claim. No pseudo-national mystification can prevail against the prequirement of reason. . . . For many months my conscience has been the seat of unpardonable debates. And their conclusion is the determination not to despair of man, in other words, of myself.[65]

In January 1957 Fanon's letter of resignation was answered by a letter of expulsion from the office of the Resident Minister. Within two days Fanon and his close associates, especially the male nurses at Blida, left. What was to be named the Frantz Fanon Hospital, "L'Hôpital psychiatrique Frantz Fanon," after 1962, was for the moment deprived of the doctor and his aides. At Blida-Joinville there was not much weeping over the doctor's departure. Political tension had infiltrated the walls of the hospital to such an extent that the departure of yet another member of the staff was no more dramatic than what had become routine. Dr. Lacaton had left after a siege of arrests and torture for his collaboration with the nationalists. To this day, the recollection of this period evokes a strained silence. For Fanon, the timing of his letter to the Resident Minister was not accidental; it marked his decision to become Algerian through his support of the Algerian struggle. Once accepted, Fanon's letter left few options. A short time later the family left for France and Lyon, the home of Josie's family. In France, Fanon was put in touch with one of the leaders of the French network supporting the resistance, and arrangements were made for his transferal to Tunisia. The contact was made through Francis Jeanson, who had already figured in Fanon's life as the reader of his first book, and a man who came to personify the depth of commitment of the French left to the Algerian cause. It was a subject about which Fanon was to write bitter pages, but if there was anyone whose sincerity and seriousness in this matter were beyond doubt, it was Jeanson.

Fanon's arrival in Tunisia was the beginning of the most politically active phase of his life. It was not only the time when he wrote for the FLN-ALN organs, *el Moudjahid* and *Résistance algérienne*, it was the period of his most intense collaboration with the political leadership of the Algerian nationalist movement. Before turning to his continuing work as a psychiatrist at the Manouba clinic and at the Centre Neuropsychiatrique de Jour de Tunis, associated with the Hôpital Charles Nicolle, it is of interest to consider an aspect of Fanon's Tunisian life that is little known. I refer to his period of teaching at the Faculty of Letters at the University of Tunis.[66] Fanon offered courses for hospital interns, for psychiatrists of the Maghreb, and for political cadres of Africans under colonial domination. He gave a course in "The Social Psychology of the Black World," at the University in 1959. Bertène Juminer, who had seen Fanon lecture, recorded the impressive effect which his presence had on the audience that attended his lectures. Speaking without notes to overflow crowds that hung on his words, Juminer recalled, Fanon spoke brilliantly, continuously, and with complete conviction to those whom he already considered "the wretched of the earth." He would come carrying books by Chester Himes in the French *Série Noire* edition, and his citations suggested that he knew the material well. Once the hour had passed, the course would continue informally in the halls of the lecture building until some Algerian bodyguard assigned to Fanon would come and whisk him away. Very soon the courses were dropped, at the request of the Tunisian government. Juminer claims that according to Fanon, it was the effect of pressure applied to the Tunisians by the French government. He did not add what he doubtless knew, that the French government was incensed by the aid offered the Algerians by the Tunis government that had so recently won its own independence.

Less controversial—at least politically—was Fanon's work at

the clinic to which he had been assigned. But there too, he did important work which he considered a milestone in his thinking, and which is currently considered an important concept in the reform of hospital treatment. The two related studies which he and Charles Geromini wrote together on this subject, and which are discussed at length below, do not convey the intense political passion and activity which marked both men. Nor would a reading of the material on day-care centers convey a sense of what Fanon was doing or thinking in the military hospitals in which he also worked in this period; an experience which fed the anguished reflections on the human cost of colonization and decolonization that appear in *A Dying Colonialism* and in *The Wretched of the Earth*.

When Fanon went to Tunisia he agreed to work at the government's Psychiatric Hospital at Manouba, using the pseudonym of Dr. Fares.[67] He occupied the position of Chef de service, and filled a post which along with many others had been hastily vacated by the French when they left following Tunisia's independence. Fanon was directly responsible to the Tunisian Ministry of Health, which, in spite of harassment by some of the hospital staff, supported his innovative work and refused to allow him to be pressured by jealous colleagues. At the Manouba clinic and later at the Centre Neuropsychiatrique de Jour de Tunis Fanon returned to the ideas of Tosquelles and the need to humanize and improve psychiatric hospitals. Judging from comments made by Fanon's friends the work was difficult because of the resistance of the hospital staff to this foreign doctor who insisted on changing things.[68] But Fanon enjoyed some success and he was able to continue writing up his research. In the collection of works produced after the move to Tunisia, the most important article was that on day-care treatment for psychiatric patients. There are two parts to this study, one written by Fanon alone, the other jointly written by Fanon and Geromini.[69] With this study, Fanon returned to a subject that had preoccupied him at Saint Alban and later at Blida. Once again he was thinking of the community uses of psychiatry, the responsibility of the doctor to the entire community, and the need to maximize therapeutic treatment in hospitals. He referred frequently to the need to maintain a connection between the patient in hospital and the outside world, the family and society to which he would eventually return. If the prospect of such integration had been canceled out in Algeria as a result of the schisms brought about by colonialism, in Tunisia the problems were of a different order. Working with Algerians, Tunisians, and other North Africans he found in his hospitals, Fanon concentrated on problems of a less urgent nature than he had encountered in his last days at Blida. In Tunis, he could concentrate on day-care treatment, which he came to feel offered a near perfect solution to the limited resources available for a growing hospital population. His reasons for favoring it were of a theoretical as well as a practical nature. Concerned with diminishing the depressing effects generally brought about by hospitalization, Fanon came to believe that partial hospitalization such as that offered by day-care centers allowed the patients to retain some of their private sense of self, to preserve what hospitalization often destroyed, a sense of dignity. In addition, on a practical level, the transformation of hospitals into day-care centers might allow more treatment for more patients. In Tunisia the experiment worked well.

There were two aspects of the day-care centers that were important to Fanon and Geromini: the fact that the psychiatric hospital was connected to a general hospital; and the concept of partial hospitalization applied to psychiatric treatment. In the first instance, the advantage of having access to specialists as well as to materials indispensable to the treatment was obvious, but the integration of psychiatry into the overall conception of treatment as envisioned in a general hospital was equally significant. It was in order to overcome the sense of the patient in a psychiatric hospital as "mad" and needing or deserving to be isolated, and of doctors who specialized in this branch of medicine as equally out of the ordinary, that Fanon and Geromini urged the association of the psychiatric with the general hospital scheme. Partial hospitalization allowed more patients to be treated in the same place, but it accomplished something else. Under normal conditions of hospitalization, treatment, whether by doctors or nurses, occurred at specified hours, and the rest of the time the patient often had the feeling of being abandoned. Under the day-care-center plan, he was offered maximum treatment in concentrated doses and he was not required to stay at the hospital longer than the prescribed hours. The hours for patients to come to the hospital extended from 7 AM to 6 PM. Where essential, exceptions were made, and doctors were on call. But the protection of the patient from the loneliness of the institution was not ignored; neither was the relationship of the patient to his family. Where there was a tendency to regard the patient as somehow fallen by virtue of his illness, hospitalization had the advantage of simply taking the aggravating presence out of the family. But for the patient, the sudden break created an unrealistic situation which was therapeutically harmful. To maintain a relationship with the family, not through visits but through normal life relations, was a continuing process of education for all concerned. The various forms of isolation and exclusion which hospitalization reenforced were thus abrogated and where possible entirely done away with. Sensitive to the impact which this might have on a patient who carried his own inner forms of exclusion and isolation, the two doctors insisted that the day-care centers were not only more practical, they were psychiatrically beneficial. The problems of dismissal and reentry, which reversed the problems of exclusion and isolation, were just as much under surveillance and less likely to occur in an extreme form, under this kind of treatment. Since the break with the outside world was never complete, reintegration into it, which was after all the ultimate objective of treatment, was likewise facilitated.

Fanon and Geromini were pleased by their experiment. In their eighteen months of work they were impressed by the number of patients who had been able to take advantage of their experiment, and they knew that no other case of partial hospitalization had been tried outside of Europe. It must be said that credit should also go to the Tunisian officials who encouraged the men and did not allow less imaginative colleagues to destroy their initiative.

At the same time that he worked at the various hospitals with which he was associated, Fanon volunteered his services to the FLN-run refugee and medical centers that operated along the borders on both the Moroccan and Tunisian frontiers. Here theoretical problems were irrelevant. The only constant worry was the lack of adequate facilities and the lack of doctors; for the rest, it was a matter of doing as much as possible under difficult circumstances. For Fanon personally, this experience marked him as much as that in Blida, where he had first come to see this aspect of colonial rule and the resistance to it, which so many of his colleagues could shrug off but which remained to haunt

him. It was no longer a question of arguing whether or not
doctors in their capacity as members of a particular profession
had the right and responsibility to be partisan. It was a matter
of caring for those men, women, and children who were the
victims of the war. This material was not meant for scholarly
journals. In fact it was only at the end of *The Wretched of the Earth*
in the section on colonial war and mental illness that Fanon
wrote up some of his cases. There he indicated that "the observations noted here cover the period running from 1954–1959.
Certain patients were examined in Algeria, either in hospital
centres or as private patients. The others were cared for by the
health divisions of the Army of National Liberation."[70]

The cases are discussed here in the context of Fanon's continuing psychiatric work and as a further illustration of his own
conception of the intimacy that exists between the doctor and the
citizen. When he introduced these cases at the end of *The
Wretched*, Fanon noted that perhaps some people would object to
the inclusion of such material. He was referring to the primarily
political nature of his book. He could also have referred to those
psychiatrists who distrusted his motives because of his inclusion
of what they regarded as politically loaded material in the presentation of his cases. Fanon's position was less complex than either
group imagined. He had long since come to realize the futility of
ignoring what was clearly the predominant obsession in Algerian
life, the nature of the colonial relationship, and the impact that
relationship had on the personalities of both Frenchman and
Algerian. Whether he wrote as a political theorist or as a psychiatrist, the elements of politics and personality were inextricably
mixed and those who chose to ignore this did so at their own risk.
The point has been made earlier and it is worth repeating. Fanon
was not crude in his analysis, he did not ignore ambivalences that
existed in the colonial situation. But he was honest enough to see
that to maintain the myth of the "separateness" of a man as a
patient and citizen was a delusion. Those who will take the
trouble to read all of his psychiatric writings will see that he was
fully capable of making the distinction between those cases that
could be considered outside of this framework and those that
could not.

When he decided to work in the refugee camps and in the
health centers, he was in constant touch with the human consequences of the war raging in Algeria. That the war aggravated,

distorted, and transformed what might have been troubled individuals, that it had differing effects on people, these are banal
observations which other post-war studies have shown. But what
Fanon showed was that the colonial relationship had deformed
relations and self-images before the war occurred; when it did
occur, what transpired could not be explained except by an
awareness of that previous conditioning. It was not merely the
adage that war is not good for people. It was an exposé of what
colonialism did to people, and what colonial wars accomplished.
The victims were clearly both the colonized and the colonizers.
In his presentations Fanon tried to show what had happened to
both groups of people. Those who wished to draw their own
conclusions, irrespective of the author's efforts, could of course
do so. In practice, Fanon probably disappointed both politically
oriented and psychiatrically inclined readers. To the former, his
inclusion of the case studies may have appeared excessive and
out of place. To the latter, the case studies were inadequate and
their political intention was equally disturbing. In fact, it is to be
regretted that Fanon did not write up the case studies with
greater care if only to disarm those adversaries who used his
example as proof of the impossibility of mingling politics and
psychology. A judicious evaluation of the case studies was offered by Dr. Paul Adams in December 1970.

> The mental disorders to which Frantz Fanon gave most attention,
> inaptly translated as "reactionary," were those that in North
> America are known as reactive and situational disorders. What-
> ever our disdain for Fanon's tendency to oversimplify intra-
> psychic experiences, we can only respect his inclination to em-
> phasize the importance of the social structure in the genesis of
> mental disorder. The cases of madness that were presented in
> Black Skin, White Masks and in The Wretched of the Earth are lacking
> in psychiatric sophistication but they are rich in recognizing what
> society and culture can induce in human beings.[71]

There is something obscene about writing about the case
studies. It is not that they are difficult to write about; in fact the
reverse is true, and therein lies the difficulty. To reduce to
well-ordered words that are socially acceptable, events that are
naked testimony to man's descent into hell, a hell of his making,
is so gratuitous an act as to be unredeemable. Whatever position
one takes as to the wisdom of Fanon's having included this data

in his political tract, the material is not fiction and one is forced to deal with it. Yet a reading of the cases cannot take place without considering the political question of terror, the place of random violence in the Revolution, and the ethical questions which this raises. Fanon dealt with these matters directly and indirectly in *The Wretched* and elsewhere. But the case studies were presented for other reasons, not as documentations of certain political acts, but as illustrations of the violence done to man by the colonial system.

> It seems to us that in the cases here chosen the events giving rise to the disorder are chiefly the bloodthirsty and pitiless atmosphere, the generalisation of inhuman practices and the firm impression that people have of being caught up in a veritable Apocalypse.[72]

The term "apocalypse" is entirely appropriate, not only to the world Fanon was describing but to any world-without-end atmosphere that is common to men caught in the grip of terror and random death. The important qualifications that come to mind in a discussion of these cases must not be passed over, but they belong to the consideration of tactics and strategy. Here, the emphasis is on the nature of the human legacy which Fanon saw as a product of this labyrinth of destruction.

The man who emerged from the colonial system, or more precisely, from its degeneration, was a divided man. If he was a *colon*, he was divided against himself to the extent that he became sympathetic to the Algerians. The Algerian, on the other hand, was a man faced with the choice of paying the price for his decision to redefine his identity according to his own criteria, or to remain a "subject" as others saw him. Those who chose the former way and who were actively engaged in the process ran the risk of being caught and punished by the forces of the system designed to contradict this decision. It is these people, French and Algerian alike, that Fanon wrote about in his section on mental illness and colonial war.

In presenting his material Fanon categorized the cases at the end of *The Wretched* according to the following terms: Series A involved "cases of Algerians or Europeans who had very clear symptoms of mental disorders of the reactionary type"; Series B involved "cases or groups of cases in which the event giving rise to the illness is in the first place the atmosphere of total war which reigns in Algeria"; Series C brought together "affective-intellectual modifications and mental disorders after torture"; and Series D included "psycho-somatic disorders."

In the first series, A, the reactive disorders, a number of cases of Europeans and Algerians are presented. All involve incidents that grew out of the political situation in Algeria: the Algerian soldier who suffers impotence on learning of the rape of his wife by French soldiers; the "undifferentiated homocidal impulses found in a survivor of a mass murder"; and the cases of the European policemen who suffer bizarre after-effects brought on by their strenuous work. In addition, there is the account of what appears to have been a random act of murder committed in the course of war. It is the murder of the wife of a French colon by a young Algerian working with the FLN whose own mother was previously killed by the French because of his connection with the underground. In the sequence of events leading from his entry into the resistance, to the knowledge that his family is subjected to pressure because of his action, to his mother's death and the seizure of his two sisters by the French, to the final act of the murder of the wife of the settler who had been the original object of the FLN search, there is a long path uneasily traveled. There is no inevitability in this tale, and had Fanon's notes on the individual in question been complete we might have known more about the nature of the man's attachment to his mother, his cultural and socio-economic background, his commitment to the FLN, and his action vis-à-vis the woman who reminded him of his mother. There is much that is evoked by the brief study: the question of responsibility, the motivation of the individual, and the nature of the guilt he bears. What does it mean to "cure" such a man, and such a case? Fanon offered little discussion of this save to explain that he had treated the young man for several weeks and that the most obvious symptoms, such as his recurring nightmares, had disappeared. But the associations that returned to haunt him did not. "Though it may appear unscientific, in our opinion time alone can bring some improvement to the disrupted personality of this young man."[73] It is questionable whether time is enough, or indeed whether it ought to be enough by itself, to produce a "cure."

In Series B a case that bears some resemblance to the one discussed and that is a prime example of the effect of "the atmosphere of total war which reigns," is that of the murder by two young Algerians, aged thirteen and fourteen, of their European playmate. Fanon had been called in to give medical advice. He interviewed both youngsters and he reproduced a part of these interviews in his text. Given the situation under which he encountered them, one may say that Fanon's job was not to produce a comprehensive psychiatric examination, and even less was this to be expected in the summarization of the case. Nonetheless the report is scanty and no reader can be satisfied that he has understood the psychological dynamics involved. The children appear numb, as they may well have become. But if numbness is the appropriate reaction to their situation, it does not constitute an explanation for their act. To demand less is to become numb to the conditions that make such an act possible.

The thirteen-year-old boy spoke first and described his playmate who was killed.

> We weren't a bit cross with him. Every Thursday we used to go and play with catapults together, on the hill above the village. He was a good friend of ours. He usn't to go to school any more because he wanted to be a mason like his father. One day we decided to kill him, because the Europeans want to kill all the Arabs. We can't kill big people. But we could kill ones like him, because he was the same age as us.[74]

The fourteen-year-old friend of this boy was more frightening in his testimony because he accepted the senselessness of this act as well as the personal innocence of the murdered boy. There was not a hint of sentimentality in his reaction. He explained that two members of his own family had been arbitrarily killed by the militia at Rivet in 1956, and that no Frenchman had been arrested after the incident.

> He did not deny having killed either. Why had he killed? He did not reply to the question but asked me had I ever seen a European in prison. Had there ever been a European arrested and sent to prison after the murder of an Algerian? I replied that in fact I had never seen any Europeans in prison.
> 'And yet there are Algerians killed every day, aren't there?'
> 'Yes.'
> 'So why are only Algerians found in the prisons? Can you explain that to me?'
> 'No. But tell me why you killed this boy who was your friend.'
> 'I'll tell you why. You've heard tell of the Rivet business?'
> 'Yes.'

'Two of my family were killed then. At home they said that the French had sworn to kill us all, one after the other. And did they arrest a single Frenchman for all those Algerians who were killed?'

'I don't know.'

'Well, nobody at all was arrested. I wanted to take to the mountains, but I was too young. So X—— and I said we'd kill a European.'

'Why?'

'In your opinion, what should we have done?'

'I don't know. But you are a child and what is happening concerns grown-up people.'

'But they kill children too . . .'

'That is no reason for killing your friend.'

'Well, kill him I did. Now you can do what you like.'

'Had your friend done anything to harm you?'

'Not a thing.'

'Well?'

'Well, there you are . . .'[75]

There is no "explanation" offered by Fanon. In a sense which is too limited, he sought to make it comprehensible by presenting a portrait of the environment in which this act occurred. But it can hardly be understood simply as the acting out of children warped by the hostile world in which they grow. It is, in the end, the few who commit such acts, although it may be the many who experience the degradation and despair of growing in such a climate. *Les Temps Modernes* in October 1969 published an article entitled, "A quoi rêvent les enfants d'Algérie?" (What do Algerian Children Dream About?). There is violence expressed in the dreams of virtually all the children who yearn to avenge themselves and their parents for the suffering they have endured. But the violence is contained in the dream. The child, like the adult who commits the act of murder in his life—as opposed to his fantasy—has acted on the basis of more pronounced and different psychological reactions.

For Fanon the connection between such acts and the environment of war was so obvious that he no longer felt it necessary to record the detailed history of each man under conditions of stress. If his descriptions of the individual case studies, insofar as they were meant to be that and not merely descriptions, were inadequate, his more generous image of the Algerian situation and its impact on the human environment was ample. The benign nature of colonialism was exploded as a myth. Fanon's essay was not isolated in providing the evidence for this. Those familiar with the clandestine literature published by the Editions de Minuit, for instance, cannot but be impressed by Fanon's restraint. The Vergès-Arnaud testimonial, *Pour Djamila Bouhired* (1957), Alleg's *La Question* (1958), Vidal-Naquet's *L'Affaire Audin* (1958), and finally *La Gangrène* (1959), were all seized by the French government when they appeared because of their accusations of the use of terror by French authorities. Having read these accounts, the request that Fanon provide convincing psychiatric data to demonstrate why men acted as they did appears to be luxurious and somewhat irrelevant. But this is only to underline the extraordinary political circumstances of the time.

- 4 -

From Psychological Observation to Political Action

The concept of neutral men as just men, in the sense in which Aimé Césaire used it in his play *Une Saison au Congo,* is peculiarly fitting to Fanon. Except that for him neutrality and justice appeared more often as mutually exclusive rather than as complementary. He contended that neutrality in the sense of standing somehow above the melees, as in the Algerian case for instance, was not possible. Then neutrality became an excuse for the status quo. Justice, in this situation, meant a firm commitment to Algeria and a condemnation of the colonial system. This was what Blida had taught, it was what working in the refugee camps had confirmed, and it was what participation in the FLN had finally endorsed. Before he transformed his commitment to a political decision to participate actively in the resistance movement, Fanon had concentrated on his medical-psychiatric work as we have seen. Out of this there emerged the attempt to produce or at least to describe the psychology and the pathology appropriate to colonialization.

It was Fanon's contention, on the basis of his experience in Martinique, France, and Algeria, that colonialism reproduced relations between the rulers and the ruled that existed in minority-majority situations, and that for this reason it was possible to speak of a psychology common to both. He had explored this in *Black Skin, White Masks,* but he took it further in his study on Algeria in revolution, *A Dying Colonialism.* The complex economic and political factors that underlay the colonial expansion were not ignored. But Fanon wished to emphasize a dimension of colonialism that had been overlooked, even by its most virulent enemies. It was not economic dislocation or the politics of imperialism which he abstractly studied. It was the human consequences of a system that determined the limits of men's actions. In Fanon's Algerian study, it was the confrontation between Frenchmen and Algerians, and the internal, psychic effect which this confrontation produced, that were examined. In *A Dying Colonialism,* two groups were analyzed, the colonizers and the colonized. But there was no pretense that this was done under the umbrella of some nonexistent objectivity. Fanon's thesis was that the Revolution was transforming individuals as well as relations between them. The evidence for this appeared in the situation of women, in the family, in attitudes towards the colonizer as expressed in areas where the two met—whether it was in medicine, in communications, or in direct human relations. Albert Memmi summed up the situation in the colony by referring to it as one of privilege—and he generalized this so that it did not mean only economic or political privilege. His own study of colonialism has been referred to frequently in this essay, as have his occasional references to Fanon.[76] He did not approve of what he considered the excessive romanticism of Fanon, or his exaggerated conceptions of the goodness of the colonized as opposed to the colonizer. The manicheanism implicit in Fanon's view he attributed to the author and not to the situation he was describing.

In discussing his own approach he wrote:

> I have also demonstrated that the notion of privilege was not a purely economic one but was psychological and cultural too. My own effort has consisted of taking this foundation, or this critical dimension which is the economic relationship, and trying on that basis to describe the socio-cultural phenomena peculiar to colonization. Some are apparent in the colonizer, others in the colonized. This yields two complete portraits, each governed by the other and arranged by the objective colonial condition.[77]

Fanon in effect drew two complete portraits which he agreed were related to one another, insofar as they were integral parts of the colonial dialectic. The governance of one by the other he referred to as the dynamic of the laws of the psychology of colonization. The term promised more than he produced. What it meant in practice was that "in an initial phase, it is the action, the plans of the occupier that determine the centers of resistance around which a people's will to survive becomes organized."[78] In an active sense, it is the initiative taken by the colonizer that produces the reaction in the colonized. The use of the veil was analyzed in this fashion. But the concept of a dynamic of the "laws of the psychology of colonization" meant more. It referred to the entire network of relationships fixed by the system. Fanon emphasized the purposefulness of these relationships as a product of the system of colonialism, while Memmi chose to refer to the accidental nature of the relationships that were the products of a situation and not a system. There was more pessimism and more tolerance in Memmi's view. Fanon was intensely optimistic, in the long run, intolerant as a matter of principle and committed to the possibility of implementing the changes in which he believed. It was a political outlook for a man considered by some to have no faith in politics, in contrast to what was perceived as romanticism, subjectivism, or a form of chiliastic ecstasy.

In *A Dying Colonialism*, in his passage on the use of the veil, Fanon gave one example of what he meant by the law of the psychology of colonization.

> It is the white man who creates the Negro. But it is the Negro who creates negritude. To the colonialist offensive against the veil, the colonized opposes the cult of the veil. What was an undifferentiated element in a homogeneous whole acquires a taboo character, and the attitude of a given Algerian woman with respect to the veil will be constantly related to her overall respect to the foreign occupation. The colonized, in the face of the emphasis given by the colonialist to this or that aspect of his traditions, reacts very violently. The attention devoted to modifying this aspect, the emotion the conqueror puts into his pedagogical work, his prayers, his threats, weave a whole universe of resistances around this particular element of the culture.[79]

Repeating the same proposition in his chapters on medicine, the radio, and the family, Fanon illustrated his conception of this process of weaving a web of resistance—which was the way in which the colonized responded to the threat posed by colonization. But it would be oversimplifying colonialism to accept this proposition as the only valid one. Assimilation of new techniques, for example foreign technology, did in fact occur. Colonialism was not without its profound impact on the colony. But the Algeria Fanon was describing was one which had decided to resist and which refused at this point in its history to accept any further. This was the affirmative essence behind the great refusal. It is not difficult to understand why it is that Algerians tend to be most enthusiastic about this particular book by Fanon as opposed to any of the others. Its portrait of Algeria is a continuous eulogy, and it is written with a fervor that is difficult to resist.[80] It is only when one compares the heroic period with the realities of post-independence Algeria that there is a letdown. Not only is this true with respect to what Fanon wrote about women, but remaining within the confines of his sociological study, it applies as well to his discussion of the family and the concept of the "new man." The most generous and perhaps the only realistic assessment is that it takes more than one generation and more than purity of intention to create the product described. The new man, after all, does emerge from the "old man" of pre-revolutionary days, a proposition that in itself did not have much appeal to a man like Fanon.

Fanon's conception of the laws peculiar to the psychology of colonization was based on the contention already expressed by Memmi that there existed a preferential relationship in the colonized-colonizer syndrome. The activity of the former was determined by the initiatives taken by the latter; but all action of both groups could be understood only as a function of their place within this system. The Revolution, by promising to break this system, freed the individuals within it to reorder their relations with one another. It would be preferable, and I would argue, more accurate, to describe what Fanon wrote, not as the laws of the psychology of colonization, but more simply, as a highly perceptive account of the psychological condition common to colonizer and colonized. It is more accurate to consider this a sociological essay than to suggest that it has the qualities of rigorous evidence that permit us to consider the products as "laws" of the system under observation.

A number of themes were constant. The lack of communication in a meaningful sense, between colonizer and colonized, was accepted as a matter of course, with rare exceptions. Hence, in something like medicine, assumed to be a neutral, value-free area of cooperation between Frenchmen and Algerians, it was a shock to learn of the attitudes on both sides and how these affected cooperation. It was no longer possible to talk simply in terms of medicine or health or illness without taking into consideration the persons and places, within this system, of those involved. Likewise, the material on the radio, whether the French-operated radio or the Algerian radio, was symbolic of more than technological progress or a mere method of communication. The lack of communication between the peoples involved meant, invariably, mistrust and fear. The decision to resist colonization and to affirm the community and its values upset the imbalance in existing relations, attempted to nullify this fear and temporarily sought to break communications to be able to rebuild them on the basis of other criteria. Internally, within the Algerian milieu, the process of revolution galvanized the energy of the population to such an extent that it broke down traditions, or seemed to, at least for the duration of war. Fanon's study could more properly be labeled a study of "relations," within the Algerian milieu and between Algerians and Frenchmen. Fear and mistrust on the one hand illustrated one aspect of non-communication; the desire for self-assertion, individually and collectively, and ultimately nationally, reflected a transformation within the Algerian sector that was to affect the factor of communication in another manner. Self-consciousness gave rise to action, and it was through this praxis that the new man, the man of the Revolution, came into being. The process paralleled Fanon's coming of age, his own transition from consciousness to action on the Algerian issue, a transference to a public plane of a private, internal transformation as well.

It is clear from *A Dying Colonialism* that this book marked a transition for Fanon from a period in which he had concentrated on psychiatric problems and work, to one in which he committed himself to more direct political action. It has been the object of the present section of this essay to demonstrate that Fanon's decision to engage in political action grew out of his psychiatric work. It was a product of what he saw and experienced in the domain of psychiatric practice that convinced him of the futility of continuing in that profession if his objective was to form men who were not alienated from their society. That this is implicit in the writing on Algerian society and on colonial society in Algeria, in this book, is fairly obvious. The evidence of a political interest of a more overt kind was also present in *A Dying Colonialism,* as the sections on the French left, the European minority, and the position of Jews in Algeria make clear. These sections constitute the next phase of Fanon's thinking and action. Strictly speaking, they do not belong in a sociological study, and much less in what was purportedly a psychological study. This was the writing of a committed man who urged a very particular kind of political commitment on his readers. There was not the kind of discussion Memmi indulged in on whether or not there can be a good colon. Nor was there the corrosive pessimism, though conditions have made it impossible to ignore it, about the possibility of the colonizer ever being genuinely accepted into the world of the colonized. For reasons that have much to do with personality as well as politics, Memmi emphasized the inherent limitations in the best-intentioned of colonizers, while Fanon wasted no time on such questions and insisted on the need for collaboration and on the possibility of bringing about a new dawn. Yet the questions raised by a skeptic like Memmi were not foreign to Fanon, as he himself demonstrated in his own subsequent discussions of minorities and the more general considerations of the national question.

By 1959 when *A Dying Colonialism* appeared, the Algerian Revolution had been going on for five years, and the more disastrous extremes to which Frenchmen and Algerians were to go in pursuit of their respective goals had already become a part of the national histories of both peoples. Fanon, in conformity with his views, had decided to become engaged in the struggle. It has been suggested that he knew of the decision to open the struggle in 1954 although he himself did not join the FLN until two years later.[81] Within two years of the appearance of his sociological study, Fanon died, in the winter of 1961, hailed as one of the martyrs of the Revolution and lauded for his many contributions to Algeria. It is to this part of his life that we must now turn, to assess the controversial question of the role of the man in the Algerian Revolution and to consider the many aspects of the complex nature of his political legacy.

-III-

THE MILITANT, 1956–1961

"Frantz Fanon!

Ton exemple restera toujours vivant. Repose en paix! L'Algérie ne t'oubliera pas."

Extract from speech delivered at Fanon's funeral by the Vice-President of the Provisional Government of the Republic of Algeria, Belkacem Krim.

El Moudjahid, No. 88, December 21, 1961

-1-

The Travail of Independence

Fanon had been in Tunis for two years when *A Dying Colonialism* appeared. He had come in 1957 after being expelled from Algeria. The expulsion was directly related to his political work, and specifically sparked by his letter of resignation which was sent to the French Resident General of Algeria in 1956. In that now famous statement Fanon deplored conditions in Algeria which he claimed made his work as a psychiatrist meaningless. The political implications were clear and it is not a tribute to the French administration that they understood its charges. Within the space of two years Fanon became a militant supporter and member of the FLN, and by 1959 he was engaged in serious work with the exterior delegation of the FLN in Tunis. In the same period of time, from 1957 to 1959, the activities of the National Liberation Front had so expanded that they were radically altering the course of Algerian history, disrupting French life and affecting the nature of Franco-Algerian relations. By 1962, the victory of the FLN and the achievements of its goals were to make Algeria independent. The nearly eight years of war produced extraordinary results, even if the post-war situation threatened them almost immediately. But the history of the eight years cannot be understood without an appreciation of what had transpired before. With respect to this point contemporary Algerian critics are correct when they indicate that Fanon was generally ignorant of the nature of the Algerian nationalist activities of the pre–1954 period. The criticism must be understood in the context in which it is made, however, which is to diminish Fanon's stature as a dominant figure in the revolutionary period.

But in 1953 when he arrived in Blida-Joinville, Fanon did not need a history lesson in order to understand what was going on, any more than illiterate Algerians needed a civics course in order to know of what they were deprived. The colonization of Algeria that made of that North African country what the French called a part of metropolitan France had begun in 1830. Algerian historians and nationalists maintain that resistance to foreign, French, rule began virtually at the same time that it was installed. But the periods of resistance had been met on each occasion with an effective force and France remained in Algeria. By the time of the First World War, France had also installed itself in the neighboring countries of Tunisia and Morocco. Across the Maghreb, the legacy of French rule marked the northern part of the continent and affected its independence movements. The enemy, France, that strange enemy that continued to be loved and imitated at the very time it was being so strenuously fought and rejected, found itself the object of three separate decolonization efforts that culminated in the independence of Tunisia, Morocco, and eventually, Algeria. By all odds, the struggle for independence in Algeria was the most bitter and the fighting, the most severe. Ironically, it had been the one colony among the Maghreb protectorates that France considered to be a part of the homeland, and the promise of assimilation was to seal this compact relationship. But assimilation and the granting of full citizenship rights to Algerians, or French Muslims as they were occasionally called, did not come to pass. The hesitations expressed in the French National Assembly were mild in comparison with the stubborn refusal with which these proposals were met in Algeria among the colon population. To each there was a logic that was not to be disturbed, and underlying the opposition in France and in Algeria was a barely muted fear that the balance between the Algerian and French populations might be upset in an unfavorable direction.

Whether or not assimilation was possible in any colonial situation was not an academic matter. To maintain a colony in its dependent status and simultaneously promise equality with the citizens of the mother country is something of a feat. What did it mean politically if not that the colony would no longer be treated as such, but on the contrary, that it would be integrated with the colonizing state? In retrospect, what is remarkable about the Algerian situation is the extent to which Algerians wished to be assimilated into France; the extent to which they supported such legislative proposals as the 1936 Blum-Viollette Bill that would have admitted certain categories of Algerian Muslims to the practice of full political rights in France. The discussion and controversy roused by the Blum-Viollette Bill in Paris was symptomatic of the complexity behind French colonization policy. But the substantive issues were not difficult to discern. The ultimate end of assimilation, if it was indeed the goal of colonization, would have ended it. Among Algerians reactions to the bill were varied. But all of the organized parties of the day, whether around Ferhat Abbas, Messali Hadj, or Ben Badis and the orthodox *ulema,* had something to say on the matter. Abbas was the most vociferously in favor of the project. Messali rejected it and the *ulema* group offered a support that has been described as tactical rather than ideological. For those who had aspired to assimilation, and the name of Ferhat Abbas is simply the best-known among them, the promise and the failure of the Blum-Viollette Bill in the French Assembly constituted a turning point in their expectations of French policy.

If one takes 1936 as a critical date in the recent history of Algerian-French relations, then the conclusion one must come to concerning the debacle of the Blum-Viollette plan and the supplementary recommendations proposed in the Assembly, is that the most optimistic and liberal of French colonial options had been destroyed. If the wishes of assimilationists among Algerians could not hope to be satisfied, then what kind of support, if any, could be expected from the Algerian population? It may be a crude and simplistic answer to suggest that no support was desired from the bulk of the population, only a tacit approval or even the absence of an active discontent. From certain favored minorities among ethnic and religious groups, favorable support was expected because favors had been granted. But the bulk of the population, illiterate and assumed to be apolitical, was expected to remain silent. If the only intermediaries or spokesmen for Algeria were the French of Algeria, and among them the loudest were the confirmed anti-assimilationists, then the obstacles in the way of communication and liberalization may be seen to have been vast. One observer of Algerian events had this to say: "Before 1940, I knew a number of Algerian intellectuals; those I met were militantly in favor of integration; for this reason they were assiduously persecuted by the French administration and by colonial circles who were revolted by such an insupportable claim."[1]

The promises of integration were not equally appealing to all Algerians, and if colonial circles were revolted, as Tillion remarks, then one must add that some Algerian circles were equally revolted, for other reasons. Assimilation meant that qualified Algerians could become French. They did not have to abandon their Muslim status, an earlier condition, and they could acquire French citizenship. But not all Algerians were such enthusiastic supporters of France. Traditionalists and non-assimilated Algerians had no illusions as to what the choice offered. It is not an accident that the categories to whom citizenship was offered were those most prone to favor assimilation. The entire assimilation argument touched on the heart of the colonial question. It was not even a matter of discussing the very essential question of needed economic reforms—which various forms of cooperation seemed to guarantee. The question was a political one. Ought Algeria to remain a part of France, or ought it to be autonomous or even sovereign? Was there an Algerian personality that was not assimilable to that of France? The assimilated minority was precisely that, but what of the majority? If Algerian nationalism was forged out of the organization of discontent provoked by French colonization and the frustrations of false hopes, it was, nevertheless, a reality to be dealt with. The paradox is that even modest assimilationist offers could at one time have answered the demands of Algerians who were not prepared to ask for independence but who wished to see the programs they believed the French were sincerely offering implemented. By refusing to act where there was still a margin of action possible, the French administration unintentionally provoked Algerians to a full realization that reform and assimilation were illusory promises and that what they promised was not enough.

Long before the goal of independence was recognized as the only just end of political action, discontent with the nature of French policy in Algeria was rife. Unemployment, the concentration of industrial and commercial activity in the hands of European elements, the redistribution of agricultural land that favored the colonizer: these are but a few of the well-docu-

mented aspects of colonial life that accounted for the slow swell-
ing anger of the indigenous population. On the cultural level the
story is even more well known. Education was not encouraged
for the Algerian masses, and there was no official attempt to
promote the teaching of Arabic. On the contrary, the native
language was taught as a foreign language, while French was
taught to those students fortunate enough to go to school. The
argument of depersonalization and the excesses of post-
independence life which sometimes appear to justify an inordinate pride in Algerian history and in Algeria's specifically
Arabo-Muslim personality, must be understood against this extended background. And yet the creation of organizations dedicated to loosening France's hold on the country, not to speak of
direct political action against France, were comparatively slow in
emerging. The possibility of reaching agreements with France
and of instituting reforms seems to have been a more common
reflex among Algerian political leaders than the push to create
nationalist movements that would put an end to French rule.

Still the FLN declaration of November 1, 1954, that called for
the recognition of the Algerian personality and the recognition
of its sovereign status, did not arise without some earlier experience. As early as 1925 Messali Hadj, the remarkable charismatic
and tyrannic leader of Etoile Nord Africaine, the first of the
modern political organizations in the pre-FLN period, became
active in France. Given the regular emigration of Algerian workers to the French capital and the important numbers of Algerians resident in France, the establishment of such a movement
in Paris is not altogether surprising. It was not Messali's locale
that made his movement suspect among later Algerian nationalists, but his arrogant sense of exclusive leadership and eventually, after 1954, the sentiment that he was susceptible to French
pressure. It was to the successor of the Etoile, the PPA, the Parti
du Peuple Algérien, founded in 1937, that some of those pro-
assimilationist Algerians who became disillusioned (to return to
Germaine Tillion's phrase) turned after 1936. Ten years later,
after intermittent jail sentences, yet another party was created
by the same man, this time the MTLD, the Mouvement pour le
Triomphe des Libertés Démocratiques. Contemporary leaders
in Algeria who recall the effect that Messali had on them are
quick to admit the attraction which he exercised among those
Algerians who did not identify with the assimilated minority and

who looked forward to independence. For all his domineering behavior, Messali came out in favor of total independence very early. At one time a member of the French Communist Party, but solidly loyal to his Algerian personality and its complex components, Messali provided a political education for substantial numbers of future nationalists.

In 1931, Sheikh Ben Badis organized the association of *ulema*, nominally a non-political affair but one that contained very explicit political assumptions. Ben Badis concentrated his efforts, and those of his collaborators, on the construction of mosques and the propagation of Arabic language and culture. The objective was to prohibit the gradual alienation of Algerians from their cultural heritage; to prevent them from becoming assimilated Europeans. To those who did not share the cultural and religious orientation of Ben Badis, Ferhat Abbas offered the example of an Algerian politician in favor of Franco-Muslim cooperation. The path from religious traditionalism to secular modernism was long, but it ultimately led to a political merger and to a reordering of priorities in order to achieve the same end. Abbas was active from the mid–1930's until he emerged as a member of the FLN in 1956, and eventually as the first President of the GPRA, Algeria's Provisional Government established in 1958. In 1938 and again in 1944 and 1946, Abbas founded a number of parties with increasingly nationalist demands. But their characteristics were still cooperation and reform rather than immediate independence. Still even the moderate Abbas, in his 1943 Manifesto of the Algerian People, called for self-determination and the recognition of Arabic as the official language of Algeria. From this to the demand for an independent Algerian state, even one that would continue to be close to France, was not a long step to take.

In 1944 after having been jailed by the Governor General of Algeria, Georges Catroux, Abbas formed the AML, the Amis du Manifeste de la Liberté. In the spring of 1945 when a congress of the party was to meet, tensions arose among the three political groupings described above. But the difficulties of the congress were entirely superseded by the Setif massacres of May 1945. There seems to be a general consensus among nationalists and historians who have written of this period, that Setif was a critical event in the development of an Algerian national consciousness. It marked the beginning of a new phase of Algerian aspirations. On the 8th of May, the Allied powers were celebrating their victory, marking the end of hostilities. In Algeria, celebrations and manifestations were taking place, with authorization, in numerous cities and towns. Setif was but one of them. There, demonstrations by partisans of the Abbas and Messali Hadj parties took on a more energetic turn than had been anticipated. Abbas had called for calm and the order of the day was for a controlled action. But the mood appears to have been one of tension and nationalist agitation. There are variations on the precise nature of the beginning of the riots that led to the massacres, but the end result was that police fired on the participants, and in the process innocent people as well as partisans were killed. The reprisal against Europeans was strong, and one source suggests that after the entire affair was over no less than 103 Europeans were dead (including the 29 killed at Setif) and 110 were wounded.[2] But if European losses were important, the counterattack by the French was remarkable for its severity. French sources claim that some 1,165 Muslims were killed; Algerians say that the figure was closer to 45,000; other observers set the number in between.[3] The impact of Setif, as a symbol of the entire wave of reprisals which lasted some eight days, is difficult to overestimate. Coming as it did after the termination of the Second World War, during which Algerians had fought with Frenchmen and shared in the traumas of war, Setif was an ugly reminder that France and Algeria were not, after all, equals in peacetime. Rabah Bitat, one of the original partisans in the FLN struggle, noted in retrospect, in March of 1956, when he was testifying before the Military Tribunal of Algiers, that after Setif he knew without the shadow of a doubt that he was one of the colonized.[4] He described May 1945 as having created a veritable abyss between the Muslim and European populations in Algeria.

From Setif to November 1, 1954, there is a comprehensible logic if not the thread of inevitability. Success for the nationalists, at any rate, was never guaranteed. In 1947 a more liberal legislation introducing a two-college Algerian Assembly was put into effect. That it continued to be dominated by the Europeans of the country and that the elections held in 1948 were widely recognized as fraudulent did not help matters. But meanwhile among Algerians who had lost faith in the efficacy of legal action, other options seemed desirable. Studies have been made on the gradual developments leading away from reliance on the parliamentary, legal political system, as a way of promoting change, to the direct military and subsequently revolutionary order of events.[5] It is a sad commentary on the possibilities that existed but remained unrealized, that legal methods of change were tested without success. It was not for lack of effort on the Algerian side, and for this the political biography of Abbas is the most convincing piece of evidence.

In 1947 a clandestine organization that operated in paramilitary style and that did not bother itself with trivial legalities came into operation. It was the first step, organizationally, in the construction of the CRUA, the Comité Révolutionnaire pour l'Unité et l'Action, that was established in 1954 and that was the direct predecessor of the FLN. The Organisation Secrète (OS), formed in 1947, operated under the generous umbrella of Messali's support, without his knowledge. When it was uncovered three years later its leaders were jailed, but the momentum was not stopped. Ahmed Ben Bella, Algeria's first President after independence, was among the OS members, and when he escaped from the Blida jail where he was held he made his way to Cairo, a landing place that was to cause great consternation in France. Mohammed Khider and Ait Ahmed, two other members of the OS who subsequently joined their efforts in the creation of the FLN, also fled to Cairo. Those who remained in the Algerian capital went into hiding while others dispersed in the Aures. The secret CRUA was formed in an effort to pressure existing organizations, specifically the MTLD, to turn to revolutionary action as opposed to their ineffective reformist attempts. In the summer of 1954 a reunion known as the Reunion of the 22 brought together the participants of the OS and the members of the CRUA. In the process of their discussions the clandestine leaders divided the country into districts, *wilayas,* which were to serve as bases of operation for the duration of the struggle. It was in the fall of 1954, in October, that the last meeting of the CRUA took place. On that occasion the name FLN, the National Liberation Front, was adopted and the decision for action on the morning of November 1 was taken. In retrospect, the statement issued by the FLN in November was extraordinary in its optimism and its arrogance. Without a mass following to speak of, with a scarcity of arms that was almost crippling, with no program save independence and collective leadership, the National

Liberation Front issued "demands" and later referred to this initiative as the first gesture of compromise for peace with the French government.

"On the 1st of November 1954 at zero hour, forty raids of armed commandos of the CRUA occurred at different points in Algerian territory. At the same time a tract was issued in all of Algeria. An appeal 'to the Algerian people, to the militants of the national cause,' it declared the onset of the period of revolutionary struggle against a colonial system that was invulnerable to reformist actions."[6] The tract that was described in *el Moudjahid* was not only an appeal to the Algerian people; it contained an invitation to the French authorities to discuss the goals of the nationalist movement.[7]

> . . . We propose an honorable program of discussion to the French authorities if they are animated by good faith and if, once and for all, they recognize the right of those whom they rule to self-determination.

> 1) The recognition of Algerian nationality by an official declaration abrogating edicts, decrees and laws making Algeria French territory contrary to history, geography, language, religion and the customs of the Algerian people.

> 2) The opening of negotiations with authorized spokesmen of the Algerian people on the basis of the recognition of Algerian sovereignty, one and indivisible.

> 3) The creation of a climate of confidence by the liberation of all political prisoners, the lifting of all extraordinary measures and the stopping of all efforts directed at the pursuit of the fighting forces.

As against these demands, the FLN offered the following program that was prophetic in its choice of subjects. It treated the matter of the European minority and the long-term nature of relations with France. Minority rights and the need for a continued economic relationship were two features which were to reappear in virtually all subsequent discussions and eventually in the Evian negotiations between the FLN and the French government concluded in 1962.

> 1) French cultural and economic interests, honestly acquired, will be respected as well as individuals and families.

2) All Frenchmen who wish to remain in Algeria will have the choice between (retaining) their nationality of origin—which (if kept) will make them strangers in relation to existing laws, or they will opt for Algerian nationality, and in that case, will be considered as such in their rights and obligations.

3) The ties between France and Algeria will be defined and will constitute the object of an accord between the two powers on the basis of equality and mutual respect. . . .

French reaction to the outbreak of war in Algeria was tempered by domestic problems that were a result of the difficulties directly attributable to colonial wars elsewhere. In 1954 the French efforts in Indochina were ended by the inglorious defeat at Dien Bien Phu and subsequent negotiations in Geneva. In the Maghreb France was in trouble in Morocco, and within one year both Morocco and Tunisia had been granted virtual independence. The prospect of abandoning Algeria, regarded as an integral part of metropolitan France, was highly unlikely. The liberal Premier Mendès-France, who had dealt honorably with the Indochina affair and had extricated France to save it from total defeat, was not prepared to contemplate any such activity closer to home. In January 1955 Jacques Soustelle was named Governor General of Algeria and by the spring of that year he had introduced measures designed to effect a final control of the rebellion. But Soustelle was moved by the desire for reform as well as the need to control the FLN actions. Even though he was checked in the former wish by the conservative pressures of the colon population of Algeria, he eventually bowed to their wishes and impressed by their expression of concern and solidarity, he gradually became their spokesman in Paris. The beloved and suffering Algeria of Soustelle was the Algeria of the colon. While the French sent in reinforcements and established detention camps, denying that they were doing anything of the sort, the FLN and its military branch, the Army of National Liberation, the ALN, were making progress. It is estimated that by 1956 the FLN had increased its mass support, had established a relatively complex organization on Algerian territory, and had succeeded in effecting a unity among former political competitors. Algerians claimed that the ALN had grown from a force of 3,000 to close to 50,000 men by August of 1956.[8] By that time other innovations were also in evidence: Algerian students organized themselves in the UGEMA, the Union Générale des Etudiants Musulmans Algériens; Algerian workers left the French trade union to form their own, UGTA, Union Générale des Travailleurs Algériens; and an Algerian Red Crescent was organized in secret. In November 1954 and again in the following year, efforts to have the Algerian question discussed at the United Nations were made. They were of course unsuccessful in this period, but the attempts themselves generated interest and with interest came an awareness of what was happening in the country. At Bandung in April of 1955 and in September of the same year, delegations presented their case before friendly governments. In the fall of 1955 it was to the neutralist leaders, Nasser, Nehru and Tito, that the FLN sent a memorandum. But in addition to this growth of support, the greatest victory of 1956 and, in retrospect, one of the most important events of this two-year period of the war was the meeting in the valley of the Soummam.

In France the government of Guy Mollet took a determined stand on Algerian developments. But neither Mollet nor his appointee in Algeria, Robert Lacoste, seemed able to control the situation in the North African departments. What was to become painfully clear as time went on was that any French Premier and later de Gaulle himself, had to cope not only with the FLN and the ALN, but with organized and unbending French and European settlers in Algeria who looked unkindly at any efforts at reform. From the point of view of the colon population anything short of total liquidation of the FLN rebellion was unsatisfactory. In retrospect the years 1956 through 1958 were to mark a gradual erosion of French control and authority in Algeria—not the control by the colon population and its administrators, but the control exercised from the mainland. Yet, to read the pronouncements of the French Premiers and their Governors-General, it is difficult to imagine that they were regarded as appeasers. Experienced listeners came to equate any toleration of nationalist demands with defeat. Hence, it must have been something of a consolation when Guy Mollet, the Socialist Premier designate in 1956, declared that he need not insist "on what France would become without Algeria [and] Algeria without France."[9] The unthinkable was uttered as a negative. "To both Europeans and Moslems, I once again solemnly declare," stated Mollet, on another occasion, "that the union between Metropolitan France and Algeria is indissoluble. The Government will fight to keep France in Algeria, and she will remain there. There is no future for Algeria without France."[10]

In the early winter of 1956, Robert Lacoste was named Resident Minister of Algeria. It was to Lacoste that Frantz Fanon addressed his letter of resignation in the same year. Given Lacoste's orientation, it hardly came as a surprise that he did not welcome its contents. Lacoste, in an address before the armed forces in the spring of 1956, reminded the men before whom he spoke that "the inalienable rights of France and Algeria do not, in my opinion, admit of any equivocation." He went on to speak of the need for a revision of the outmoded and unimplemented statute of 1947. His recommendations were for reform, but within the existing context. He went so far as to remark that the French Parliament had recognized the existence of an Algerian personality and he asked his listeners, on whom the burden of peace and pacification would fall, to do no less. In the same speech he made the following remarks:

> It has been said and reiterated that every conflict is, basically, a conflict of ideologies. But contrary to what may happen in other places, and even if behind them the disturbing Communist propaganda and the conquering passion of Islam may be discerned, our adversaries of today, the terrorists, the rebels, have no ideology other than the wish to evict France from Algeria.
>
> In this 'internal' conflict which they want to transform into an 'external' conflict, they have no valid theory or framework. They are trying to make up for the absence of any political doctrine by a real racism (which the unconscionable action of certain Frenchmen has, unfortunately, sometimes encouraged). They are seeking to justify, on the grounds of religious kinship, the inadmissible interference of foreigners.
>
> Against this absence of ideology, we can offer not any particular political ideology but that which the present crisis may reinvigorate, the 'national' ideology, the love of France. Our country's enormous resources of culture and generosity have indeed been barely tapped for Algeria. It is up to you to help me draw them here. For we shall build a new Algeria only by giving this Franco-Moslem population, often still backward, complete equality of rights and duties with Metropolitan France in order to satisfy its dignity and legitimate self-respect.[11]

Two days before the Soummam meeting was held, Lacoste announced that two hundred thousand men had arrived from France to aid in the process of pacification. This nearly doubled the figure already present in Algeria. Would these new recruits also be tapping the culture and generosity of France for the benefit of the underdeveloped Algerians? Between 1956 and 1958 the entire face of the struggle changed. If the French were deeply committed, militarily and certainly politically, on the Algerian side much had transpired to reflect how poorly timed Lacoste's good wishes were. The ALN dug itself into the countryside, reaching the entire territory, including the South. The city of Algiers became the target of direct action, and from December 1956 until the fall of 1957 the period of the Battle of Algiers was on. The terrorism of the French was an excuse and a justification for the terrorism of the FLN. International commissions were sent to investigate and endless commentaries and exhortations to good behavior accomplished little. In Paris Germaine Tillion returned again to Algiers with one such investigatory commission and in the same trip managed to meet clandestinely with Saadi Yaacef, the feared FLN activist in the Algiers zone. Her interviews with him are a model of sanity in an insane situation.[12] The year 1956 ended badly; five FLN leaders including Ahmed Ben Bella had been kidnapped by the French as they were on their way to Tunis from Rabat. Algerian unions were forcibly dissolved, and the population, military and civilian alike, suffered heavily under the repressive hand of the administration.

In the spring of 1957 Lacoste was no longer thinking in terms of inspiring love and friendship or even fraternization. The discovery of oil in the Sahara had effected a change in attitude.

An event of paramount importance, finally, is likely substantially to change the destiny of Algeria and France: the discovery of considerable mineral—especially petroleum—deposits in the Sahara. These discoveries, which are significant in terms of the world market, will bear out our country's mission in Africa and justify even further all the efforts of Metropolitan France to restore calm to Algeria, which is the key to the Sahara.

As a matter of fact, the Algerian Sahara, where up to now almost all the new discoveries have been made, will become part of a vaster French economic community whose expansion will considerably help the development of northern Algeria.

This will enable our country to recover the elements of power and independence which it has lacked for a long time. With this new power and independence, it will be able to resume the place that rightfully belongs to it in Europe and the world.[13]

If oil and the prospects of oil were cause for a serious intensification of the fighting, the combination of oil and France's strategic interests in Bizerte and Mers el Kebir were equally compelling. These interests were not presented to the informed public as relevant to France alone; they were relevant to the entire NATO network. The argument that France was fighting in defense of French interests was expanded so that France became the guarantor of European interests against communist expansion and the stealthy advance of Arabism. The arguments of the OAS in 1962 were not substantially different. In essence their propagators had no interest in Algeria per se, and certainly not in its population. What hypnotized them was the larger perspective, the manichean vision of the world in which the forces defending French integrity in Algeria suddenly loomed as the defenders of Christendom against the secular allies of men bent on jihads.[14]

It was not only in the ranks of the OAS, between 1960 and 1962, that such imaginative reconstructions were proposed. In the French Assembly after the bombings of Sakiet Sidi Youssef in Tunisia, an event that enraged international opinion and caused scandals at home, the dimensions of the debate on the Algerian question were mightily expanded. By then the military administration had come to play a role of considerable importance in Algeria. It was widely known that Lacoste in his invitation to General Massu and the 10th Parachute Division had increasingly handed over security and police responsibilities to the military. The reformist interests and efforts of the military in Algeria, the diversity of policies, and the variety of men and attitudes added up to a complex picture that generalizations can but distort. The policies of a government that had been essentially taken over by the military were not in absolute accord with those of the homeland. In Paris, the view from the National Assembly was not the same as that seen from Algiers. And in Algiers the army and the police forces were soon to reveal splits in their own ranks that had grave implications for the future. The allegation that the government at home was sabotaging the efforts of the army in Algeria was used as an ugly reminder of other days when the government had also not been energetic enough in its support of its military. Indochina was not forgotten; nor was 1940. But how were the arguments used? What was being defended at any cost, and why? The acrimony that marked the debates in the press and the Assembly left few men unscathed. Meanwhile in Algeria, cabinet crises were interpreted as signs of weakness, and defeatism was seen as the inevitable end of interminable discussions. The Supreme Commander of French forces in Algeria, General Salan, took a dim view of these proceedings in May of 1958. He called on his supporters in Algeria and Frenchmen on the mainland not to abandon their troops and not to abandon their Muslim friends who were expecting protection from the rebels.

On the 10th of May the vigilance committee that represented the association of veterans, patriotic groups, and political parties active in Algeria called on the Algerians to express their opposition to the choice of a government by the National Assembly. Within three days General Massu sent a telegram to President Coty informing him that a civilian and military committee of public safety had been created. The objective was to create a responsible authority that could deal with the goal of French policy, to keep Algeria French, and to put a final end to defeatists and reformists who were wasting the nation's youth and the army's pride by undermining it from across the Mediterranean. Less than one month later, after the threat of a direct putsch on Paris, General de Gaulle was persuaded to take over the direction of the government in exchange for the extraordinary powers he made a condition of his return. The Fifth Republic was thus born out of the chaos and internecine strife caused by the Algerian Revolution, an event that symbolized yet another step in the dissolution of the French empire. It was out of the confrontation between the generals in Algeria who had threatened the authority of civilian rule in France and hence the life of the Republic itself, and the men of the Fourth Republic and eventually de Gaulle, that the decisive step was taken to allow de Gaulle to return on his own terms. For the duration of these days, the FLN was quiet. It was understood that the course of events in the motherland was important for the outcome of the Revolution. But an important step was soon to be taken.

In Tunis, on September 19, 1958, the first Provisional Government of the Algerian Republic was created with Ferhat Abbas as its President. The decision to create the GPRA was of the utmost importance. That it had to reside in exile presented obvious difficulties, and the separation of the GPRA from the fighting forces who were largely concentrated within the country created the split between interior and exterior which has loomed so large in Algeria's politics. But a number of decisions to concentrate and organize the military, first on the east and west in the areas adjacent to the Algerian frontier in Morocco, at Oujda, and at Ghardimaou in the east, represented attempts to consolidate power in two and eventually in one center. Communications between the interior, the military on the frontier, and the headquarters of the civilian government in Tunis were not always excellent. Differences of political outlook, the difficulties of coping with an impossible military situation, and the inherently distinct views of the military and the civilian members of the FLN-ALN family, produced splits that lasted after independence. It is vital to understand the internal political differences as much as they can be understood, given the fact that we must still wait for an Algerian account of the Revolution and this aspect of its history. But whatever difficulties may have been increased or even created by the establishment of the GPRA, in retrospect the benefits seem to have been greater. Relations with countries in the Arab world, in the African continent, and in Asia immediately followed. By 1960 some 19 countries had offered de facto or de jure recognition. The situation of the FLN delegation in New York at the United Nations was enhanced. The obvious advantage was that there now existed a governing authority that could speak for the FLN and Algeria.

In October 1958, one month after the GPRA had been constituted, de Gaulle offered the FLN his Peace of the Brave, something less than the immediate independence the FLN wanted, and under conditions of continued siege which made acceptance intolerable. But the mood was clear and in spite of the continued destruction of life and property, it seemed obvious that a point of no return had been reached. In 1959, de Gaulle went a step further and offered Algerians three options: identification with France, association with France, or outright secession. Some officials in Algeria today claim that peace had been possible in 1959 and the three years of war that continued and worsened in intensity might have been avoided if the French government had been sincere in its offer. It has been indicated that had this been the case, the nature of Algero-French relations in the post-war period would of course also have been different, and perhaps the circumstances leading Algeria to take a socialist path would have been altered. This assumes that Algeria's decision to follow a socialist line of development was dependent on the degree and nature of French cooperation that could be expected. It is an argument that leaves much unsaid. In 1959 at any rate, the GPRA did not succeed in bringing about the conditions it considered as a prerequisite to accepting the self-determination offer, and the fighting continued. It is probably more accurate to say that both things occurred simultaneously: the pursuit of the war and the submission of offers for cease-fire and discussion. In their declaration in response to the self-determination proposal, the GPRA pointed out that it was meaningless to talk of elections and public opinion in a country in which the army of occupation was close to half a million and where there as many gendarmes, militia, and police. When those men would be withdrawn and when political prisoners would be liberated, then free discussions with the GPRA might be possible.

There were other situations which the GPRA also recognized as intolerable and these seemed to be worsening. Generally speaking the 1958–1960 period was described as among the most difficult of the war. The number of Algerian refugees was increasing and the camps in Morocco and Tunisia were filled with men, women, and children in various degrees of destitution. Inside the country, detention camps and the policy of forcibly moving populations in order to disrupt loyalties and what potential there might have been for organized resistance, created a mass of uprooted men whom independence could not easily rehabilitate. As if this was not enough, the accounts of torture, in Algeria and in France, multiplied to the amazement of a numb population. Clandestine publications revealed the brutalization of the French forces, and the hopeless arguments of who was to blame for the onset of terrorism did nothing to help those who had been murdered or those who lived as broken human beings.[15]

If the FLN was discontent with what de Gaulle offered, the army in Algeria was equally unhappy and prepared to act. The demonstrations of the week of January 1960 (known as "Barricades Week") were meant to impress the government in Paris with the strength and solidarity of the French military spirit in Algiers. The military claimed to speak on behalf of the European population and for those Muslims who were opposed to the FLN. The numbers of Muslims who preferred French military support and the guarantee of a continued French presence were doubtless less numerous than the inflated figures which General Massu publicized, but the French population and its extremist fringe were clearly allies. It was the Algérie française movement that provided strong backing for this military resistance to de Gaulle's policies. And it was the same milieu that offered support for the organization of the FAF, the Front de l'Algérie française, created in June of 1960 in order to unite and represent the European minority and its anti-FLN Muslim supporters. It was in June of 1960 that de Gaulle renewed his invitation to the FLN for direct talks, a step that ended in failure but that marked another attempt on the road to reconciliation. It is in this context, with the military-civilian tension on the one hand, and the FLN struggle against the French military on the other, that the events of 1960–1962 must be regarded. On December 11, 1961, the counter-demonstrations held in Algiers by the FLN massed thousands of supporters of the movement and had a decisive impact on French observers, particularly those in the government at home. But it also enraged and frightened the clandestine opposition to de Gaulle and marked yet another reason for the organization of the forces against independence. The polarization of forces and reactions intensified the brutality of the struggle but it also cleared the air for those who had any misconceptions as to what was possible.

It is impossible to overestimate the importance of December 11. French historians are nearly unanimous in pinpointing it as the turning point of the entire Algerian War. The psychological jolt was enormous. The counterdemonstrations graphically drove home the lesson that the Moslems could, if they chose, play at the Europeans' game and win it, for they far outnumbered the Europeans; and suddenly they realized their own force. The pied noir ultras more than ever distrusted the Army, which had let them down once again, as during Barricades Week. Within the Army, many officers experienced second thoughts about the great hope of May 1958. Integration, it seemed, had never existed, or it had been outstripped by events. The ensuing despair of some soldiers and civilians led, stage by stage, to the formation of the OAS.[16]

De Gaulle had begun to work towards negotiating a settlement with the FLN in 1961, prior to the December demonstrations. In fact, it was the knowledge that he was working with the GPRA that angered those who felt cheated by the actions taken in Paris. But the sailing was not smooth at either end of the line. Although the Algerians recognized that much headway had been made between the abortive talks at Melun held in June 1960 and those inaugurated at Evian in May 1961, it took time and effort to arrive at a common understanding of how to approach negotiation, let alone the negotiation itself. From deploring the impact of independence on the Algerian economy, a veiled allusion to the idea that Algeria could not survive without France, to a recognition that independence might lead to cooperation between the two countries in another spirit, the path was long and arduous. It was in March, on the 7th, that a cease-fire was announced and the Evian phase of the negotiations began.

El Moudjahid summarized the pre-negotiation talks that lasted between March 7 and 18 in the following way:

A cease-fire is concluded. It will be applied pending the cessation of military operations and armed struggle on Algerian territory, on the 19th of March 1962, at 12 o'clock.

Guarantees relative to the operation of self-determination and the organization of public powers in Algeria during the transition period have been defined by common accord.

The formation, at the end of the self-determination [phase] of an independent and sovereign State in conformity with Algerian realities, and under these conditions, the cooperation of France and Algeria in response to the mutual interest of the two countries (is envisioned). The French government and the Provisional Government of the Algerian Republic believe that the solution of independence for Algeria in cooperation with France is the appropriate solution to this situation. The French government and the Provisional Government of the Algerian Republic have therefore, of a common accord, defined this solution in their declarations which will be submitted to the approval of voters during the balloting on the self-determination issue.[17]

In the March 19, 1962 issue of *el Moudjahid*, the last one to be included in the special three-volume series that brought together most of the wartime issues of the newspaper, the last line of the last article read as follows:

> The cease-fire conference is being held at Evian from the 7th to the 18th of March; on the basis of political agreements reached at Rousses, then at Evian, the Algerian Revolution attains the first part of its objectives and decides to stop the armed struggle.[18]

The important passage here is the one that indicates that the political agreements of Rousses and Evian marked the first stage of the Algerian Revolution. The implication is that there was more involved in the ultimate aims of the Revolution. The point is an important one because the Evian agreements were vital in shaping forthcoming Algerian-French relations. The criticisms that have been leveled, in retrospect, at the Algerians for accepting such accommodating accords must be seen in this light. Economic ties and military bases are two sensitive areas that have been open to question after the event. But in other respects, with regard to the situation of French residents in Algeria, the question of citizenship, the question of cultural exchange and the delicate matter of continuing the communication, culturally, between France and Algeria, while attempting to introduce Algerian and Arab educational systems and structures, all of these matters were—with the exception of the last item—spelled out in considerable detail in the Evian talks. They were not as sensitive, in a direct sense, as the questions of retaining French bases or encouraging a close economic relationship with the former mother country. But if Evian was meant to end the war and no more, these critical and difficult matters were of the essence in subsequent post-war years. In fact, Algerian economic development was closely tied to and affected by the French economy and the nature of economic and political relations between the two states. The oil discussions, which became so embittered in the summer of 1970 and which eventually led to the nationalizations of February 1971, reflected how much of the spirit of Evian was still present in the French attitude towards Algeria and how much Evian may have prejudiced relations against the long-range interests of Algeria.

In terms of Algeria's situation in 1962, after close to eight years of vicious war, it was a remarkable tribute to all concerned that Franco-Algerian relations were as cordial as they were. It was also a tribute to pragmatism that those responsible for Algeria's future realized that political independence would be of little use without abundant economic help. It was not altruism or even sentimentality that was responsible for French interest in undertaking this help. It was understood that second to being present in the old sense of a colonial power, such aid and the elaborate conceptions it gave rise to provided another opportunity of guiding Algeria in an economic direction that would sustain French interest. Oil and the Sahara were not forgotten. Nor was the prospect of alternative sources of aid forgotten. As for Algeria, as was indicated above, the choices that existed for recovery and development were limited and the imperatives were great.

- 2 -

A Committed Press:
el Moudjahid

The discussion of priorities and the analyses of problems of independence and post-independence struggles were very much a part of Fanon's thinking. The more he became involved with the FLN, the more he witnessed the conditions of the Revolution, and the more he became aware of the needs and the extraordinary limitations that countries like Algeria faced. *The Wretched of the Earth* is hardly the litany of a disappointed man, as one Algerian official has tried to point out.[19] On the contrary, it is the sum of Fanon's thinking on those very problems which the FLN grappled with during the Revolution, and which the heirs of the FLN are facing now. Written in 1961, it contained a distillation of the experience Fanon had obtained in the political phase of his life; that is to say, in the years when he committed himself most directly to the FLN and the struggle for Algerian independence. It is the phase that coincides with his move to Tunis and his decision to become a formal member of the FLN.

A number of facts related to the exact date of Fanon's departure from Blida, the precise details of his reception by the FLN, and even the story of the contact between Blida via Paris and Tunis, remain less clear than one would wish. According to an article written by his wife in *Révolution africaine* in 1963, Fanon left Blida in 1956.[20] From the account of his life which forms part of a dossier commemorating his death in *el Moudjahid* (written in 1961), Fanon began his "exile" in January of 1957; more precisely on the 28th of the month.[21] Although the period of Fanon's formal membership in the FLN would seem to date from 1957, his collaboration in a spirit of solidarity had begun two years earlier. Pierre Chaulet, the pied-noir who was to become Algerian after independence, was the man who first made contact with Fanon at Blida. Through Chaulet, Fanon began to learn what the National Liberation Front was about, and he started to write for some of the underground periodicals for which Chaulet was working and writing.[22] Pierre Chaulet and his wife are considered to have been the first French militants of the FLN in Algeria. According to Mohamed Lebjaoui, the dissident Algerian exile, Chaulet was part of a group known as the Mandouze group in Algeria. André Mandouze, professor at the University of Algiers and closely allied to the partisans of the FLN without being a member of the organization, belonged to another category of Frenchmen involved in the Algerian experience. Chaulet was a French colon in Algeria. Mandouze was and remained French. Lebjaoui claims that it was through another key figure among French supporters of the FLN, Francis Jeanson, that Pierre Chaulet demonstrated his usefulness in Algerian circles. It was through Chaulet, at Jeanson's request, that contact was made with an FLN official from whom Jeanson could obtain information he wanted for the important book he and his wife were writing on the Algerian situation.[23] Through his associates and friends Chaulet was able to make the necessary contacts. It was Chaulet who obtained the interview with Abane Ramdane, one of the key thinkers of the FLN prior to his death in 1958. And it was to Abane that Chaulet declared that he considered himself to be a militant of the FLN. "Abane, sufficiently well informed of Chaulet's personality not to doubt his sincerity, immediately accepted. From that day on, Pierre Chaulet, his wife and Anne-Marie (his sister), began their political work in certain European circles, actively joining the Mandouze group along with others, and assuming all of the forms of the militant's responsibilities (liaison work, providing refuge, arms, etc)."[24]

It is perfectly plausible then that Chaulet sought out Fanon and tried to bring him closer to FLN circles. In addition to his political sympathy, Fanon must have appeared attractive because of his medical training. Chaulet and his wife and sister were especially active themselves in caring for the wounded maquisards brought in from the countryside, and they must have known of the shortage of men equipped to do this kind of work. As of 1955 then, Chaulet and Fanon struck up a friendship that was personal as well as political. After the order of expulsion from Blida, Fanon went on to Tunis, via France, Switzerland, and Italy.[25] Belkacem Krim, in the funeral oration which was published in *el Moudjahid*, recalls that Fanon answered the call of the "responsables," and joined the "exterior delegation of the FLN" in Tunis.[26] Francis Jeanson, in his postface to the second edition of *Peau noire, masques blancs*, describes Fanon as joining "us" in Paris for a few days, "in transit for Tunis, where he would rejoin the political-military état-major of the Algerian Revolution."[27] The reference is to those Frenchmen around Jeanson who were active in their collaboration with the FLN. It is clear from these texts that Fanon did not go to Tunis as a tourist, nor merely to be near the FLN leadership. He was invited to come and the arrangements for his transit were assuredly made by cooperation between the Paris-based FLN supporters and the FLN delegation in Tunis.

What were Fanon's responsibilities as assigned by the FLN? It was doubtless assumed that in addition to his medical work in Tunisian hospitals, he would contribute his services to the ALN centers for soldiers and refugees. In addition, he was to work for the FLN press organs, first *Résistance algérienne* and then *el Moudjahid*.[28] He was eventually assigned to the Ministry of Information of the Provisional Government, after its creation in 1958. Before that, he worked for the Commission de Presse, the press division of the FLN headquarters. El Mili, who has been quoted here earlier in connection with Fanon, maintains that Fanon joined the FLN in a formal manner only in the spring of 1957.[29] But his contributions to the FLN press did not await formal collaboration. The published material that appeared under Fanon's name during his lifetime, and after his death, most notably the essays included in *Pour la révolution africaine (Toward the African Revolution)*, are all taken from the *el Moudjahid* period. The nature of unpublished material which may be available, or material that appeared anonymously but is indeed Fanon's, remains to be investigated. Some material that is in *el Moudjahid* and is signed by Fanon has not been cited or included in the printed editions of his works. I refer here not only to excerpts

from what later became *A Dying Colonialism*,[30] but to the text of
his statement at the conference held in Accra in 1958, which is
omitted from *Pour la révolution africaine* and the American edition, *Toward the African Revolution*. The material in question is
signed, which makes its omission that much more surprising.[31]
In addition, there is the omission of his lecture, or rather an
excerpt from it, delivered on the occasion of the Second Congress of Black Writers held in the spring of 1959 in Rome.[32]

Fanon wrote for *el Moudjahid* between September 1957 and
January 1960. At the beginning of his apprenticeship, the newspaper and indeed the FLN press in its entirety, were undergoing
a process of reorganization. From the beginning of the period
of armed resistance in 1954, the FLN had recognized the importance of keeping the population informed of the progress of
events, and of the position of the FLN and the ALN in the
process of the struggle. The press, or more simply the use of
tracts to fulfill this function, was regarded as a vital task of
information and education. It was only in June 1956 that *el
Moudjahid* first appeared, issued in both French and Arabic, as
the earlier publications had been. *El Moudjahid* came out irregu-
larly until the press was transferred to Tunis, which occurred
only in the fall of 1957. Before that, the first and second issues,
which appeared in June and July 1956, appeared in Algeria.
From then on they appeared in Tunis: the third came out in
September; the fourth in November, to mark the Soummam
Congress; and the fifth appeared in December of the same year.
In the special edition of *el Moudjahid* published in Yugoslavia in
1962, the editors of the Algerian newspaper noted that the fifth
and sixth issues of the paper, published in January 1957, are no
longer to be found. This has been contradicted, at least in private, by an FLN official. But the entire collection of *Moudjahid*,
for this period, remains in private hands even in Algeria. The
three-volume edition published by the Yugloslav government is,
for the public, however, the closest we can come to a reading of
the complete texts until the material held in private becomes
available.

In any event, it was a feat that the editors of the early *el
Moudjahid* were able to edit their newspaper on Algerian soil.
Prior to moving the press to Tunis, however, *el Moudjahid* was
supplemented outside of Algeria, for foreign consumption, by
Résistance algérienne. This newspaper, which is the one Fanon

wrote for, was edited in three series, in three different places. It appeared in series A, B, and C, in Paris, Morocco, and Tunis. To my knowledge Fanon's contributions to *Résistance algérienne* have not been identified. While these papers were being edited, the intensification of the struggle, especially during the extended period of the Battle of Algiers, was making the continuation of publication of *el Moudjahid* in Algeria extremely difficult. In 1957 the equipment of the paper was destroyed and the staff dispersed. The seventh issue of the paper was lost in the melee and the eighth was to appear in Tetouan, Morocco, where temporary headquarters were established between August and September of 1957. It was the November 1957 issue that first came out in Tunis, although after that time, Tunis was the headquarters of the FLN press corps until June of 1962. With the move to Tunis, *Résistance algérienne* ceased publication, and the central organ of the FLN, *el Moudjahid,* took over. Internal publications continued to appear, but they were informational bulletins for internal distribution.

On the basis of this information, we can deduce that Fanon began contributing to *el Moudjahid* while it was still being edited in Morocco, since his first article appeared in the September 1957 issue. It was characteristic of the editors and staff of the paper that they generally did not publish signed articles. Anonymity was not only a way of protecting the identity of writers, who might after all have resorted to pseudonyms. It was an expression of revolutionary solidarity; of the collective effort that underlay the entire revolutionary task. From a practical point of view this has made the identification of articles that much more difficult. But there are enough Algerians alive today who participated in this period of the Revolution and in this aspect of its work, to determine the particular authorship of an article. More important than this detective work is the matter of determining who was responsible for the formulation of editorial policy. Technically, *el Moudjahid* was under the direction of the Ministry of Information, or its equivalent, prior to 1958. In any event, it was regarded as the central organ of the FLN and reflected its policy. Mohamed el Mili claims that he and Fanon worked together in the reorganization of what became *el Moudjahid* in Tetouan, Morocco, in 1957.[33] Insofar as M'hammed Yazid was involved in information and press matters before he assumed the title of Minister of Information, he was another key participant in this task. After the move of the newspaper to Tunis he was in charge, and he has spoken of Fanon as being responsible to him.[34] What is still difficult to establish is the degree of responsibility that Fanon actually had in editorial policy. When one realizes the intimate connection between the FLN and the newspaper, the question of editorial policy and initiatives becomes that much more important. On the basis of the articles that appeared during the period 1957–1960, when Fanon was active in *el Moudjahid,* his own contributions are rather small. I refer to the number of articles he wrote and not necessarily to the influence he may have wielded in the background. It is revealing that among the detractors of Fanon's influence in the Algerian Revolution today, Reda Malek and M'hammed Yazid may be counted. In all fairness to them it must be said that working outside of Algeria, Reda Malek until recently in France, and Yazid until 1971 in the United States, both men have been exposed to the exaggerated portrait of Fanon's influence in the Algerian Revolution which is so common in the West. Their attempt to put Fanon's role in a less exalted perspective may in part be attributable to this phenomenon. But there is the question of politics and internal pressures and orientations in Algerian politics today, which is also relevant.

What is striking about Fanon's writings in *el Moudjahid* is the remarkable congruity between his choice and range of subjects and those of the newspaper. Whether or not there was also a congruity in political outlooks is a more difficult matter to determine. For Fanon, the years of his journalistic work coincided with a period in which political questions were uppermost in his mind.

The FLN was undergoing difficult crises with the increase of French troops in Algeria and the intensification of battle. Sectarian differences existed among FLN members and the creation of the Provisional Government in 1958 did not eradicate these differences. The terrain was fertile for thought and action, and Fanon seems to have indulged in both. On the newspaper, he dealt primarily with matters of external policy. Questions of internal policy involving what we might call domestic matters were not generally in his domain. In a sense it is difficult to divide internal and external concerns in any firm fashion, and almost every one of the subjects with which Fanon dealt had some bearing on a position adopted by the FLN with regard to

Algeria's internal future. But it would appear that he was assigned to handle those problems that involved the exterior
primarily. That he himself was interested in internal questions
of the most sensitive kind is obvious from a reading of his last
book. It is also clear from the nature of the material selected
from his last work at the time of his death and published in *el
Moudjahid*—it was his analysis of the relation of the party to the
masses—that his understanding of critical internal issues was
appreciated.

In his *Moudjahid* phase, Fanon concentrated on four principal
themes: 1. French colonialism in Algeria; 2. the response of the
French left, including the Communist Party, to the Algerian
question; 3. the position of the FLN on minorities; and 4. relations between developments in Algeria and the Maghreb and
Africa.

The articles that can be classified under the first subject were
in fact an eclectic collection of polemical essays. There was not
yet an analysis of colonialism. In its place, there was a description of some of the worst aspects of French colonization, i.e. the
question of torture as practiced in France and Algeria. There
was an attack on reformist attitudes which tended to undermine
the political goals of the nationalists, or of their antagonists, in
France. And there was considerable attention paid to the Cold
War and its impact on Algeria. What can be considered as a
tentative analysis of colonialism, in this *el Moudjahid* period, was
motivated by the desire to expose colonialism as a total system
and to undermine the habit of partial assessments and moderate
evaluations that, to Fanon's way of thinking, ignored the holistic
character of the system. The emphasis on torture served this
purpose well. To those who maintained that this was an excess
which, if curbed, would allow an amelioration of the question,
Fanon answered that it was not an excess but a logical end of the
system. Torture, to Fanon, was an inevitable aspect of colonialism.[35] Individual cases were more dramatic than quantified ab-
stractions, but the moral was the same. In his discussion of the
case of Djamila Bouhired and the stir caused by her case in Paris,
Fanon was extremely harsh. He was deeply critical of those
people who might forget that this was but one case and there
were other anonymous cases that were equally important.[36] And
he was bitter with those Frenchmen who appeared to be more
concerned with the moral corruption of their youth than with

the effect of torture on the Algerians.[37] In his criticism of the French left Fanon offended both Frenchmen and some of his own colleagues on *el Moudjahid* who thought that he went too far. This is a question which is discussed in some detail below, but it is appropriate to mention it here because of the Bouhired reference. Fanon was uncompromising in his writing and he apparently felt that this outweighed any tactical considerations. Thus, to those who would have been content to commend the French who took a stand, even if their positions were not absolutely identical with those of the FLN, Fanon's attacks were to seem disproportionate.[38]

There was probably less disagreement on the attitude to take towards the reformers, or to those who took the position that independence would be suicidal for Algeria. As for the former, their argument was that Algerian nationalism did not exist and hence, neither did an Algerian nation. The ills of the territory could be treated by the urgent administration of economic and political reforms. The Constantine Plan of 1958 was one such example. The question might have been asked, as indeed it was, where had such a plan been earlier, when the request for it and when the receptivity towards it would have been ample to assure it some success. Fanon argued that at this stage, reforms were disguised attempts to maintain Algeria within the French camp. They were certainly not motivated by any desire to improve the lot of the nation.[39] The argument that independence would prove economically unfeasible was frequently heard in official pronouncements. Its authors were invariably also the men who maintained that Algeria could not do without France in other respects. From this point of view, to grant Algeria independence was to condemn it to suicide. This avoided discussion of the responsibility for Algeria's economic situation and it made any discussion of economic relations outside of a colonial framework appear to be irrelevant. If the political objectives of the Algerians were rejected and if their ability to sustain a nation from an economic point of view was equally questioned, then what was left to negotiate? Under these circumstances, it was not unnatural to talk of agitation by foreigners, by communists, or by other unfriendly agents. And the conclusion was that if only these people could be singled out and contained, the problem itself would disappear.

The reference to communists as agitators was to come up on

many occasions and from different sources. Anyone with the least familiarity with the position of the French Communist Party on the Algerian question would not be prone to make such a statement. But those who saw foreigners in general and communists in particular behind the Algerian affair were prepared to blame any number of people or governments, including Nasser and Egypt, for their troubles. Fanon was to write at length on the complicated matter of the French left, including the communists, and Algeria. But he had little patience with these accusations. In his discussion of the position of the Soviet Union, Fanon was equally unsentimental. He saw that Soviet interests and support of nationalist movements was a result of its position in the cold war, even though he believed that the USSR had been more receptive to these movements than the West. The cold war was analyzed in *el Moudjahid* and to a lesser extent in Fanon's articles. It was a subject he was to pay more attention to in *The Wretched of the Earth* where the emphasis was not merely on Algeria.[40] From the point of view of the newly independent states of Africa, for instance, Fanon believed that they would do well to avoid involvement in the cold war as much as possible. Their needs were to be attended to first, and where possible, without recourse to their former colonial rulers. The expression of the wish was hardly adequate to realize it. The goal of neutralist states, Fanon maintained, was to concentrate on economic problems; to deal with hunger and to promote a self-image freed of the arrogance of western criteria. But how was this to do be done? In practice, Fanon himself realized that the economic situations as opposed to the ambitions of newly independent states made self-development virtually impossible. What were the alternative sources of economic aid; how could neo-colonialism be avoided? Critics who have been disappointed with Fanon's limited observations on these subjects may have been just. He had not developed a cure for the disease. At this stage of his own life and thinking, the emphasis was on the description of the illness.

That the preferential relationship which colonial powers had developed would not be easily abandoned hardly needed a reminder. Fanon interpreted de Gaulle's position on Algeria in this light. Fanon dealt with de Gaulle's position in an article he published in the November 1, 1958 issue of *el Moudjahid*. Aware of how radical de Gaulle appeared to French colons in Algeria, and how liberal the same general appeared in Paris, Fanon rejected both interpretations and claimed that de Gaulle was quite simply doing his best to salvage what he could of French interests in Algeria.[41] If this was true for France, Fanon went on to argue, it was equally true for other European powers, and even for the United States, which was busy forging a distinct policy for itself in the African continent. John Kennedy's remarks on Algeria before and after he became President of the United States were scrutinized by the FLN. *El Moudjahid* published a number of Kennedy's statements made on different occasions to demonstrate that what appeared to be a genuine expression of good will might be something less virtuous and more politically useful.[42] Fanon himself did not seem tempted by the thought that the United States had any different thoughts on Algeria or Africa than did France. Only the style was more appropriate and the timing was effective. The United States had realized that colonialism was becoming obsolete, but it did not wish to be absent when the new wave was inaugurated.[43] At the least, Fanon gave Americans the benefit of recognizing that the future lay with independent states. And though his skepticism about the United States was great, he took note of Senator Kennedy's anti-colonialist position as a sign, along with the position of the English trade unions, that Algeria's struggle had achieved international recognition and that France would eventually have to do the same.[44]

The real motives of French policy, as of American policy, were the subject of much discussion; not only in the *el Moudjahid* articles, but later in Fanon's last book. The threat posed by neo-colonialism and the vulnerability of the new nations were themes frequently discussed at various stages of Fanon's work. There was certainly no illusion about the economic or even political hardiness of the new states. Prior to independence, there was a tendency to deal with the multiple problems of statehood in an undifferentiated manner. The priorities were different. Fanon had learned firsthand among his Algerian colleagues that there were fundamental differences on orientations for post-war Algeria. There were none on the essential matter of its independence. In his journalistic work, he did not elaborate on his own thinking along these lines. That was to emerge in *The Wretched of the Earth*. But in a style that was peculiar to him, Fanon emphasized the difference between independence and decolonization. The former was what all Algerians were working towards. Decolonization implied, in this usage, the granting of a new status to succeed the colonial relationship. Precisely because it implied the granting of freedom by the mother country to its former colony, it was unacceptable. If there was one theme which Fanon hammered at, in his private dialogue with himself in *Black Skin, White Masks,* and now in *el Moudjahid,* and again in his other books, it was that freedom is not given, it is seized, it is fought for, it is fashioned by men and nations.

-3-

The French Left and Algeria

In his essays on colonialism, Fanon dealt mainly with the impact of colonization on Algeria; but not exclusively. He was aware of how destructive the war was for France and he knew how deeply divided the population became as time went on and a settlement continued to appear remote. What concerned Fanon and Algerians in FLN circles, was the position of the left in France. Clearly, the left was considered as an ally, or a potential ally in the independence struggle. At the least, it was hoped that it would represent a more enlightened, informed current of opinion on the Algerian question at home. In practice this was not to be the case at all. Organized parties were characterized by their conformity to the official position of the government, which saw Algeria as French. Independent leftists and government critics subsequently became centers for other positions, and in some instances for radical action. If Fanon expressed an attitude that appeared to differ from that of his colleagues on *el Moudjahid,* it was only a matter of degree. There was a tactical question involved, of course, and in the long run the differences on this subject were to be important. In a series of three articles on the French left Fanon produced a devastating attack that found some of the sympathetic left as well as some Algerians dazed. He did not write on this subject again, after the appearance of his articles on the 1st and the 15th of December 1957 and in the January 1, 1958 issue of the newspaper. Doubtless he was not asked to do so. But *el Moudjahid* continued to publish articles on the subject. As time went on, Fanon's harsh line was adopted by other writers on the paper. It was less a proof of his views than a general confirmation of the situation. The revelation of differences between Fanon and some of the *el Moudjahid* staff on how to approach this question was doubtless symptomatic of more profound disagreements, not only on the question of tactics to be adopted, but ultimately on the nature of the objective. *El Moudjahid* was hardly conciliatory in its position. But there appears to have been a strong desire to distinguish between those individuals who took a courageous stand, and those individuals or parties that in practice merely mouthed words that disguised their politics. It might have been easy enough to dismiss the entire left, and perhaps Fanon's position that the left had been inconsequential in this matter was a point of view that was widely shared. But the impression which a reading of the wartime *el Moudjahid* leaves is that those who concerned themselves with this subject were thinking of the long-term relations between Algeria and France, and they were anxious to sustain, if not to build up a repertoire of good relations for the future.

Fanon's writing on the left, as on the minorities, was not always consistent. There was an alternation between an inflexible, hard line, and a marked respect for the ambiguities that existed. Did Fanon's writing on this subject have any appreciable influence in France among the left? Influence is of course so difficult to document that even if one is tempted to say yes, particularly when it comes to the possible influence of Fanon on individual, independent critics, the answer must remain a tentative one.

On December 1, 1957, Fanon introduced a series of articles under the title, "French Intellectuals and Democrats and the Algerian Revolution."[45] He began, characteristically, with a strong and direct statement. One of the duties of members of the intelligentsia as well as democratic elements in colonialist countries, he claimed, is to support the national aspirations of colonized peoples, without reservations.[46] However, before the stage of armed struggle, Fanon noted, the support that was offered was generally ineffectual. It was limited to the holding of meetings, occasional appeals, and press campaigns. But the democratic left did not have sufficient contact with the masses in its own country to have an impact on popular opinion; it was self-centered. Even the contacts that often existed between intellectuals and members of the nationalist movement were not put to good use. Fanon recognized that as soon as the situation in the colonial territory became difficult, when armed struggle was met by repressive tactics, the attitudes of populations on both sides stiffened. For the colonized, for those who shared the nationalist goals, to exist in a biological sense meant to exist as a sovereign people.[47] But this very polarization of the situation had a very different effect on the democratic elements at home. In the first place, they were forced to realize that the struggle against colonialism was now equivalent to a struggle against the nation. Would they take this step? In the case of Algeria, Fanon reminded his readers that the decision of the French government to pursue the war in Algeria was accepted by the nation in its entirety; this included liberals and leftists. To increase support for its policies, the French government introduced the cry against terrorism, giving the impression that France was doing no less than struggling against barbarism in Algeria. By 1957, if not earlier, the French left was all but silent.

In his second article, Fanon pursued the theme that the French left, aside from being unable to take a strong stand at home, retained a paternalistic attitude towards the Algerian nationalists. The left argued, according to Fanon, that the FLN ought to be more concerned—if it wished to influence French opinion—with the nature of that opinion. Certain tactics, and the question of torture was dominant, were unacceptable. This attempt by the democratic left to influence the direction of the FLN's policy by posing conditions for its support was no better than similar attempts by the communist left. The democratic left was concerned that the FLN not turn too much towards the Soviet Union, while the communist left was just as anxious that Algerians not substitute American imperialism for French colonialism.[48] To Algerians, Fanon pointed out, this cold-war battle was of no interest. Algerians wanted none of this, all that they wished for was independence. The argument was less naive than it sounded. Fanon was well aware that the cold war had a direct effect on Africa and the third world. He nevertheless believed that it was possible to keep out of this competition.

Where Fanon hit hardest was in his insistence that the real issue blocking support by the left for Algeria was the inability of the left to face the fact that Algeria wished for total independence and nothing less. He criticized the fact that this left could not even bring itself to describe colonialism as it was, a form of conquest and military occupation. If this definition was accepted then the reaction against such an occupation would be understood. But to talk merely of colonialism meant that polite men of good will could continue to hope that reform would be productive, that racism would diminish, and that better relations on a human level would develop. Contrary to what he was to write in his essay on the French in Algeria, in *A Dying Colonialism,* Fanon maintained here that *all* Frenchmen in Algeria were the enemy. The attempt to differentiate good Frenchmen from bad ones became another way of avoiding the issue. If he did not allow for a more subtle position it was in order to bring home the point that dominated his pronouncements on colonialism: it was the concept that colonialism is a system in which relations between ruler and ruled are based entirely on force. Individual characteristics whether they be those of Algerians or Frenchmen do not alter the picture. The position of the French left therefore, should be to condemn this system as a whole, and not to seek out individuals who may appear to be exceptions to the rule. "Colonialism is the organization of the domination of a nation after military conquest."[49] That the French public, including the Communist Party, accepted the myth that this colonization had resulted in the creation of a French Algeria, was merely another example of the capacity for self-deception common to the French, and to the left in France.

In his third and final article, from which some of the above arguments have been abstracted, Fanon pursued the same line of attack, with equal lashes for the non-communist as well as the communist left. Neither one had accepted the prospect of real national liberation, he claimed. For the non-communist left, the existing colonial situation clearly had to go, but what would replace it? Fanon believed that this minority invariably thought in terms of some kind of federal system that would continue to link Algeria with France. It was this which was at the basis of the profound disagreement between the FLN and the left, wrote Fanon, and not certain tactical or even psychological considerations, as some would have it. It was not a question of means, but of the end, and the radicals of the left, minority socialists, and members of the MRP (French Catholic party), could not bring themselves to accept the end that Algerians wanted, i.e. complete and total independence from France. The communist left,

even though it paid lip service to the idea that all colonial countries must eventually achieve independence, in practice seemed
to believe that Algeria ought to remain within a French framework. Implicit was the notion that France somehow had a privileged position in Algeria, a position that did not differ from that
held by most traditional parties. Furthermore, Fanon suggested,
the communist left was as paternalistic in its assumption that
Algeria could not exist without France, without French expertise, capital, and technology, as were the democratic left and the
right.

It was somewhat anticlimactic to announce at the end of this
series of articles, that the Algerian people felt that the French
left had not done as much as it might have in the context of the
Algerian war. But Fanon insisted that his criticisms were meant
to clarify issues and to provoke a change. The subtitle of one of
his last paragraphs was, "Is it too late?"[50] The French left must
unconditionally support the effort of Algeria to free itself of
French domination, he wrote. Neither the presence of the European minority, nor Sakamody, must be allowed to affect this
support. The reference was to an instance of FLN massacre of
Europeans. But Fanon met the argument head on. He reminded
readers that the argument of barbarism was precisely what M.
Lacoste was using, and that Prime Minister Guy Mollet was
trying to instill the idea that excesses, this time in the French
army, must also be isolated and controlled. But this was designed to confuse men of the left. Their position, from the point
of view of the Algerians, ought to be as follows: to keep themselves and the masses informed about the true nature of the
Algerian struggle; to support all strikes that are reactions to
conditions that arise out of the continuation of the war; to pressure the French government to recognize the right of peoples
to self-determination; and to wholeheartedly support the struggle for peace in Algeria. Only at the end of this essay did he
indicate that the FLN saluted those Frenchmen who had had the
courage to refuse to fight against the Algerian people, and who
were now, as a consequence, in jail.

What made Fanon's attack difficult for the French left to swal-
low was that it was so undifferentiated. No distinction was made
between the organized left, the party structure, and the dissenting left outside of it. True, the difference between the communist and the non-communist left was made, but only to underline

the essential similarities in their positions. By 1957 there was evidence of considerably more awareness than Fanon gave credit for, and the verbal battle between the left, particularly around the *Les Temps Modernes* group, and the government, was severe. Individual Frenchmen such as Mandouze and Jeanson did not wait for Fanon to act, and in time, Maspéro and the men who joined to establish *Partisans*, which came directly out of the Algerian war, were deeply committed. It is true that the *Partisans* experience came much later, in 1961. But the expressions of solidarity and self-searching in *Les Temps Modernes* began in 1957. In general Fanon was correct in his analysis of the position of the left, and perhaps this explains the angry reaction to his articles. The Hungarian uprising aroused much more concern in the left than did Algeria, and this added to the sentiment that what was between the left and Algerians was something simpler and nastier than complex ideological issues. But was it so easy to brush aside the question of torture and the question of the French minority in Algeria? The FLN dealt at length with both issues in *el Moudjahid;* the first by exposing the use of torture by the French police and military, the second, in its detailed treatment of the European minority and Jews. To say that the FLN dealt with the matter of torture by bringing up instances of the use of torture by the French is of course no answer at all. There were Algerians who, prior to 1956, were not supporters of the FLN and the evidence of this is not difficult to find. The allegations of ruthlessness of some FLN leaders towards Algerians who were lukewarm in their support are likewise common knowledge. But it was the obstinacy of the French in the face of Algerian demands that gradually made supporters of cautious men, like Mouloud Feraoun, for whom political commitment was generally distasteful, and the FLN not particularly endearing. It was the gradual polarization of issues and the recognition that moderation had become irrelevant that made silent supporters of many Algerians who did not endorse the methods of the FLN when they entailed ruthless measures. Fanon was not right in pushing aside the issue of torture, nor is the only response to the question of torture to ask who is using it. But Fanon was right when he insisted that the question of torture was used by the French government to project an image of the Algerians as a nations of barbarians, and to prohibit a direct confrontation with the political facts.

As early as 1955, before Fanon joined *el Moudjahid*, *Les Temps Modernes* came out with a strong editorial declaring that "Algeria is not France."[51] If it is France, it claimed, then there ought to be 120 Muslim deputies in the Assemblée Nationale, and the salary scale as well as Social Security must be revised and unified in order to eliminate discrimination. If, on the contrary, Algeria is not a part of France, "then one must negotiate with the nationalists and recognize the Algerian people's power to administer itself." In the same issue Jean Cohen had a strong article on "Colonialism and Racism in Algeria," that was reminiscent of what Fanon said, although it was less dramatic. Mohammed-Cherif Sahli, an Algerian who was with the FLN and not particularly noted for his moderation, contributed an article to the same issue entitled "From 'Assimilation' to 'Integration': Political Mystification." It was an elaboration on the position offered in the editorial; neither assimilation nor integration meant anything substantially different from domination. But at the end of his article, Sahli had a few words to say about the French left, doubtless to honor the orientation of the journal that published his article. What Sahli said was not substantially different from what Fanon was to write later, but its style was kinder.

> [Algerians] do not ignore the fact that their [the left's] task is difficult, given the prejudices that arise out of the old myth of 'l'Algérie française.' But they believe that in order to enlighten and win over a worried and troubled [public] opinion, it is not enough to denounce the abuses and the violence of the system. If one wishes to work for a positive solution, one must free the Algerian problem from the spider's web of official lies and directly attack the system itself.[52]

In 1956, *Les Temps Modernes* called for the recognition of Algeria and for negotiations with the nationalists.[53] In the same year, Sartre, an unswerving supporter of the cause of self-determination for the Algerian people, wrote a scathing attack on colonialism. It was precisely what Sahli, and especially Fanon, called for as the indispensable statement of the problem. "Colonialism is a system," argued Sartre, and his opening remarks might just as well have been culled from Fanon's articles written one year later.

> I would like to warn you against what one can call "neo-colonialist mystification."

Neo-colonialists think that there are good colons and very bad colons. It is the fault of the latter that the situation of the colonies has deteriorated.

The mystification consists in the following: you are shown Algeria, you are complacently shown the misery of the people, which is awful, you are told of the humiliations that the bad colons force on the Muslims. And when you are really indignant, they add: "That is why the best Algerians have taken up arms: they couldn't stand it any more." If you have really been taken in, then you come back convinced that:

1. The Algerian problem is first of all, economic. It is a matter of—by judicious reforms—giving bread to 9 million people.

2. That it is then social: one must multiply the number of doctors and schools.

3. That it is, finally, psychological: you recall De Man with his "inferiority complex" of the working class. He had found, at the same time, the key to "the native personality": badly treated, badly nourished, illiterate, the Algerian has an inferiority complex vis-a-vis his masters. It is by acting on these three factors that one can calm him down: if he eats to satisfy his hunger, if he has work, and if he knows how to read, he will no longer be ashamed to be a "sous-homme" (less than a man) and we will rediscover the old Franco-Muslim fraternity.[54]

Sartre recognized that what was missing was the political dimension and this was no accident. No, he was to write with indignation, there are no good or bad colons. "There are colons, that is all."

We, Frenchmen of the "metropole," we have only one lesson to learn from these facts: colonialism is in the process of destroying itself. . . . Our role, is to help it to die. Not only in Algeria, but wherever it exists. People who speak of abandonment are fools: there is no abandoning what we never possessed. On the contrary, it is a matter of building new relations with Algerians, between a free France and a liberated Algeria. But let us not, above all, be mystified by the reformist hoax. The neo-colonialist is a simpleton who thinks that we can still operate the colonial system, or else he is a malicious man who suggests reforms because he knows that they are ineffectual. They will come in time, these reforms: it is the Algerian people who will make them. The only thing that we can and must attempt—it is essential today— is to struggle (at the side of the Algerians) in order to deliver both Algerians and Frenchmen from colonial tyranny.[55]

It is not difficult to see why Fanon admired Sartre. The feeling was obviously mutual long before Sartre agreed to write the preface to *The Wretched of the Earth*. In 1959, *Les Temps Modernes* published one of the chapters of *A Dying Colonialism*, the one on the European minority in Algeria. It was a balanced statement that carefully distinguished between those Frenchmen who supported the FLN and those who did not. This was not equivalent to talking about good or bad colons, but it was certainly far from the declaration that all Frenchmen in Algeria are the enemy. In Fanon's articles against the French left, he did not cite individuals, as has already been pointed out. To the extent that he was directing his attack at the liberals who seemed offended by the hard position of the FLN, or the parties who were solid supporters of the government position, i.e., the Socialists and Guy Mollet, his anger was shared by those Frenchmen who wanted no part in these equivocations. In 1958, *Les Temps Modernes* ran articles on the Guerroudj affair, the trial of an Algerian couple condemned to death for alleged complicity in an earlier incident that had involved the explosion and destruction of property. The affair was but another case in which militant supporters of the FLN and the ALN were tried in an effort to stamp out resistance to French rule. In the May-June 1959 issue the case of Ould Aoudia, the thirty-five-year-old Algerian lawyer who had defended Algerians and who had been assassinated, was presented by the last testament of Ould Aoudia himself.

La Question, by Henri Alleg, had appeared in 1958 and in the pages of *Les Temps Modernes* a small printed sheet carried an address to the President of the Republic protesting the seizure of Alleg's book, and calling on those in charge of public affairs to condemn the use of torture in the name of the Declaration of the Rights of Man and the Citizen. Frenchmen were asked to join in this solemn protest and to send their names to those of the signatories, care of the League of the Rights of Man. The signatories were André Malraux, Roger Martin du Gard, François Mauriac, and Jean-Paul Sartre. In this group Sartre was certainly the most vehement and the most consistent in his opposition to the war. The publications of *L'Affaire Audin* in 1958, *Pour Djamila Bouhired* in 1957, and *La Gangrène* in 1959 had exposed what no amount of censorship could hide. In explaining the motive for writing his book, Alleg had written the following:

All of this, I had to say it for those Frenchmen who will be willing to read me. They must know that Algerians do not confuse their torturers with the great people of France, from whom they have learned so much and whose friendship is so dear to them.

They must nevertheless know what is being done here IN THEIR NAME.[56]

By 1959 a great deal was known about what was being done in Algeria in the name of France. Analyses of Algeria appeared in impressive number along with the publication of tracts and manifestos that were frequently seized by the government. In the August-September 1960 issue of *Les Temps Modernes*, the editors explained that they had planned to publish the Declaration on the Right of Insubordination in the Algerian War. The text was censored and the periodical appeared with two empty pages followed by the list of names of the signatories. In the fall of 1960 the Manifesto of the 121, which reiterated the right to resist the draft to Algeria, and which called for the support of Algeria, met with the same fate. This time, *Les Temps Modernes* published the response to the declaration made by the French Federation of the FLN.[57] In Algiers and in Tunis, *el Moudjahid* was to publicize the event, praising the courage of the signatories. In the spring of 1961, *Les Temps Modernes* published an important section from Fanon's last book, *The Wretched of the Earth*. It was the chapter on violence.[58]

To cite Sartre's journal is only to recognize one of the most active periodicals, with respect to the Algerian question. But it was not the only one, nor were its contributors the only people to express sustained concerned with what was going on, in France and in Algeria itself. In the fall of 1961, *Partisans* appeared; its emergence was directly related to the Algerian struggle and to the sense of impotence inspired by the spectacle of the organized left.

We do not believe that we have a monopoly on the truth; our rage, that pushes us to action, our disrespect towards the parties of the left, is not an anti-party attitude. We believe it is false to affirm that the working class is more revolutionary than the direction of the party that expresses it. We believe also that there are periods in the history of a revolutionary movement when it is around intellectuals, with or without machine guns, that the action of the avant-garde is crystallized: 'partisan' action necessary to the dynamism of the revolutionary movement.[59]

The distinction between the working class and the party that speaks for it was a reference to the Communist Party, which had betrayed the Algerians in their independence struggle and had betrayed the working class by not explaining its solidarity with the colonial peoples. It was a subject Fanon expressed some skepticism about. The energetic and independent tone of *Partisans* sometimes sounded as though it was directed as much against other leftists involved in sectarian disputes, as with the French governments's policies in Algeria. But the contributors and editorial staff of the journal were all men whose fidelity to the Algerian cause was unquestioned. Maspéro, who was the editor and publisher of three of Fanon's books, worked with such supporters of Algerian independence as Gérard Chaliand and Maurice Maschino. It was Maschino who wrote "L'Itinéraire de la générosité" after the death of Fanon, in the same issue of *Partisans* that carried an editorial about the man and his work.

Although there were strong areas of contention between the members of the anti-party and non-party left, by 1961 there was a consensus on the need to end the Algerian war. Whether this could best be accomplished by total collaboration on the left at home was an academic question. One would have had to believe that the left determined government policy, or at least, by its veto power could affect it. Neither case was true. Nevertheless the question of collaborating with the Communist Party, or at least creating a united front with it, raised questions that had implications beyond the Algerian question. Long before the Algerian war, post-war problems and the disillusionment with the Soviet Union had already shattered the wartime ideal of collaboration. It is not a surprise that the men who were the most vocal on Algerian matters were also those deeply involved in the major political crises of the continent, Poland, Hungary, and the Suez-Sinai campaign. Among those who expressed themselves on these questions, Camus was of particular interest to those concerned with Algeria. His troubled comments on the conduct of the war and on the goals of the Algerian nationalists became a source of grave disappointment to Frenchmen and Algerians who had hoped to find support in his views.[60] His remark made in December 1957, in Sweden, shortly after he received the Nobel Prize, echoed far. "I have always condemned terror. I must also condemn a terrorism which operates blindly, in the streets of Algiers for example, and which one day may strike my mother or my family."[61] The image of random terror and the vulnerability of innocent people rang powerfully. Camus had written about Algeria, both in his fictional work and in his journalistic essays. His familiarity with the land of Algeria was well known. But as it became clear that Camus would not comment on the Algerian demand for independence; as it emerged that he not only did not support the FLN, but that he rejected negotiation with it, his position became awkward and unsatisfactory. Conor Cruise O'Brien, writing of this, recalled that much as one disagreed with Camus' views, it was essential to remember that his position "issued out of the depths of his whole life-history."[62] But how was one to explain that such a man, the incarnation of an ethical imperative in political life, the "resistant" par excellence, could not bring himself to speak on this issue? To criticize Camus' position from the vantage point of safety, and with the knowledge that the issues of which one speaks are past, is too easy. But if there is a criticism one can make, it is that Camus' condemnation of terror and violence was partial. To criticize terror was understandable; but what of the conditions that led to it? Was violence a characteristic of certain actions, or also of certain historical situations? If the latter, then were such situations not also to be condemned because of their destruction of human life?

The brief review of discussions held in France on the Algerian question is a limited account of the vast controversy that raged through all political circles, including the left. That it was of immediate concern to Algerians is obvious. With respect to Fanon, the point was made earlier, that he had a tendency to denigrate those positions which he felt to be less than complete confirmations of the Algerian demands. Others who worked for the FLN and who wrote for *el Moudjahid* appear to have had less intransigent attitudes; a reflection of differing political as well as personal predilections. But it was the consequences that mattered. After the publication of Fanon's three articles in 1957–1958, a note appeared in *el Moudjahid* explaining that the editors had sent the third of the Fanon articles to Gilles Martinet, then writing for *France-Observateur*, for comment. They hoped for a reply that would open the door to further discussions. "As for us," wrote the Algerians, "we are not closed to any debate, as long as it is frank and loyal, and as long as it takes place under the sign of the truth."[63]

Unlike Fanon's polemical pieces, *el Moudjahid* offered a more varied fare for those who were concerned with the evolution of French opinion. It published notes on individual activities and on group meetings, and statements by men whose political orientation was a matter of indifference except on the Algerian issue. In 1958, it published recommendations made by French university professors for a solution of the Algerian problem. The report recommended the negotiation of differences and it discussed the prospect of independence with candor. It endorsed independence but not without reviewing the subjects of concern to Europeans in Algeria, and to Algerians themselves, such as economic viability.[64] The university colloquia continued into 1959 and once again *el Moudjahid* took note of these discussions. In fact, it was the editorial in the Political Bulletin of the Ministry of Information of the GPRA that brought these activities to the attention of the newspaper. Support from various student movements, in France, and even in the United States, was acknowledged. But attention was riveted on what occurred across the Mediterranean. That there were internecine quarrels between the members of the left was evident. The question of draft resistance elicited a disturbed reaction in France, not only among members of the establishment, but among those members of the left who asked themselves, publicly, what it meant to be French. *El Moudjahid* took a condescending tone in discussing these matters, but its words remained measured and relatively brief. More attention was given to the establishment of strongly dissident organizations such as Jeune Résistance. In May 1960 *el Moudjahid* reported on its activities, noting that it advocated resistance to fascism in France and the termination of the war through negotiation. By the spring of 1960 there were an estimated three thousand deserters.[65] Their absence did not substantially alter the military situation in Algeria. But their action promoted another image of France. These men, wrote *el Moudjahid,* "give us an image of the French people different from that of a nation of oppressors and tyrants, and their action constitutes indirect evidence of the justice of our cause and the authenticity of our liberating struggle."[66]

On February 23, 1960, the Jeanson cell that was accused of directly aiding the FLN was uncovered; a dramatic trial followed that publicized French support for Algeria, and in addition, the position of the FLN. The trial revealed a broader range of support than had been anticipated. Press censorship, however, continued to mask the further evidence of such support. Thus, the Manifesto of the 121, along with reviews of the Jeanson trial, were publicized in the pages of *el Moudjahid*. The statement of the 121 had been barred from the pages of *Les Temps Modernes*, and instead its contents along with the names of the signatories appeared in *el Moudjahid*. The manifesto supported the rights of Frenchmen to refuse the draft in the Algerian war. It considered as justified the decisions of Frenchmen to aid and protect Algerians who were being oppressed in the name of France; and it declared that "the cause of the Algerian people, which contributes decisively to the destruction of the colonial system, is the cause of all free men."[67] In 1960 and 1961, the activities of the Jeanson group, Sartre's efforts in his journal, Jeune Résistance, and the creation of the Anti-Colonialist French Movement[68] were systematically supported. There was no illusion that these individuals constituted the majority of the French left, and when the French-based FLN decided to hold peaceful protests in the fall of 1961, *el Moudjahid* wrote about "Les manifestations algériennes en France et le silence de la gauche."[69]

The "respectable" left that urged caution, good behavior, and an implicit commitment to some form of continued Algero-French association was disturbing and disappointing. But the situation of the French Communist Party, and the behavior of the Algerian Communist Party that was regarded as its client, were worse. It was in the same issue of *el Moudjahid* in which the proposals of the university seminar on the Algerian question were published, that the editors began their critique of the French Communist Party vis-à-vis the Algerian Revolution. In this April 1958 issue, the editors reprinted a text that had appeared in the Information Bulletin of the French-based FLN. They were not interested in criticism at this stage, they were merely interested in clarifying positions. But these points of order were designed to reveal how wide the gap was between the theory and the action of the French CP. Four days after the opening of the struggle in November 1954, the French Communist Party published a communiqué in which it noted that "a problem of national character" was developing in Algeria. But it was precisely the nationalist character of the struggle that the Communist Party refused to acknowledge, and with it the predominant role of the FLN. On March 2, 1956, the Political Bureau of the Party published a statement that ran as follows:

> We are for the existence and the permanence of the specific political, economic and cultural ties that exist between France and Algeria. Policy must be resolutely changed. One must wish to establish peace in Algeria. There is no other way of achieving this than in negotiation with those with whom we are fighting. . . .

But for the French CP, negotiation did not mean talks with the FLN, it meant talks with "representatives of all currents of the nationalist movement, with all layers of the Algerian population, without distinction as to origin."[70]

That the party did not strenuously oppose the vote of Special Powers in 1956 was in conformity with its general support of the government position. The accusation that the French party and, in Algeria, the Algerian Communist Party, had never confronted or recognized the genuine national aspirations of the population explained the reticence of both groups to take a position in 1954. In reviewing the origins of the Algerian Revolution, *el Moudjahid* wrote of the reformist trends that had existed in Algeria, and that reflected a desire to find a way of accommodating Algerian needs with a continued French presence. It described the Algerian Communist Party as subordinated to its French parent, limited to a part of the working class, and operating within the sphere of continued French sovereignty. The thesis of "a nation in formation" was but another way of maintaining Algeria in French control "while awaiting the triumph of the communist revolution in France that would make of the French empire a new Union of Soviet Socialist Republics." This hostility to Algerian nationalism had roots in the problematic discussion of the national question by nineteenth-century socialists. The hostility of the party to Algerian nationalism "was related to the attitude of those socialists of the nineteenth century who, under the color of internationalism, were opposed to the liberation of oppressed nations, and whom Marx and Engels condemned in severe terms, accusing them of making themselves into champions of French imperialism."

The discord between the French Communist Party and the Algerian nationalists was not affected by the clarification that *el Moudjahid* brought to the issues between them. But the FLN

organ had successfully pointed out the crux of the issues sepa-
rating the two. Whether or not the Algerian party was or was not
subordinated to its French counterpart was less significant than
the fact that both parties continued to speak in terms of the
interests of the working class and the practices of a nation in
formation, long after it was clear that the working class in Algeria was more affected by nationalist than by class consciousness. In France, the FLN continued to call for the clarification
of the nature of the struggle between Algeria and France so
that the working class of France would not blindly rally to
the support of its government, but would understand that its
long-range interests lay in an alliance and support of Algerian independence. One could argue that the nationalist
reflexes of the metropolitan working class were also severely
aggravated by the economic dislocations caused by the trans-
formations in the relations between the colony and the
colonial power. Fanon recognized that this subject was not
adequately discussed, and while his own discussion of it
brought no resolution to the immediate conflicts he detected
as the price of the dissolution of economic ties between colonizer and colonized, he continued to believe that there was a
fundamental solidarity between the worker and the colonized.
But this optimistic note, expressed in an article written in the
fall of 1958, appeared to be contradicted by a referrence in
the series on intellectuals, the left, and Algeria published one
year earlier. There he wrote: "In a colonial country, it used
to be said, there is a community of interests between the
colonized people and the working class of the colonialist
country. The history of the wars of liberation waged by the
colonized peoples is the history of the non-verification of this
thesis."[71] On another occasion, at the conference which he
attended in Rome, in 1959, Fanon again referred to those
who considered the nationalist phase as obsolete.

> The nationalist claim, it is said here and there, is a phase that
> humanity has passed; the time has come for large unions and the
> latecomers of nationalism must, as a result, correct their errors.
> We think, on the contrary, that the error, full of grave conse-
> quences, consists in wishing to skip the nationalist stage. If cul-
> ture is the expression of national existence, I would not hesitate
> to say in the case that interests us, that the national conscience
> is the most sophisticated expression of culture.[72]

Fanon's comments revealed a contradiction in his position that he, in effect, never fully resolved, between the wholehearted endorsement of nationalism, and his hope that it would nevertheless produce a nation prepared to transcend the limitations of nationalism. The defect is not his alone. *El Moudjahid* was not concerned with a theoretical discussion of the validity of nationalism in the socialist dictionary. There was no attempt to excuse the nationalist ambitions of the FLN. There was a wish to expose the hypocrisy of the Communist Party position that was, in practice, merely a copy of the official French government policy. That it too disguised one of the fundamental problems in socialist experience, the nationalist question, is another matter. The FLN in practice, refused any organizational collaboration with the Communist Party in Algeria and allowed cooperation with members of the CP only on an individual, unaffiliated basis.

The position of *el Moudjahid* towards the Soviet Union and the Soviet bloc bore little resemblance to the policy adopted by the FLN towards the French and Algerian Communist Parties. If the Soviets became more pragmatic after the Twentieth Party Congress of 1956, the FLN matched them in the flexibility of its own attitude. It is doubtful however that the writers on *el Moudjahid,* who analyzed the changing Soviet position towards Algeria and France, were aware of the relationship between these changes and internal Soviet discussions. On the basis of the articles published in the FLN organ, Algerians appeared to draw conclusions largely on the basis of their own experience. Bloc politics interested the FLN and the writers of *el Moudjahid* made serious attempts to educate their public as to the realities of post-war international relations. It was recognized, for instance, that the Soviet Union had flirted with France and the government of Guy Mollet in an effort to persuade France to adopt a less anti-Soviet stance in continental affairs. According to the writers of *el Moudjahid,* it was only after the friendly hand extended by the French Communist Party was rejected by Guy Mollet's Socialist Party, and especially after the Franco-British and Israeli collaboration on Suez and Sinai, that the position of the Soviet Union towards France stiffened. ". . . the USSR and the popular democracies increasingly presented themselves as the champions of the Arab cause in the face of western imperialism. The consequences of such a development were soon felt in the Algerian affair, in which the eastern bloc did not hesitate to formally condemn France's policy of force, and to insist—unequivocally—on the total and complete independence of Algeria."[73]

The FLN, expressing itself through the medium of *el Moudjahid*, noted that in August of 1956, at the Soummam Congress, the FLN had taken the position that it was time to look for the help of nations and peoples of Europe, "including the northern [states] and the popular democracies." Help from this sector already exists on a moral plane, wrote *el Moudjahid* in the spring of 1958, "and perhaps it will be extended to other spheres. The FLN will perhaps one day have to have recourse to this if the West does not decide to radically alter its policy, and to understand in all of its dimensions, the explosive aspects of the tension created in North Africa as a result of the Algerian war."[74] This might lead to a revision of the FLN position, noted *el Moudjahid*, comparable to that which led Churchill and the English to ally themselves to Stalinist Russia against Hitler's Germany. The prospect of this change was contemplated but the orientation of the FLN was not substantially altered. When the Soviet Union began to take a more sympathetic attitude towards Algeria and the Maghreb states, its policy was praised. But there seems to have been a certain distance in relations between the FLN and the Soviet Union. With the formation of the GPRA, the USSR extended de facto recognition, but the element of calculation was never far, or so it appeared in the eyes of the FLN.

With Yugoslavia, as indeed with a number of the other Eastern bloc states and with the Far Eastern states whose political orientation was socialist, the FLN enjoyed warm relations. In these instances, whether Yugoslavia, or Indochina, the common understanding and experience of nationalist struggles created a strong bond. It was further strengthened by a socialist orientation. In the case of Cuba, and in the more dramatic case of China, the common tie was less the nationalist struggle than the anti-capitalist and anti-western aspect of the policies of both states. The men chosen as envoys to these states, with the exception of the formal visit to Yugoslavia by President Ferhat Abbas in the summer of 1959, were chosen for their political sympathies. Ben Khedda, Omar Oussedik, and even Belkacem Krim were not random selections; the two choices of Ben Khedda and Oussedik who visited China were particularly telling since these were the more radical leaders in the inner FLN circles. That their vision of the nationalist struggle, in its long-range goals, differed from that of some of their colleagues was not unknown. In the period when all efforts were subordinated to the nationalist struggle these critical differences still appeared tolerable.

-4-

The Minority Question

Recognition of Algerian nationalism was the demand made by the FLN to the French government. On the other side of the Mediterranean, this demand elicited a sharp reaction not only because of its threat to continued French control, but because of the dilemma posed by the presence of a sizable French minority in Algeria. However much the government concerned itself with the Algerian question, Algerian-based Frenchmen came to believe that they were persistently misunderstood and eventually betrayed by the mother country. It is not enough to say that Algeria's Europeans regarded the prospect of Algerian's independence with fear because it so obviously threatened their privileged position in any future state. Nor is it enough to recall that those Europeans who traced their ancestry in Algeria back three or four generations considered themselves to be as much "at home" as the Algerians. The predicament of the Europeans had as much to do with nature of their relations with Algerians as it did with their peculiar identification with France. It is this phenomenon, summed up in the desire for legitimation by the French government, i.e. support for their position, that may account for the apparent intransigence of their position. One author has expressed the sentiments of this minority in this fashion:

> The racialism of Algeria's Europeans was thus a complex phenomenon, undercut by a deep yearning for reconciliation. It constitutes one psychological root of the doctrine of integration.
> The other was a deeply felt emotional identification with

France, stemming, it would seem, partly from the insecurity of
doubtful social origins and of a very mixed ethnic background,
partly from provincial isolation and partly from the enforced
solidarity of a European minority in a colonial environment.[75]

Integration held its own economic threats, specifically terminat-
ing the economic privileges of Europeans. Hence, some, a small
number to be sure, considered total independence as preferable
—assuming that their own activities would continue. Others
turned to the extremist positions which the OAS came to represent, a politics built on despair. In any event, the European
minority, some 800,000 strong by Algerian estimates in 1954,
was not a monolithic group. Not only did it contain sizable
numbers of non-Frenchmen, its interests were identified with
those of Algerian Jews when it was convenient to do so, although
the Algerian Jews were not part of the European minority, as
were the French or European Jews. The policy adopted by the
French government and its Algerian representatives towards the
European minority and the Jews in particular, is difficult to sum-
marize with any degree of accuracy. It may be sufficient to indicate that colonization had a direct hand in creating conditions,
built on the initial mode of colonization itself, which were designed to keep the ethnic and religious minorities of Algeria
apart. Divide and rule had been common practice in Morocco
between Arabs and Berbers, and it often seems to have been the
practice in Algeria in the relations between Jews and Muslims.
But further investigation of the situation of Jews in Algeria dem-
onstrates that here too there were significant differences in the
situations of the European Jews who identified with the colons
and who were indeed part of the colon group and the Algerian
Jews, the "indigènes" who by language, culture, and historic ties
formed part of the Algerian community. To classify these as one
undifferentiated mass might serve a political purpose, polarizing
sentiment around Jewish vs. Algerian Muslims, but it distorted
a complex past.

That the "minority question" excited opinion at home, in
France, as much as among Europeans of Algeria is hardly a
surprise. But analyses delivered at the eleventh hour were not
always marked by historical accuracy. The FLN confronted the
minority question as directly as possible. That there was occasional evidence of tactical opportunism, which meant putting

the best foot forward in dealing with French leftists and liberals on sensitive issues, will not come as a surprise. In any event there were enough differences of opinion in the ranks of the FLN to make it possible to select the appropriate spokesman for the appropriate occasion. Fanon himself may well be considered to have been an apt spokesman for the FLN on the French front —a man whose articulateness and whose political orientation equipped him for the purpose of communicating FLN ideology to the French left. The FLN position on the minority question was expressed in the 1956 decisions reached at the Soummam Congress, and reiterated and altered on later occasions. In 1961, at the time of the Evian talks, the subject was reviewed at length. *El Moudjahid* reflected the party's position on these matters, revealing differences when they occurred even when these were not meant to be recognized as such. Fanon, in conformity with his position in Tunis, spoke out on behalf of the FLN. When he wrote on the minority question—and when his essay was reproduced in *Les Temps Modernes* of 1959—it may be assumed that he was not speaking for himself alone. But his thinking on this problem formed part of his book *A Dying Colonialism*. Whether or not he wrote any material on this question for *el Moudjahid* is not known.

Judging from the material in *el Moudjahid*, particularly from the period of the Soummam Congress, Fanon was in tune with the views expressed on that occasion. Whether or not he knew Abane Ramdane well, a controversial subject in Algeria today, Ramdane's hand is generally believed to have been instrumental in composing the Soummam program, and it was a conception with which Fanon was essentially in harmony.[76] Between the Soummam program of 1956 and the declarations made in 1961, on the question of minorities, there were some differences. The choice offered remained the same. That is, Europeans were invited to become Algerians or to remain foreigners in an independent Algerian state. Algerian Jews were invited to assume their Algerian citizenship, recognition being made of the special legislation that had granted them French citizenship under the Crémieux decree of 1870. This was not where differences occurred. It was in the description of the nature of the Algerian state. The Soummam statement did not mention the religious character of the future state. But the statements that appeared in 1961 were of another kind altogether. Then, the future state was frankly described as being of Arab-Muslim character. No one can argue that this description denied reality, since the majority of Algerians were indeed of Arab-Muslim culture and religion. But it hardly requires effort to understand the difference between a state whose religion is defined and formally written into a state document thereby endorsing a close link between the political and religious character of the state, and one in which the constitution omits the same. Fanon belonged to that element in the FLN milieu which opposed this direction. Had he been alone one might well consider him to have been inexcusably naive or misinformed or ignorant of Algerian realities; which is more or less the official position on Fanon's politics held in Algeria today. The ruling elite today has opted, indeed emerged from the very traditional element, or else agreed to compromise with it, for its own political reasons. The radical wing has been, with a few exceptions, curbed in political life. And with it, the question of the religious character of the state is no longer subject to discussion. Privately, much is said; but publicly, Algeria is an Arab-Muslim state.[77]

Fanon wrote about both the European and the Jewish minority. El Moudjahid ran articles on both subjects from 1954 until 1962. Between Fanon's position and the changing views expressed in el Moudjahid, the evolution of the FLN position, from Soummam to 1961, is revealed. It is difficult to escape the view that Fanon was useful in propagating a liberal position before French and European audiences. In France, Fanon's writing on the minority question did not arouse the indignation caused by his critique of the left. On the contrary, the section on the minority published in Les Temps Modernes, excerpted from A Dying Colonialism, conveyed a sense of moderation. Whereas in the 1957 articles on the left, Fanon wanted to impress readers with the hypocrisy of distinguishing between good and bad colons, in the 1959 essay Fanon made every attempt to prove the opposite. His position on colonialism had not changed. He continued to see it as a system in which all colonialists shared in the original sin of exploitation legitimized by their situation. But there were some colons who rejected their privilege and who had thrown in their lot with the Algerians. These were the men whom Albert Memmi would describe as colonialists with a conscience, in his own analysis of the colonial situation, The Colonizer and the Colonized.[78] Unlike Memmi, whose

pessimism Fanon did not share, Fanon believed that such political commitment would serve to erase the differences dividing Algerians from Europeans of Algeria. Memmi, on the
other hand, was skeptical both of the possibility of Europeans identifying with Maghreb culture and about the prospect of Tunisians (or Algerians) ever really accepting
Europeans as their own. The case of Fanon in Algeria would
seem to bear out Memmi's pessimism.

Like Memmi, Fanon understood that the situation of the liberal French colon was extremely precarious.[79] Could there be a
good colon; could he survive as such? If he had a conscience,
then he would be drawn to the nationalists. If he joined them
he would be disowned by Frenchmen. But would he be accepted
by the nationalists, or would he remain an outsider always under
suspicion? Fanon agreed that the Frenchman with a conscience
faced a choice, but he did not raise the question of whether or
not such a choice would find acceptance among the nationalists.
In terms of political action, Fanon's position was effective,
whereas that of Memmi seemed to guarantee political paralysis.
In any event, in practice, even though Fanon regarded the
French democrats of Algeria as minimally effective politically, he
urged them to join with the Algerians. Comparing their situation in Algeria and in France, Fanon conceded that there was
more freedom of movement in France. In Algeria, it was debatable as to whether there was such a thing as a French left, at all.
In spite of his denunciations of the Communist Party, Fanon
concluded that there was no other place for a dissident Frenchman in Algeria to go than to the CP. In any event, he was in
accord with Memmi, in agreeing that any dissenting Frenchman
was forced to live in clandestine fashion and under great psychological strain. As far as he was concerned that ought not to
preclude action, and for Fanon, action ultimately involved collaboration with the FLN.

In Fanon's account, Frenchmen who joined the FLN did so on
a par with other Algerians. The extent to which they helped was
a decision for which they accepted full responsibility, while on
the Algerian side, there was no attempt to impose difficult conditions. Fanon knew that the FLN had decided to work with
reliable Frenchmen in Algeria, and he noted that similar decisions had been made prior to 1954 by parties such as the MTLD,
and UDMA. If little publicity was given to this fact after 1954,

it was in order to protect the parties concerned. What was important was that the FLN did not discriminate between Algerians and Europeans in its plans for the future; at least, this was what Fanon believed.

> For the FLN, in the new society that is being built, there are only Algerians. From the outset, therefore, every individual living in Algeria is an Algerian. In tomorrow's independent Algeria it will be up to every Algerian to assume Algerian citizenship or to reject it in favor of another.[80]

The decision to cooperate with Frenchmen, or rather to seek out their help, was made very early as Fanon had written. In the Soummam declarations of the summer of 1956, the FLN had elaborated its positions on a number of the essential aspects of its program. With great care and precision in a document whose importance cannot be overestimated, the FLN defined its objectives, its methods, and the problems facing it in Algeria and abroad. Under the heading of the transformation of popular sentiment into creative energy, i.e. political action in favor of Algerian independence, the party noted that contacts with French liberals were desirable.[81] Furthermore, it declared, political action, like military science, teaches that no element be neglected, no matter how unimportant, in the pursuit of victory. For this reason, the FLN would not neglect Europeans, either in Europe or in Algeria. The Soummam statement then went on to distinguish three positions common to Europeans on the Algerian question: neutralism, which meant letting the extremists defend their interests against the Algerians alone; an intermediary position that favored the creation of double nationality; and finally, the recognition of Algerian independence. The existence of these three trends was proof enough of the diversity of views among Europeans, and the FLN warned against the "unpardonable error of putting all Algerians of European or Jewish origin in 'the same bag.' "[82] The objective, which was to end colonialism, must not be lost sight of, and its nature must be explained to Europeans.

> The Algerian Revolution does not have as its goal to 'throw into the sea' Algerians of European origin, but to destroy the inhuman colonial yoke.

The Algerian Revolution is neither a civil war nor a religious war.

The Algerian Revolution wishes to conquer national independence in order to establish a democratic and social republic guaranteeing true equality to all citizens of the same country, without discrimination.[83]

Elsewhere, the Soummam declaration stated that the Algerian Revolution

is a national struggle to destroy the anarchic regime of colonization and it is not a religious war. It is a march forward in the historic sense of humanity and not a return towards feudalism.

It is, finally, the struggle for the rebirth of an Algerian state in the form of a democratic and social Republic and not the restoration of an obsolete monarchy or theocracy.[84]

Aside from wishing to be precise about the nature of the Algerian state in order to undo the image of that state perpetrated in Europe, the FLN set out to clarify the term minority in such a way that Europeans and Algerians would know what was meant. The FLN did not like the French habit of referring to Algeria as a region made up of large numbers of distinct communities, as opposed to minorities. The former term seemed to dispel the fact that there was an Algerian nation and to substitute in its place a set of communities each distinct from the other. The Algerian position was that there was not one minority, but many minorities, and that among them one could distinguish at least three major groups. The total number of non-Muslim Frenchmen, according to the FLN, was, as of October 31, 1954, 1,033,000. Of this number, there were some 60,000 Europeans from Italy, Spain, Greece, Switzerland, Germany, Malta, and the Scandinavian countries. These people were subject to the regulations of their respective consulates. Then there were about 150,000 Jews, "theoretically confused with 'Frenchmen' and with 'Europeans' since the Crémieux decree of 1871 [sic]. But they are neither French nor Europeans. 'Natives,' often of Berber origin, their place in society, their political reactions, and particularly the racism of European Algerians have conferred a unique position on them. It is a minority apart."[85]

The French of Algeria numbered about 800,000. But of this

number some 50 to 60 percent were not of French origin; They were Europeans who became French as a result of their birth in Algeria (according to a law of 1889). The total number of Frenchmen of French birth was then reduced to some 400,000. Still the FLN recognized that this category of native-born Frenchmen of France, and Europeans largely of Mediterranean origin who had assumed French citizenship, could be considered as a single bloc. "It is they who call themselves, 'the French of Algeria,' and who, in order to preserve their advantages, have committed France to a fascist course."[86]Although this disparate group acted as a bloc in its economic interests and in its political attitudes, in fact, the number of people who were actually large landholding colons was considerably smaller than the total number of Europeans and French Algerians. The FLN assessed the number of important colons at 28,000; pointing out that of these there were roughly 5,000 "gros propriétaires" who were involved in vineyards, alfa, or grain. Still, the active minority was not insignificant since it possessed roughly a third of the land and three-quarters of the irrigated perimeters. The rest of the Frenchmen of Algeria, who were not in agriculture, were in industry, commerce, the liberal professions; they were technicians, specialized workers, and members of the bureaucracy. Whether or not they shared exactly the same political opinions, they were assumed to be in accord by those who were responsible for forming French Algerian opinion among this segment of the population.

The FLN position on the European minority, in a general fashion, had been stated at the Soummam Congress. Then, in 1959, the President of the GPRA once again touched on the minority problem. "Once again, through the voice of the President, the Algerian Revolution affirms that the minorities are 'already Algerians,' and that they 'will be so increasingly' 'with all the rights of citizens' with respect to their language, their culture and their religions.' "[87] There is no insoluble problem in this situation, noted the *el Moudjahid* writer. The only problem that exists is one of attitude. It is not the legal situation that is difficult to agree upon, but the readaptation process. And those who cannot readapt will have to go the way of the minorities of Morocco, Tunisia, Libya, and Egypt. Of those who choose to stay, their integration will be facilitated by the commitment of some to Algerian independence, by the collaboration offered by

Europeans to the work of the FLN, by these "multiple gestures of concrete solidarity," and by the doctrinal position of the Algerian Revolution itself. While these clarifications were useful, they did not satisfy the questions that were being raised on all sides as to the future of Frenchmen of Algeria. In January 1961, *el Moudjahid* devoted a good part of its issue to this matter. The result was important and differed, in a subtle but critical manner, from some of the earlier statements made in the name of the FLN. With its usual directness of style, *el Moudjahid* noted that one of the distinguishing characteristics of Algeria as a colonial country was that it had been a colony of settlement, and that this settlement was important in numbers. Furthermore, the impact of that settlement had served to obscure the fact that there was a native population that continued to exist and that was not French. Now that the process of demystification had begun, it was no longer necessary to cater to these myths. The time had come for men and women in Algeria who were members of this minority of settlers to think of their future not in relation to France, but in relation to Algeria.[88]

In the Soummam declarations that were reproduced in *el Moudjahid*, in other references to the future Algerian state, and in Fanon's discussion of the future state, the emphasis was on the democratic and social Republic. Now, however, a further refinement was added.

> First of all, when one talks of the European minority a question comes to mind. Minority with respect to whom? With respect to the majority of the inhabitants of Algeria, of course. But to brush away any equivocation on this, this majority must be defined: it is essentially made up of the Algerian people who, as a nation, possesses its own characteristics that are defined in a national culture that is Arab-Muslim.[89]

At the end of the article in question, the author spoke of the principal motive force of contemporary Algeria and referred, once again, to the bases of integration of the minority in the Algerian majority. The guiding line was that all men who willed themselves to be Algerians on the basis of a "homogeneous and unifying patriotism," were welcome to the fold.

In what way did the 1961 statement add anything new or different to the previous statements on the subject? In the context of *el Moudjahid* and in the formal declarations on the question of the minority in Algeria, the 1961 statement underlined what earlier pronouncements had not emphasized with as much directness. While the Revolution was identified as a nationalist and not a religious movement in western declarations, the Islamic factor was more emphasized in other areas. In a pamphlet published by the Organization for Afro-Asian Peoples' Solidarity (1961), the author discussed the objectives of the National Liberation Front. He defined one objective as the "restoration of an integral and sovereign Algerian State, democratic and social within the framework of Islamic principles" and the second, as the "respect of all basic freedoms without any racial or religious discrimination." In March 1961, in an interview he gave to the newspaper *France Observateur*, Saad Dahlab, then Secretary General in the Ministry of Foreign Affairs of the Provisional Government, dealt with the same issue. Asked about the status of the minorities in an independent Algeria, he answered as follows:

> The Algerians of European origin or of Jewish religion have had and will have different reactions to the transformations taking place in Algeria. Some have already courageously taken a stand in favor of the Algerian Revolution. Of course, they are not many, but their presence in our ranks or by our side takes on a symbolic character. It shows that no insurmountable obstacle exists to their integration in the Algerian nation.
>
> Others, who have not participated in the Algerian Revolution, have an attachment for Algeria which makes it possible for them to become full and equal Algerian citizens. Of course they will want to continue speaking French, but don't we ourselves speak French as well as Arabic? We will continue tomorrow to teach French along with Arabic in Algeria and we understand very well that Algerians who are Catholic, Jewish or free thinkers will not want to submit their disputes to the cadi (Moslem religious leader), but we have never considered imposing this. Our revolution is a national revolution, not a religious one.[90]

It is as foolish to deny the importance of Islam as a factor in the national reaction against foreign occupation, as it is to deny the fact that there was obviously a solid understanding of where and when to underline the Islamic factor in FLN statements. Nevertheless, the essential question remained. Those who had spoken of the need to define the majority in clear terms, the better to situate the minority, had been direct and to the point.

Did their clarification and the recognition that for some Algerians the future state ought to be an Islamic-Arab state have any consequences as far as the relations of Algeria with minorities was concerned? It is incorrect to regard the development between 1956 and 1961, with regard to this question, as one affected by the pressures of the Revolution, or in any way a function of chronological developments. It is more accurate to see those differences as expressive of different political orientations which coexisted, at times uneasily, in the movement of the FLN as a whole.

For Fanon, a non-sectarian democratic and social Republic as opposed to a theocratic state was essential. For the authors of the Soummam declaration, no mention was made of the essentially Arab-Muslim nature of the future state. Was this a denial of the Arab-Muslim majority? Was it assumed unnecessary to elaborate on the obvious? Or was this a way of indicating a different orientation in the future state? The question that arises after reading the 1961 *el Moujahid* statement is to what extent citizenship was to be determined by the characteristics of Arab-Muslim personality. Formally and legally the content of Algerian citizenship for all applicants would be the same. "It is not a question in fact, of practising, in the name of the absurd cult of identity, a reverse 'integration' in independent Algeria, or of reviving the politics of assimilation in a new form."[91] For those Algerians and for men like Fanon who accepted the reality of the nationalist aspirations of the Algerians, there was still a considerable difference, however, between a Muslim-Arab Algerian state, and an Algerian state in which the majority of people were Muslim-Arab.

The March 1962 issue of *el Moudjahid* that carried the detailed discussions of the Evian talks, had a section on the minority question in which these problems were again discussed. There, the earlier tone was adopted and the term Arab-Muslim did not appear. On the contrary, one of the statements dealing with this matter read as follows:

> If the Revolution addressed itself distinctly, to Jews and to the Europeans of Algeria, it was in order to take into account a human reality, one that is psychologically and sociologically subtle. But it is clear that in the hour of decolonisation, the men and women of Algeria do not define themselves by race or religion, but by their civil status and by their political choice. This is why

in the Franco-Algerian accords, there is only a question of the "French minority of Algeria."[92]

Those Frenchmen who chose to become Algerians

> would be integrated into the Algerian nation, with absolute respect for their own individual circumstances (language and culture, religion, personal status) and they would have access to all positions open to Algerian nationals (diplomacy, government, high administration . . .) in conformity with their competence.[93]

The Evian statement is close to that of the Soummam in spirit but does either one reflect what the majority of the FLN and the ALN believed in? In practice, it is the description of the Algerian state as Arab-Muslim which today conforms to the reality of Algeria.

The Jewish question which was handled as part of the minority question was nevertheless not identical with the problem posed by the European of Algeria. Fanon discussed the Jews of Algeria in the same essay devoted to the European minority, in *A Dying Colonialism,* and he recognized the difference in status of the two groups without discussing the genesis of these differences. He distinguished between those Jews who were closely tied to the French colonizers—the element involved in business and trade and administration, and the vast majority, according to Fanon three-fourths of the total, who were arabized and Algerian.[94] He was primarily interested in writing of the Jews who had joined in support of the FLN and in exposing the position of the FLN on the basis of the August 1956 declarations. What Fanon excerpted from the Soummam statement on the Jews was the request that they join the Revolution and reclaim their Algerian nationality along with other Algerians. "Jewish intellectuals," wrote Fanon

> have spontaneously demonstrated their support of the Algerian cause, whether in the democratic and traditionally anti-colonialist parties or in liberal groups. Even today, the Jewish lawyers and doctors who in the camps or in prison share the fate of millions of Algerians attest to the multiracial reality of the Algerian nation.[95]

Singling out those examples of Jews who had taken an open stand in favor of the FLN, Fanon quoted at length from a statement of a group in Constantine, written in August 1956.

One of the most pernicious maneuvers of colonialism in Algeria was and remains the division between Jews and Moslems. . . . The Jews have been in Algeria for more than two thousand years; they are thus an integral part of the Algerian people. . . . Moslems and Jews, children of the same earth, must not fall into the trap of provocation. Rather, they must make a common front against it, not letting themselves be duped by those who, not so long ago, were offhandedly contemplating the total extermination of the Jews as a salutary step in the evolution of humanity.[96]

Fanon then cited the statement by Algerian Jews written in January 1957. Fanon's selections are as much an indication of the position of those Jews quoted, as they are indicative of his own views.

It is time, today, [the 1957 statement read] that we should return to the Algerian community. Attachment to an artificial French nationality is a snare and a delusion at a moment when the young and powerful modern Algerian nation is rapidly taking shape. . . . Jews have joined the ranks of the Algerians fighting for national independence. . . . Some have paid with their lives, others have bravely borne the foulest police brutalities, and many are today behind the doors of prisons and the gates of concentration camps. We also know that in the common fight Moslems and Jews have discovered themselves to be racial brothers, and that they feel a deep and lasting attachment to the Algerian fatherland. In proclaiming our attachment to the Algerian Nation, we put an end to the pretext used by the colonialists when they try to prolong their domination by making the French people believe that the revolt here is only the result of a medieval fanaticism. . . .[97]

The FLN at the time of the Soummam Congress addressed itself to the Jewish minority in Algeria, as Fanon had indicated. On this occasion, as later, the FLN distinguished between the position of the Jewish and the European minority. It recognized that the French had bestowed special privileges on the Jews in the form of the Crémieux decree and it recognized that this measure had effectively widened the gap between Algerians of Muslim persuasion and the Jews of Algeria. The FLN did not enter into the history of the Jewish minority and its relations with the French, which would have complicated matters a good deal more. The Crémieux decree of 1870 "had made naturalized French citizens of the Algerian Jews."[98] It had fulfilled a wish for closer ties between Jews in Algeria and France. But the decree cannot be understood without considering the experiences of Algerian and European Jews prior to 1870, which in turn requires a consideration of their relations to both Muslims and other Europeans. If relations between Muslims and Jews were generally smooth, there were also bleak periods.[99] On the other hand, evidence of anti-Semitism, particularly during the Dreyfus period and later, in the twentieth century during the Second World War, expressed by Europeans against Jews, is as striking. To consider the Crémieux decree as a political act designed to alienate Jews from Muslims is an error, even though in practice this was one of its results. To consider it as the expression of a wish for protection and privilege on the part of a certain segment of Jews in Algeria who identified with France and not with Algerians, is closer to the truth, even if it is an abridgment of it. To produce a balanced portrait of Jews in Algeria, it would be necessary to distinguish between the arabized Jews who identified with Algeria, the European Jews who identified with France and with the colon administration in Algeria. In what way economic factors underlay this elementary partition is an essential part of the story. Suffice it to point out that to speak merely of Algerian Jews or European Jews, or worse still, to adhere to the Muslim-Jewish polarization in the Algerian context, is a simplification which approaches distortion.

In their campaign to win over the Jewish minority, the FLN exposed the racist and anti-Semitic character of French colonialism and of some of the ultra, extremist circles in Algeria, who fought to keep Algeria French. They noted that the Jewish minority had taken no part in the May 13, 1958 ultra manifestations. But they also recognized that for most Jews, the wait-and-see attitude was the policy adopted.[100] In November 25, 1959, the FLN of France issued an appeal to Algerian Jews in which it declared:

> You are an integral part of the Algerian people and it is not a matter of your choosing between France and Algeria, but of becoming active citizens of your true country. Either you want to fully exercise rights which no one will again be able to question, in this country whose future will be what all of its children will make of it in a free and democratic manner, or else you agree to live under the reign of scorn and you content yourselves with a

citizenship granted by your oppressors in a context which is the
very negation of the most elementary rights of the human personality. . . . At the moment when our struggle is entering a
decisive phase, we are waiting for you to affirm, in your capacity
as Algerians, your adherence to the ideal of Independence, and
from then on, that you take a greater and more active part in the
struggle of your people—so as to dissipate an equivocation that
risks compromising our future relations in order that tomorrow
may live, equally for all, the Algerian democratic and social
Republic.[101]

When attacks against the Jewish synagogue of Algiers took place
in December of 1960 the FLN was quick to denounce the event
and to call for common collaboration in an effort to investigate
those responsible. Once again, the FLN took the opportunity to
expose the divisive efforts of the French and to appeal to Jews
for solidarity in the national struggle. The attitude of a handful
of Israelis in Paris, on behalf of the Algerians, attracted some
attention from FLN circles. "According to an AFP (Agence
France Presse) communiqué, Belkacem Krim and Boumendjel
appear to have judged the formation of this committee as of
'considerable importance.' "[102] The committee referred to was
the "Committee for a Free Algeria," established by the Israelis
in question. More important, however, was the general mood of
apprehension and confusion which led French Jews and European Jews in general, to place events in Algeria in the context
of Middle Eastern developments. With allegations of Egyptian
support, if not direct instigation of the FLN, which were heard
in France, this mood appeared to be justified. In fact, Egypt was
hardly a guiding light in the Algerian affair nor was Algeria
directly involved in the Middle Eastern tangle. But the international scene did not make such prospects entirely fanciful. By
her collaboration with France on Suez, Israel in practice abandoned any intention—if she had had any—to speak out critically
of France on Algeria. Algeria, in turn, supported Egypt in the
Suez crisis. As to the Arab-Israel question, Algerians remained
neutral, although interest ran high and feelings were not indifferent. Present in the Arab League as an observer, Algerians
were nevertheless far more involved, necessarily, in their own
situation than in developments in the Middle East.

In the opinion of one observer, A. R. Abdel-Kader, a controversial personality who was exiled from Algeria after inde-

pendence, the Algerian Revolution was one of the only movements of national liberation to have taken a decisive and anti-
racist stand on the Jewish question.

> Among all of the movements of national liberation that have
> appeared in Muslim and Arab countries since the Second World
> War, the Algerian Revolution is the only one that has taken
> vis-à-vis racism in general and the Jewish question in particular,
> an unequivocally anti-racist position, in conformity with its scien-
> tific and revolutionary conceptions of social history, and has not
> allowed itself to be dragged into the Judeo-Arab conflict, inher-
> ited from the English colonial period.[103]

By 1969 the number of Jews remaining in Algeria, by Algerian
count, was somewhere between 3,000 and 4,000.[104] In 1954,
according to Algerian sources, there had been roughly 150,000
Jews in Algeria.

-5-

The Maghreb and Africa

―――――――

While the Jewish question was pressing for the Jewish minority in Algeria and for Jews in France who watched apprehensively for the outcome of the Algero-French struggle, for the FLN other issues were as important. Fanon in his *el Moudjahid* period concentrated on the questions of colonialism, the French left, the minorities, and finally, the relation of the Algerian Revolution to the Maghreb and to Africa. In this, as in the other issues he treated, he concentrated in areas that were of particular importance and interest to him, but always within the broader context of the interests of the FLN. Between the Maghreb and Africa, Fanon was clearly more interested in Africa. Whether or not this was related to his feeling of greater solidarity with black Africans as opposed to North Africans is an open question. The FLN not only recognized Fanon's interest, they positively encouraged it by sending him on missions in Africa. In 1960 Fanon went to Cairo to consult with the Provisional Government's representatives on the proper policy to be pursued in Africa.[105] That he wrote in *el Moudjahid,* and later in his last book, on his African experiences, was clearly the fruit of the labor of this period. At the time of his funeral, Fanon's African missions were singled out for special citation by the ALN speaker who delivered a eulogy at his burial, and by Belkacem Krim, who, at the time, was Vice-President of the Provisional Government.[106] In *el Moudjahid* as well, Fanon's work in Africa on behalf of the Algerian cause was noted with great appreciation.

In contrast, Fanon wrote little on the Maghreb. But still, at the time of the French bombings of Sakiet Sidi Youssef, the Tunisian border village, Fanon called for the withdrawal of French bases from Tunisia, and emphasized the need for Maghreb unity in the face of French colonialism. The incident in Tunisia had caused a great stir in Algeria, in the United States and Great Britain, where attempts were made to mediate between France and Tunisia, and in the United Nations. For Fanon, this was but another occasion to denounce the brutality of France, to condemn the policy of force, and with reference to the concern expressed in the United States, to explain that the dominating motive and sentiment in Maghreb policy was anti-colonialism, and not pro-communism or pro-westernism. The reference was brief and very much to the point.[107] In *el Moudjahid* as a whole, the Maghreb was a far more important area of concern than it was for Fanon. Maghreb unity was not a mere slogan, and the organization of conferences in Tangiers, in 1958, for instance, had as its aim the political cooperation of the North African states and their declaration of support for Algeria. At least two extensive studies were published dealing with the oil policies of the western powers in the Maghreb, and the problem of capital investment in the same region.[108] The need for a common economic policy supported by a common political policy was underlined with great persuasiveness. French interests in the Sahara, the realization that western states looked to North Africa for continued use of oil resources in the event of a lessening of Middle Eastern oil, or in the event of changing conditions which might affect their Middle Eastern privileges, were taken to be the factors motivating western interest in the resources of the Maghreb.

It was clearly understood that the overpopulation and unemployment in the Maghreb, coupled with its paucity of capital and its inability to continue relying exclusively on agricultural development, inevitably led it to turn to those states that could provide the requisite capital investment for industrialization. The Algerian trade unionist, identified as the author of the study on industrialization and neo-colonialism, recommended borrowing from a variety of countries to prohibit reliance on any single state. In addition, he recommended "Planning" in the Maghreb as a whole, in order to treat the economic problems of the region with maximum efficiency. To date planning has been adopted by virtually every state of the Maghreb, but not yet synchronized; and diversification of sources of capital has become, in Algeria, at least, a cardinal principle. If Fanon did not write about these questions in *el Moudjahid*, that he was thinking about them is evident from a reading of his last book. The question of neo-colonialism and economic dependence was a subject which haunted him to the end.

While some Algerians focused on the Maghreb, others, including Fanon, looked south and thought in terms of cooperation with African states. Fanon's discussion of Africa revolved around two themes: the central, guiding role played by Algeria and the Algerian Revolution in Africa; and the need for concerted efforts to oust France and Europe from the continent. At Accra in 1958 and again in Monrovia in the same year, at every conference held in Africa that involved countries of Black Africa as well as the Maghreb, the Algerian question was raised and the opportunity was not lost to cite it as a model for the continent. Fanon played a role in this process, having been named the representative of the Provisional Government in Accra, in March 1960. From that time on he was preoccupied with the dual tasks of surveying the possibilities of opening a southern front to ease the delivery of arms to the FLN through the southern frontier; and with the larger task of awakening Africa to its revolutionary mission.

Fanon had few illusions about the political conditions prevalent on the continent. In *el Moudjahid* he had been critical of those Africans, like the Ivory Coast's Houphouet-Boigny, whom he regarded as a French agent, and of the Senegalese poet-President, Léopold S. Senghor, whose pro-French cultural politics served to reenforce the French presence in Africa.[109] But these were merely the most overt champions of France. There were others who were more subtle and more dangerous. France, for all of its difficulties in dealing with sporadic instances of revolution in Africa, could still count on reliable friends. African unity was so far from existing that the ideal of a vast African march into Algeria in order to help the FLN combat France and free Algeria, was as chimeric as the prospect of Africa uniting. There were nevertheless striking exceptions to this grim picture. Guinea, under Sekou Touré, was one example of an independent course; Ghana under N'Krumah was another, and Mali under the leadership of Modibo Keita was a third. With Algeria,

Fanon regarded these countries as the most promising states of the continent. In the Congo, Patrice Lumumba stood out as a revolutionary leader, but Fanon recognized early that the colonial and regional difficulties would combine to undo what Lumumba had tried to create.

> Lumumba had once proclaimed that the liberation of the Congo would be the first phase of the complete independence of Central and Southern Africa and he had set his next objectives very precisely: support of the nationalist movements in Rhodesia, in Angola, in South Africa. . . .

> The enemies of Africa realized with a certain fear and trembling that if Lumumba should succeed, in the very heart of the colonialist empire, with a French Africa becoming transformed into a renovated community, an Angola as a 'Portugese province,' and finally Eastern Africa, it was all up with 'their' Africa, for which they had very precise plans.[110]

What was at issue, according to Fanon, was the future of imperialism in Africa. "Let us be sure never to forget it: the fate of all of us is at stake in the Congo."[111] Lumumba's position was heard in the circles of the FLN in Tunis, and when Lumumba visited Tunisia, he made a point of seeing the members of the Provisional Government. M'hammed Yazid, Belkacem Krim, and Ferhat Abbas received him, and *el Moudjahid* ran an editorial statement inspired by the visit. In the August 5 issue of *el Moudjahid*, Lumumba was quoted on the Algerian question and its relationship to the future of Africa.

> The Algerian problem for us, is the problem of all of Africa that is struggling for its liberation. Africa is not opposed to the West, Africa has no hatred for the white man, Africa has its right to dignity and liberty in the same fashion as all the countries of the world.
> For us there is no French Algeria. There is Algeria, that is all, and this Algeria is in the African continent.
> It is in the name of the very civilization which the Europeans themselves taught us, that we demand the end of the injustices and humiliations that exist in Africa.
> The West must make a choice today: either to free Africa and to live in friendship with her, or to refuse the hand of friendship which Africa extends to her.
> We do not wish to isolate ourselves, neither do the United

States, France or Great Britain. But we wish our relations with the West to be conducted in the framework of economic and technical cooperation between free nations. It is only under these conditions that cooperation is possible.[112]

In accord with the FLN, and with Fanon on this matter, Lumumba counseled against any involvement in the cold war. Neutralism, if it allowed the states of the Maghreb and of Black Africa to achieve their independence, was eminently desirable. The ultimate goals of such states would require generations of men and a heady accumulation of capital in order to save the wretched of the earth. What had cold-war politics to offer such men and nations?

Before Lumumba's assassination, and even before the poisoning of Felix Moumié of the Cameroons, another man in whom Fanon believed, he had become convinced that in certain parts of Africa, only armed struggle would succeed. In Kenya, in South Africa, in Algeria, in areas of massive colonial settlement, the colonial power would not be dislodged save by force.[113] For every moment that he allowed himself to dwell on the character of the new Africa that would emerge after the revolutions had rid the continent of European colonialism, Fanon remembered that the African and Maghreb states had their own differences to settle and that these were also serious obstacles to unity and cooperation.[114] "Here Algeria at war comes to solicit aid from Mali. And during this time Morocco is demanding Mauritania and a part of Mali . . . Also a part of Algeria."[115] The lesson was not lost. But how to undo this internecine rivalry? Even when he was at Accra, on the occasion of the All-Africa People's Congress held in 1960, he was forced to realize that being African did not mean that there was a comprehension of the issues at stake—even of those in Algeria. Peter Worsley, who attended the Congress, recorded his souvenirs of Fanon's presentation and reaction.

> In 1960, I attended the All-Africa People's Congress in Accra, Ghana. The proceedings consisted mainly of speeches by leaders of African nationalism from all over the continent, few of whom said anything notable. When, therefore, the representative of the Algerian Revolutionary Provisional Government, their Ambassador to Ghana, stood up to speak, I prepared myself for an address by a diplomat—not usually an experience to set the pulses racing.

I found myself electrified by a contribution that was remarkable not only for its analytical power, but delivered too, with a passion and a brilliance that is all too rare. I discovered that the Ambassador was a man named Frantz Fanon. At one point during his talk he appeared almost to break down. I asked him afterwards what had happened. He replied that he had suddenly felt emotionally overcome at the thought that he had to stand there, before the assembled representatives of African nationalist movements, to try and persuade them that the Algerian cause was important, at a time when men were dying and being tortured in his country for a cause whose justice ought to command automatic support from rational and progressive human beings.[116]

Fanon may have been disheartened by the official representatives of the African nationalist movements, but he never abandoned the strong faith he had in the African masses. Lyric in his praise of the African struggle to be free, Fanon wrote of Africans in the same heady tones that he wrote of the suffering masses in Algeria. Beneath the discouraging evidence of hypocrisy and betrayal, there was another dream.

> The Africa of everyday, oh not the poets' Africa, the one that puts to sleep, but the one that prevents sleep, for the people is impatient to do, to play, to say. The people that says: I want to build, to love, to respect, to create. This people that weeps when you say: I come from a country where the women have no children and the children no mothers and that sings: Algeria, brother country, country that calls, country that hopes.[117]

What Fanon described may have been Africa; it was also Fanon identifying with the struggle for liberation he saw in Africa. It was this vision to which he returned when he reflected on the question that preoccupied him: the help which Africa might give to Algeria. What was involved, specifically, was the possibility of opening a southern front. The southern front would involve all of the African peoples who had agreed to collaborate in this adventure. They would march together into Algeria, gradually advancing into the heart of the country and then into its northern reaches, the colonial stronghold, "continental Algeria." Together with their Algerian comrades they would rout the French and the war would be over and won. In his notes, written in this period, Fanon considered the various possibilities—supplying forces already in existence in the Sahara; supplying *wilayas* I, V, and the remains of VI, or creating a "series of lines of attack perpendicular to the Tellien Atlas which could possibly meet up with and work with the already existing *wilayas*."[118] Having made a decision on this question, he then proceeded to ask how it might be implemented. What was involved was the recruitment of troops and their training and introduction into Algeria. It was not only a military success that was important, it was the political work which this army might accomplish, and the reenforcement of the political mission of the ALN which it was responsible for endorsing.

Fanon's situation and residence in West Africa, his travels across southern Algeria, and his contact with Black Africa marked him in an entirely different way than had his Algerian experiences in Blida, or in the Tunisian period after 1956–1957. In Algeria Fanon was involved in an active and constant struggle to assure the acquisition of arms, to convince international opinion, and to keep Algerian opinion informed about the progress of the war. He was a true believer in the cathartic impact of the Algerian Revolution, and if he erred in his evaluation of its long-range effect on the country and its people, it was out of a total and unrestrained enthusiasm and commitment to the Algerian cause. But in Africa, Fanon's involvement was different. He had the occasion to see men and movements with whom he felt in some instances a great solidarity, and in others, a hostile revulsion. The role of the bourgeoisie in the continent became an important subject in his thinking. That regional tensions could assume the proportions he found angered him and brought him to a pitch of despair. "What must be avoided," he wrote, "is the Ghana-Senegal tensions, the Somali-Ethiopia, the Morocco-Mauritania, the Congo-Congo tensions. . . ."[119] In the last year of his life, it was the combination of the lessons of Algeria and the experiences of Africa that dominated his thinking.

-IV-

THE SUMMING UP:
THE WRETCHED
OF THE EARTH

The philosophers have only interpreted the world in
various ways; the point, however, is to change it.
Marx, *Theses on Feuerbach*

-1-

The Question of Violence

In 1960 Fanon learned that he had leukemia. At the time of his death, Belkacem Krim linked an earlier accident in which Fanon had been involved, with the subsequent cause of his death.[1] It was not suggested in a scientific spirit, nor as evidence of any conspiratorial theory, but merely as further proof of the selfless devotion of the man. Fanon had not sought to protect himself from the dangers involved in collaboration with the FLN, and even when he knew that he was fatally ill, he did not spare himself. The accident occurred on the Moroccan-Algerian frontier. The car in which Fanon was riding was blown up, but as Geismar tells us in his account, the precise details of what occurred remain unclear due to conflicting reports. "Miraculously escaping death, he [Fanon] had twelve fractured spinal vertebrae. The lower half of his body was almost totally paralyzed. He was flown back to Tunis, then to Rome for more specialized medical treatment."[2] In Rome, there were more incidents, this time less mysterious in origin and purpose. The Red Hand, a right-wing group of Algerian pieds noirs, was responsible for blowing up the car of the FLN representative designated to meet Fanon as he arrived in Rome. Later, in the hospital to which he was sent, another attempt was made, this time directly on his life. He escaped, but the incident convinced him of the determination of the enemies of the Revolution.

It was when he was in Ghana that Fanon began to discern symptoms which would later be diagnosed as those of leukemia. Dr. B. Juminer recalls that when he returned to Tunis from Mali

and Ghana, Fanon was already seriously ill, had lost a considerable amount of weight, and was markedly weaker. Colleagues
who examined him were soon shocked when they realized the
nature of his illness.[3] Tests were repeatedly made, only to
confirm the diagnosis. Treatment was begun in Tunis, then in
the Soviet Union, and in the end, in the United States. In the
USSR, Fanon improved sufficiently to be able to travel and to
look into psychiatric institutions, which he reputedly found
disappointing. But more important, he felt able to return to
Tunis and to his work. At the time, instead of continuing a study
he had begun on the Algerian Revolution and Africa, Fanon set
to work on what became *The Wretched of the Earth*. Between March
and May 1961 he completed the bulk of the manuscript, with an
interval to consult with Sartre on the introduction that Sartre
agreed to write. In the summer he worked on the section dealing
with national culture, and it was only in the fall—in November
while he was in Washington, D.C., where he had finally agreed
to go for treatment—that he read the proofs.

The meeting between Sartre and Fanon in Rome has been
well described by de Beauvoir in her memoirs. It was through
Claude Lanzmann of *Les Temps Modernes*, that Fanon managed to
get his manuscript of *The Wretched* to Sartre. De Beauvoir wrote
that Sartre had become convinced of the truth of Fanon's analysis when he was in Cuba. "He (Sartre) was in agreement with his
book: a manifesto of the Third World, extreme, whole, incendi-
ary, but also complex and subtle; he willingly agreed to preface
it."[4] Sartre's opinion of the book, as related by de Beauvoir, is
a far more sober statement than the near hysteria which it was
to provoke in France, England, or the United States. The account of the meeting in Rome provided de Beauvoir with an
opportunity to observe Fanon, and her remarks are not only
useful for the information they provide on Fanon's where-
abouts, but as a guide to the personality of the man. It was a
sympathetic and critical portrait which de Beauvoir sketched of
a man tortured by the injustice and violence of the world around
him, and consumed by the passion to rectify what he found. He
wanted Sartre to be committed to the Algerian cause in a more
total fashion; to stop writing, for instance, as a mark of protest.
But it also appeared to de Beauvoir that he was deeply troubled
by what he had seen and knew from the inside. ". . . on the
dissent, the intrigues, the liquidations, the oppositions which

were later to openly provoke such a stir, Fanon knew much more than he could say. These somber secrets, perhaps also his personal hesitations, gave his remarks an enigmatic turn, one that was prophetic in a strange and troubled way."[5] She quotes Fanon as saying that "I have two deaths on my conscience which I will not forgive myself for: that of Abane and that of Lumumba." While this caused de Beauvoir to wonder whether he was not assuming too great a responsibility, giving himself too much credit for these events, the remark is nevertheless an important one. Algerian officials are at pains to point out that Fanon barely knew Abane Ramdane, the key figure in the Soummam meeting in 1956 and a radical revolutionary. His remarks on the subject of the man and particularly his liquidation in 1958 must not, therefore, be taken seriously.[6] There may be too much protest in the warning. Whether or not Fanon was directly responsible, as his statement quoted by Simone de Beauvoir suggests, is not the decisive question. It would have been in keeping with Fanon's exaggerated sense of responsibility, particularly within the revolutionary milieu, to speak as though every man was responsible for every event of the collective whole. The death of Lumumba—like the death of Ramdane—was something which responsible men who knew better, ought to have been able to prevent or to anticipate. That is perhaps the meaning of his remark. It suggests that the responsibility for the death of both men was broader than later accusations and defensive explanations would demonstrate.

Fanon's somber knowledge of the inner workings of the Algerian Revolution had a good deal to do with the mood in which he wrote *The Wretched of the Earth.* But for all of his deception with the difficult process of revolution, in Algeria and even more in Africa, Fanon's study reflected his persistent faith in the liberation movements of both Algeria and Africa. *The Wretched of the Earth* is certainly Fanon's most important book from a political point of view. There is little that affects political development in developing countries that it not discussed here. And for all of its well-publicized treatment of the question of violence, it is not the critique of violence that is the principal contribution of the work. It is the analysis of political development in the third world, specifically Algeria and Africa, in which the question of violence plays an important role. Under this classification one has to include the penetrating discussion of political organiza-

tion, and the genesis and degeneration of nationalist movements and parties.

The question of violence, however, if not the main contribution of Fanon, is obviously an extremely important aspect of his
writing. It is hardly surprising that it has attracted as much
attention, and that it has been the pretext for a facile praising
or damning of the author. Hence, those who believe that Fanon,
like Che and Mao, was more interested in the process of violence
than where it led, can only be said to have missed the point.
Fanon was clearly concerned with the process because he believed the objective to be critical to human existence. That he
did not consider it to be a marginal aspect of the political life
he dissected in the third world, had a great deal to do with his
own espousal of a revolutionary counter-violence. One may
argue that it is doubtful that the violence which Fanon advocated for the individual could possibly fulfill the psychological
functions which he claimed. And one may publicly regret that he
mingled existential notions with political recommendations. But
to consider the discussion of the cathartic effect of violence in
the national and international contexts as nothing more than an
expression of Fanon's personality is a gross distortion unwarranted by a reading of his work. The governing assumption, for
Fanon, was that violence was not limited to the battlefield, nor
was it an aspect of international relations, only. The entire
colonial enterprise was built on a foundation of force and conquest, hence, the primary role of violence. Lest this appear too
abstract, Fanon made every effort to demonstrate that the implications of this situation affected human relations and the
self-image of both colonizer and colonized. Fanon's thesis, as
expressed in his notion of the cathartic effect of violence, was
that decolonization could only occur successfully where the
colonized not only seized their freedom through a liberation
struggle, but participated in violent action to individually ex-
punge themselves of the colonial heritage of inferiority and
submission. It is this aspect of his concept of violence which, so
graphically expressive in words, is considerably less convincing
as a policy.

The development of the idea of the cathartic effect of violence
appears in the conclusion of Fanon's discussion of violence in
the colonial context. There, in keeping with an analysis which
was apparent in embryonic form in the *Moudjahid* essays and

even in *Black Skin, White Masks,* Fanon described the colonial world as a manichean world, a compartmentalized world. Beginning with the realization that the parts of the city inhabited by the colonizer and the colonized were radically different, Fanon came to see these physical differences as symbolic of the two species of humanity resident in each. What was essential in the argument was that the process of colonization was a process realized by force, that force remained latent if not in actual use in the colony, and that force and the threat of force were the prerogatives which the colonizer held over the colonized. The partition of cities was merely a formal expression of the partition of humanity in the colony.

Nor was a Marxist analysis adequate in explaining the character of colonial life. "The governing race is first and foremost those who come from elsewhere, those who are unlike the original inhabitants, 'the others'."[7] Fanon remained perpetually in flux between a Marxist analysis which he rejected because he felt it ignored the racist aspect of colonialism, and the tendency to apply psychiatric categories in the discussion of the human consequences of colonialism. But the latter merely provided a description of the human situation produced by the colonial system. It did not explain the genesis of that system nor how it operated. It was not enough to identify the governing race with the "others." The question was not who the "others" were, what religion or race, but how they came to be governing and what prerogatives that entitled them to. Fanon moved away from an emphasis on race, as his discussion of negritude demonstrated. It is a move for which he has been discreetly if persistently criticized among some black militants in the United States today. But if he was generally sympathetic to a Marxist analysis, he did not consider himself to be a Marxist, and he did not appear anxious, politically or intellectually, to explore the possibilities which such a rigorous analysis might offer.

In the colonial milieu, the colonizer encouraged the aggressiveness of the colonized against his own kind. He erected a system of prohibitions which assured the frustration of the colonized population and guaranteed regular explosions which were carefully directed against members of the colonized group. Eventually this circle would be broken and the colonized would emerge to challenge the colonizer's contention that he was less than equal. From the assertion that colonialism implies the creation of a manichean world in which the colonized is reduced to a permanently inferior status, to the assumption that a radical reordering of this situation involves and presupposes a change in the personality of the colonized, is the long step that leads from consciousness to action. It was the step which Fanon chronicled in *A Dying Colonialism,* and it was to constitute a major theme in *The Wretched of the Earth.* Where did violence and the concept of its cathartic effect fit into this framework?

Fanon used the term violence in different contexts, and to describe different phases of a process. The process under discussion was decolonization. Decolonization, according to Fanon, would occur only through violent means. The reasons for this were implicit in the nature of colonialism and the vested interests of the colonial country, and in the relationship of the colonizer to the colonized. Decolonization meant the destruction of the colonial system. It also implied the possibility of reconstructing human relations and so producing a new society. Decolonization, achieved through the use of violence and armed struggle, would give birth to the new man. Violence, then, appeared in the following contexts: it was critical in the process of decolonization, specifically in the armed struggle sustained by the peasantry; it was instrumental in the success of the Revolution in that complex combination of armed resistance and individual action from which would emerge the new man. Violence was presented as a tool in the process of decolonization, as organized force; and on an individual level, as the indispensable means to experience the Revolution. It was from this second concept that Fanon derived the notion of violence as a cleansing force. He introduced the idea that violence was the absolute form of praxis. He attributed to violence, conceived in this manner, distinct from its use in armed struggle, a virtue and a promise which it did not otherwise possess. And by associating the cathartic effect of violence with the individual use of violence, he raised the obvious possibility, that it could have the same effect on a group. In this way individual acts of violence committed in concert were believed to bestow new life. The moral justification of violence was based on the assumption that it transformed man psychically. That one could speak of its moral justification was a reminder of its ultimate purpose as well as of its character of retribution in the cause of justice. The oppressed regained their dignity in this traumatic process. In *The Wretched of the*

Earth, Fanon spoke of violence as a "royal pardon," and as a "cleansing force."

> At the level of individuals, violence is a cleansing force. It frees the native from his inferiority complex and from his despair and inaction; it makes him fearless and restores his self-respect. Even if the armed struggle has been symbolic and the nation is demobilised through a rapid movement of decolonisation, the people have the time to see that the liberation has been the business of each and all and that the leader has no special merit. From thence comes that type of aggressive reticence with regard to the machinery of protocol which young governments quickly show. When the people have taken violent part in the national liberation they will allow no one to set themselves up as 'liberators.' They show themselves to be jealous of the results of their action and take good care not to place their future, their destiny or the fate of their country in the hands of a living god. Yesterday they were completely irresponsible; today they mean to understand everything and make all decisions. Illuminated by violence, the consciousness of the people rebels against any pacification. From now on the demagogues, the opportunists and the magicians have a difficult task. The action which has thrown them into a hand-to-hand struggle confers upon the masses a voracious taste for the concrete. The attempt at mystification becomes, in the long run, practically impossible.[8]

To justify violence as part of the need for armed struggle in a process of national liberation is one thing; to justify individual acts of violence in the belief that they cleanse those who so act, is something quite different. Struggle was the critical concept and process more than the violence which might mark it. It is doubtful that the attempt at mystification which Fanon believed would "in the long run [become] practically impossible," would indeed become impossible thanks to the illuminating effects of violence. Revolutions and coups in Africa are not evidence of such a result. The Algerian experience is hardly more encouraging. Few if any Algerians in the FLN have been known to justify the Battle of Algiers, for instance, on the ground that it would cleanse its participants of the humiliations of colonialism. On the contrary, those Algerians who are willing to discuss Fanon —from a sympathetic point of view—make it clear that this is one aspect of his analysis which they do not believe Algerians shared. It is not the need for armed struggle which they question, but the concept of the cathartic effect of violence. In practice, one looks for evidence that individual acts of violence do metamorphose the individual. That the desire for violence exists is another matter; the question is of its efficacy and, in Fanon's case, of its morality as well as its potential political harm. It would appear to be a measure of Fanon's failure to remain loyal to his own complex analysis of the roots of the colonial inferiority complex, that he was capable of turning to such a solution. It is clear that decolonized man is not entirely free of his colonial past or of some of the complexes that it has bred into him. Nor has the practice of violence on the individual level raised individuals to a level of responsibility where they may challenge their leaders when these seek to lead them astray. The objective, in Fanon's terms, of the cathartic effect of violence was not only to transform men, it was to make them capable of creating a better society. In retrospect, it is hardly possible to claim that it is the absence of adequate illumination by violence that is responsible for the political tragedies of post-independence nations. It is the prohibition of politics and the inadequacy of political organization that have robbed yesterday's partisans of their rewards. That Fanon knew this himself is clear from *The Wretched of the Earth*.

It is tempting to conclude that Fanon's concept of the cathartic effect of violence does not belong to the realm of politics. On an individual level, it appears to synthesize the wish for retribution and the hope of redemption. Fanon himself was an example of a man who longed to bear witness to his own rebirth as a free man, to have justice done and to be saved and reborn. But he himself never engaged in any act of violence of the type he considered a prerequisite to this situation.

The attempt to discover the philosophical roots of Fanon's conception of violence, not the primacy of violence in armed struggle, but violence in the sense in which it is mystified by Fanon, is an effort to place Fanon's thinking on the subject in a larger intellectual and historical framework. It is not this type of analysis that has produced the most serious critique of the question. That has been done by political commentators for whom violence is not an armchair alternative but an instrument which has the potential for self-destruction as well as constructive revolution. But the question of Fanon's antecedents in the intellectual sense is worth considering, if only because it has attracted considerable attention. The comparison with Georges Sorel's *Reflections on Violence* has been made, but there is no evidence that Sorel was a formative influence on Fanon's thinking. Hence, the following statement by Hannah Arendt seems unwarranted. "Fanon, who had infinitely greater intimacy with the practice of violence than either [Sorel or Pareto], was greatly influenced by Sorel and used his categories even when his own experiences spoke clearly against them."[9] On the basis of discussions with men who knew and worked with Fanon, and who maintain that they entertained extended discussions with him on this very subject, the influence of Sorel was totally absent.[10] Neither Sorel, nor Engels' study *The Role of Force in History*, which Fanon was given by Reda Malek, appears to have been critical in the development of his thinking. Reda Malek, who worked with Fanon on *el Moudjahid* in Tunis, in reminiscing about conversations with Fanon recalled that he had brought Fanon a copy of Engels' work and that he had been astonished by Fanon's disappointment on reading it. It was too mild, and perhaps inappropriate to his interests in the Algerian situation. In *The Wretched of the Earth,* Fanon quoted passages from Engels' *Anti-Duhring,* parts 11, chapter 111, on the theory of violence, but only to repudiate it. Engels did not understand that the "violent reaction of the colonized introduced a qualitatively new element" in the struggle.[11] Renate Zahar, in her discussion of Fanon, Sorel, and Engels, suggests that Fanon may have felt that by his emphasis on the disparity between the technological superiority of the colonizer and the blatant inferiority of his adversary, Engels was prejudging the potential of the latter and of the entire violent confrontation.[12] It was not that Engels was unfamiliar with colonial wars. Referring to the Napoleonic wars, Fanon remarked that the Spanish resistance to Napoleon was based on a strong national faith, and the revival of guerilla warfare. What disturbed Fanon was the similarity he sensed between the position of Engels and that of the national-reformist parties that feared the outcome of the violent confrontations because they were uncertain that this activity of the masses was in their best interests.

The comparison with Georges Sorel is obvious although what Fanon and Sorel had in common is less so.[13] The two polemicists functioned in two very different contexts and societies. Sorel's emphasis on syndicalism finds no parallel in Fanon, nor does his attitude toward the proletariat. It is in the area of violence that the comparison is most often made, but here too Sorel's concept of the role of violence as an essential myth is not comparable to Fanon's view of violence as a cathartic instrument in the process of decolonization. However dangerous and apolitical one may consider Fanon's concept of violence in the service of colonized men, it does not appear similar to Sorel's apocalyptic visions, drowned as these are in a violent rage at the anti-militarist mood of his time and at the recession of heroism. Fanon concentrated on racism and colonialism and he developed his ideas on armed struggle in the context of the Algerian war. He did not write about the reconstruction of society in terms of permanent class antagonisms which would be perpetuated by violent means. He was far more skeptical of the proletariat's vanguard role than was Sorel, and he did not consider violence as an essential aspect of socialism when he discussed the political character of Algerian society after independence. For Sorel it was the essential component of the political milieu, either striking by the aversion it inspired, or critical by the power it bestowed on its proletarian users. For Fanon, violence was indispensable to the process of decolonization but it was inadequate to it, and it was not raised to the status of a permanent policy either in the decolonization process or after. In sum, violence did not occupy the same function for Fanon as it did for Sorel.

In her discussion of Hegel and Fanon, Renate Zahar explains that "on the theoretical level, Fanon's concept of violence is implicitly derived from Hegel, through Sartre's philosophy."[14] For Sartre, violence is considered as a reaction, and the violence of the colonized is necessarily a reaction to the violence of the colonizer. Zahar points out that the colonial situation represents a new historical instance of the master-slave relationship conceived by Hegel. For the latter, emancipation for the slave is through the process of labor, a process which has rendered him indispensable to his master and which therefore constitutes the instrument of his own salvation. The liberation of the slave takes place through a struggle with the master for the reward of recognition. But Fanon, as we saw earlier, did not believe that the colonized was in a position vis-à-vis the colonizer even to benefit from such a confrontation. Fanon used the concept of work as a liberating instrument. But, and this is the great difference between the meaning of the term labor for Fanon and for Hegel, for the former, labor was identified as violence. Absolute praxis is represented by violence, according to Fanon, and the militant is the man who works—in this sense. It is at this point that Fanon introduces his examples of the Mau Mau in Kenya, and the suggestion that in Algeria, militants are asked to commit an irrevocable act which reflects and seals their commitment to the revolutionary struggle.

While she endorses Fanon's view that spontaneous action, including violence, must be organized and channeled to be effective, Zahar does not seem particularly critical of the theory that violence can accomplish the internal cleansing and psychic transformation which Fanon believed possible. Others, with a different experience, more political than theoretical, were to take up the question from a more practical perspective.

-2-

Peasants, Parties
and Spontaneity

It is the Vietnamese Communist Nguyen Nghe, in the periodical *Pensée*, who has pursued this question of violence in Fanon's work within the larger context of political movements. Nguyen Nghe's critique is based on his experience and that of the Vietnamese Communist Party, and it is important to bear this in mind in considering his severe criticisms of Fanon. Nevertheless, in comparison with most analytic efforts aimed at Fanon, this one is so clearly superior that it deserves the most careful consideration. Nguyen Nghe's objections to Fanon range from the use of inflammatory language, which he finds poetic and moving but not an effective substitute for political analysis, to an excessive individualism which he links with the influence of French existentialists. For Nguyen Nghe, national liberation is primarily a political process and the eulogies of violence, particularly the descriptions of peasant violence which he found in *The Wretched of the Earth*, marked Fanon in his eyes as politically immature. "When one neglects this political ideological work," he wrote, "in order to concentrate exclusively on the military art, one must expect disappointments—especially when conditions of peace are restored, even in victory."[16]

To evaluate the validity of Nguyen Nghe's criticisms depends in the first place on a reading of Fanon, and particularly on how one interprets his discussion of violence, armed struggle, and the general question of political organization. It is only in this light that the highly polemical position of Nguyen Nghe can be studied.[17] Fanon's conception of violence and the role of violence, not the idea of its cathartic effect but its political importance, can be understood only if one follows his analysis of existing political parties in the colonial context. It was as a result of his disaffection with traditional, reformist parties, his conviction that they were profoundly alienated from the masses, that Fanon developed his ideas about the "illegal party" and its eventual identification with the peasantry. The combined efforts of these two groups, the former playing the role of the ideological vanguard and the latter informing and broadening the base of the illegal party men, produced a new symbiosis that became a potent political force. When the pressure of this force was applied in the direction of the cities, another element in Fanon's revolutionary hierarchy emerged, the lumpenproletariat. The lumpenproletariat became politicized and active—therein lay the novelty of its position in Fanon's analysis. It played a role for which it had previously been considered ineligible. What is absent in Fanon's description and discussion is the traditional proletariat. The working class in the colonial milieu, according to Fanon, is not the vanguard of the Revolution, it is the rearguard of the establishment. There is not only an overt skepticism about the revolutionary nature of the proletariat, there is little patience with the international left, the workers of the world, or their alleged solidarity. Fanon had said as much in his *el Moudjahid* articles and in *A Dying Colonialism*. The most searing aspect of Nguyen Nghe's criticism, that Fanon ignored the question of the political education and organization of the peasantry, and hence had no conception of how revolutions are made or carried out, is quite simply a misreading of Fanon's text. That there are contradictions in the original and that it suffers from disorganization is not much help. But it is not the content of Fanon's analysis with which Nguyen Nghe argues in his brilliant attack, it is the fact that Fanon did not conform to the framework of revolutionary action which he believed to be beyond debate.

Fanon made it plain in the first part of his essay in *The Wretched of the Earth*, that he was profoundly disappointed in existing nationalist parties in the colonies. One may assume that he was generalizing from his experience in Algeria and in Africa. But it was in the section on spontaneity, which in effect is a critique of parties and political organization, that Fanon spelled out his position. He criticized existing parties for being poor and inappropriate imitations of continental parties derived from the metropolitan territory. He criticized them for importing attitudes towards the countryside and the peasantry that were taken from Europe and that had no place in the countries to which they addressed themselves. He criticized nationalist parties for being more interested in bureaucratic administration than in what they were meant to accomplish. But the most important defect they exhibited was in addressing themselves to the proletariat, the skilled workers, and the civil servants.[18] In other words, they neither spoke to nor for the majority of the population, the peasantry.

From this initial observation, Fanon developed a number of themes which remain central to his political thinking. First, that the proletariat in underdeveloped countries is the most favored class. "It cannot be too strongly stressed that in the colonial territories the proletariat is the nucleus of the colonized population which has been most pampered by the colonial regime. The embryonic proletariat of the towns is in a comparatively privileged position."[19] The men whom Fanon put into this category —tram conductors, miners, dockers, interpreters, nurses, and taxi drivers—functioned like a bourgeoisie in the colonial milieu. Secondly, the principal clients of the nationalist parties shared a mistrust for the rural, peasant masses of the population. Primarily urban in their appeal, organization, and membership, they tended to ignore the countryside, or else they failed in their attempt to implant themselves in it when they tried. Thirdly, the rural, peasant masses distrusted the city parties and did not need their guidance to become aware of their exploited situation. They saw the parties as unrepresentative of their interests, while the parties misread the passivity of the peasants as a sign of indifference. Finally, an important break occurred in the traditional party that reflected the strong division of opinion on these matters. A minority wing, a dissident group which Fanon referred to as the illegal party men, withdrew from the party and turned, first for its protection and then out of a new-found solidarity, to the countryside and the peasant masses. According to Fanon, the peasantry was the only revolutionary element in the nation, but it was galvanized into action by its contact with this dissident band of party rebels. The maquisards were the rebels formed in turn by their communion with the peasantry. Active in the countryside, they did not abandon the cities entirely. On the contrary, turning back to the cities from which they had originally come, they now found a new element of the population which they had hitherto ignored, the bidonville lumpenproletariat. It is the lumpenproletariat that would pressure the cities and act there, in the same spirit that the peasants had electrified the countryside.

The emphasis on the peasantry and the lumpenproletariat have been recognized as new departures in the analysis of the revolutionary situation as it exists in certain underdeveloped countries. When the criticism is made, as it is by Nguyen Nghe, that Fanon made the classic mistake of failing to realize that the peasantry is not inherently revolutionary and that it cannot be substituted for the politicized proletariat—not the lumpenproletariat but the working class—he was simplifying Fanon's position to the point of distortion.

> The peasant, himself, can never have a revolutionary consciousness; it is the militant coming from the cities who will have to patiently search out the most talented elements in the poor peasantry, educate them, organize them, and it is only after a long period of political work that one can mobilize the peasantry.[20]

If Fanon had suggested that the peasant developed a revolutionary consciousness alone, Nguyen Nghe's comments would be appropriate. But this is not at all what Fanon does. What has been generally ignored in the discussion of Fanon's reevaluation of the role of the peasantry and the lumpenproletariat, is the role he assigns to the deviant nationalists, the illegal elements of the nationalist party who secede from it in conformity with their just rebellion against its self-enclosed character. It is this group that plays the role which Nguyen Nghe wants assigned to the proletariat.

In Fanon's analysis, the "illegalists," as they are abysmally called, are pushed out of the city, and out of the suburban sections of the city towards the countryside. They are moved by the need to escape from their former colleagues who now collaborate with the colonial regime in tracking them down. It is this pressure which forces the non-party men to discover the peasant masses. What the dissidents learn is that the peasants have not remained indifferent, nor have they concentrated on imbibing the platitudes passed out by the nationalist parties of the cities. Instead they have come to accept that the struggle for their liberation must be in terms of violence, of an armed insurrection. They have thought in terms of the national struggle and the redemption of land. When Fanon writes that in certain instances the peasants intervene in a decisive way, it is in the domain of armed struggle for national liberation, and after independence, it is in order to influence the direction the nation should follow.

The former party men who have become maquisards learn from the peasants who protect them. But they also instruct them in political and military organization. This period is brief, according to Fanon, for the masses are moved to action and they are impatient. Fanon's remarks about the maquisards providing a political and military education are reminiscent of what the ALN did in Algeria. Far from ignoring the question of the politicization of the movements of the peasantry and the lumpenproletariat, Fanon makes it clear that while the period of spontaneity is glorious, it must be brief, else it threatens the liberation movement. There is a genuine confusion provoked by the ambiguity in Fanon's discussion of the role of the maquisards. What has become of these dissidents? In Fanon's text, they are lost in the midst of the peasant masses with whom they have joined, and they reemerge, along with the lumpenproletariat, as a distinct group when they prepare for their confrontation with the enemy in the cities. Yet there is no indication that they have organized themselves as a revolutionary party, even though it is proper to speak of the combined forces of the peasantry, the lumpenproletariat, and the rebels as constituting the revolutionary elements of the population.

Between the time when the dissidents first make their contacts with the peasantry, and when Fanon speaks of their impact on the lumpenproletariat, there is a phase of independent peasant action, the rebellions which Fanon feared would become rampant and ultimately destructive. Clearly, the dissidents have not played a role in this phase. On the contrary, what characterizes it is the absence of any organization, programs, or resolutions. The overriding objective is the disappearance of foreign colonialists. While he is aware of the dangers of spontaneity, Fanon's description of this period is so favorable that it is not surprising that he has been accused of the very dangers he himself exposes in the spontaneity of the rebellion.

Shortly after he has praised the importance of the peasant rebellions, Fanon insists that spontaneity alone is not enough and it must be condemned. The leaders, whom we are given to understand are the maquisards–non-party-men of old, are found once again. Their role is now the important one of channeling the energies released by the jacqueries into a political movement the objective of which is the implementation of the Revolution. For the leaders, the meaning of politics has undergone great change. It is no longer the process of mystification but the unique means of intensifying the current struggle and preparing the people for the leadership of their country.

> The leaders of the rebellion come to see that even very large scale peasant risings need to be controlled and directed into certain channels. These leaders are led to renounce the movement in so far as it can be termed a peasant revolt, and to transform it into a revolutionary war. They discover that the success of the struggle presupposes clear objectives, a definite methodology and above all the need for the mass of the people to realise that their unorganised efforts can only be a temporary dynamic.[21]

Simultaneously praising the peasantry for its commitment in the course of armed struggle, for its total action against the colonizer, Fanon warns harshly against the limits and the weaknesses of such a program. It is precisely because this does not constitute a program, because even hatred against the foreigner must be superseded, that the weaknesses of spontaneity must be severely condemned. The discovery that the peasant rebellions reveal a profound instability, that the colonizer continues to make inroads into the rural community and that his forces remain superior, reenforce the knowledge that it is only by organization and education of a new consciousness that the gains of the colonized must be consolidated.

> All this taking stock of the situation, this enlightening of consciousness and this advance in the knowledge of the history of societies are only possible within the framework of an organisation, and inside the structure of a people. Such an organisation is set afoot by the use of revolutionary elements coming from the towns at the beginning of the rising, together with those rebels who go down into the country as the fight goes on. It is this core which constitutes the embryonic political organisation of the rebellion.[22]

Yet in the very next sentence, Fanon reaffirms his faith in the political importance of the peasantry:

> But on the other hand the peasants, who are all the time adding to their knowledge in the light of experience, will come to show themselves capable of directing the people's struggle. Between the nation on a war-time footing and its leaders there is established a mutual current of enlightenment and enrichment. Traditional institutions are reinforced, deepened and sometimes literally transformed. The tribunals which settle disputes, the djemaas and the village assemblies turn into revolutionary tribunals and political and military committees. In each fighting group and in every village hosts of political commissioners spring up, and the people, who are beginning to splinter upon the reefs of misunderstanding, will be shown their bearings by these political pilots.[23]

The political pilots are the leaders, the dissidents whose responsibility it is to provide a political education and to direct the existing organizations of the countryside in the appropriate direction. If there is mystification of the role of the peasantry, it cannot be found by a faithful reading of Fanon's text. Even the accusation that he establishes a false dichotomy between the countryside and the city turns out to be false. Just as he is aware that the objective of the national liberation movement must not be only political liberation, so he understands that the limited outlook of the peasant masses, whose indispensability is not argued, must be stretched and expanded.

> The people will thus come to understand that national independence sheds light upon many facts which are sometimes divergent and antagonistic. Such a taking stock of the situation at this precise moment of the struggle is decisive, for it allows the people to pass from total, indiscriminating nationalism to social and economic awareness. The people who at the beginning of the struggle had adopted the primitive Manicheism of the settler—Blacks and Whites, Arabs and Christians—realise as they go along that it sometimes happens that you get Blacks who are whiter than the Whites and that the fact of having a national flag and the hope of an independent nation does not always tempt certain strata of the population to give up their interests or privileges.[24]

Nguyen Nghe considered Fanon's description of the role of the peasantry, and the encounter between the political militant and the peasantry, as quite simply erroneous. He was no more convinced by Fanon's analysis of the proletariat as the privileged class of the colonial establishment. On the contrary, he felt that Fanon had had to distort, in fact to deny all revolutionary potential to the working class in order to justify his thesis of a peasant revolution. In the first place, Nguyen Nghe believed Fanon wrong in placing all of the groups he identified as the proletariat in the same class. There is an error, he claimed, "in placing in the same social class, dockers and miners with interpreters and nurses. The first constitute the true proletariat, the industrial working class (in the colonies one must also include in this group the workers on the big plantations); the second are part of the petite-bourgeoisie, which is also revolutionary but with less resolution and less consistent in its attitude."[25] To believe that the peasants teach the militants, in the same way in which the latter educate them, is sheer nonsense.[26] The explanation for Fanon's error, according to Nguyen Nghe, was that Fanon had emphasized that phase of the revolutionary struggle which he knew best, i.e. the heroic phase of the armed struggle. But as a result he had lost his way. His perspective was out of focus. His error was not only in emphasis, but in ignoring the imperatives of the revolutionary struggle beyond this phase, imperatives which could only be ignored at the price of total defeat. What Nguyen Nghe had in mind was not only the need for national unity at a broader base, but the need for technological expertise and a familiarity with the modern world which the peasantry did not possess. It was Fanon's entire conception of the third world and the meaning of neutralism which Nguyen Nghe contested.

The issue of organization vs. spontaneity and the role of the party have proved to be key issues used by a variety of commentators to assess Fanon's position and the validity of his revolutionary stance. The criteria depend, of course, on the evaluators and what they, in turn, represent. The most interesting critiques have come from the left, and from different perspectives on the left. Renate Zahar is close in spirit to Nguyen Nghe, although as her study indicates, her own interest has not been political organization per se, nor the political assessment of Fanon's work. She is nevertheless in accord with Nguyen Nghe in pointing out the weaknesses in Fanon's political thinking, accusing him of being fixed at a prepolitical stage of consciousness. "Political praxis," she writes, referring to Fanon's conception of it,

> identifies itself with emancipatory violence, without any relation
> with its material correlation, the process of social work: it is
> conceived as a force which imposes itself on the spirit; the con-
> science of the colonised being structured in a manichean and
> auto-alienated fashion, as a result of the fact that it has been
> forged by the antagonisms of the colonial society.[27]

From her vantage point, Zahar felt that Fanon remained unaware of the complexity of the relationship between spontaneity,
violence and the forces of production. This being the case, how
could one assume that Fanon would understand how to explain,
let alone how to guide, the peasantry. It was not a matter of
taking issue with the primacy of the peasantry, which she did not
do, but rather, of questioning how its efforts might be moved
beyond the stage of mere revolt.[28] In the end, Fanon's work
provided a fine example of the phenomenology of neo-colonialism. But according to Zahar he was as incapable of explaining
relations between imperialist powers and their formerly dependent territories as he had been to explain the social and
economic bases of political praxis.[29]

The same position was taken in a pamphlet entitled, "Coéxist-
ence pacifique et 'Tiers Monde,'" published by the Algerian
review *Révolution socialiste* (*Revue ideologique, politique et culturelle du
Parti de l'Avant garde socialiste*) in August 1970. Its anonymous
authors argued that Fanon had influenced Algerian leaders who
then found themselves in an ideological current that was "pre-
Marxist" or even hostile to Marxism.[30] A more sympathetic view
came from the Trotskyist aide to Ben Bella, Michel Pablo, who
was more generous in his estimate of Fanon's role in Algerian
politics. Unlike those who anxiously sought to diminish Fanon's
impact in Algeria, Pablo noted that in 1963 the FLN had allowed
a "Frantz Fanon Marxist circle of Algiers" to hold meetings that
brought together "Algerian and European members and non-
members of the Party."[31] He referred to the Fanonist wing of
the Algerian left as "the authentic product of the Algerian Revolution and the expression of the revolutionary peasantry in its
entirety, and of the revolutionary intellectuals, the 'populists.'"
Pablo described the spectrum of the left in Algeria, immediately
after independence in 1962, as ranging from a Marxist-Leninist
wing, to a Fanonist wing and an Arab socialist Nasserite wing.

His description of this left in its broad scope represents a far more complex picture than its detractors often admit.

> It [the left] reflects, ideologically, the interests and aspirations of the plebeian base of the Algerian Revolution, which includes the peasants, the workers, the radicalised petite bourgeoisie of the cities, especially the 'educated.' Its Marxist-Leninist wing, still limited but that exists, represents the true interests and aspirations of the most radical section of the revolutionary peasantry and the emerging proletariat; the most determined elements of these two layers that seek a structural transformation, a socialist one, in traditional Algerian society that is molded by feudalism and imperialism in a unique way. This wing is already very close to the 'Fanonist' wing, the authentic product of the Algerian Revolution and the expression of the revolutionary peasantry in its entirety, and of the revolutionary intellectuals, the 'populists.' The wing of Arab socialism, of the Nasserite genre, represents, ideologically, the radical elements of the petite bourgeoisie and the 'educated', attached to Arab culture and often, to Islam.[32]

Soviet commentators have, not surprisingly, taken a less optimistic view of this "revolutionary peasantry" which Pablo labeled as constituting the Fanonist wing of the Algerian left. On the contrary, concerned with the weakening of "the role of the working class in the struggle against imperialism," T. Timefeev, Director of the Institute of the International Workers Movement at the USSR Academy of Sciences, disparagingly referred to the example of Fanon and his followers.[33] Associating Fanon with current Maoist trends, Timefeev pointed to the rejection of "the leading role of the working class in the world revolutionary movement," characteristic of the Maoists. Yet the same observer, commenting on Fanon and his Algerian supporters, claimed that they were also under the strong influence of Islam. The Soviet evaluation of Fanon may be incorrect in detail, but the thrust of the argument was accurate. If nothing else, Fanon's rejection of the position of the French and Algerian Communist Parties, and his suspicion of Soviet international politics, would have earned him the negative reputation Soviet observers chose to give him.

If there is anything worth pursuing in the alleged Maoist character of Fanon's position, it may be his accord with the Chinese Communist Party position expressed in 1956, for instance, in which the elitist notion of the vanguard party was rejected. The insistence that the party "does not have the right to place itself above the popular masses. . . . to recognize that it does not have the right to dispense favors, to monopolize all the work, to force the masses by the power of orders and commandments", conforms to the spirit of *The Wretched of the Earth.*[34] But how much further could one go successfully with such a comparison? As a final note on this question of party and peasantry, and the comments which Fanon's work has aroused, it would seem obvious to compare Fanon with Che Guevara[35] and Regis Debray.[36] Personality considerations aside—though they were certainly operative in the attraction of Guevara to Fanon—the three men agreed that traditional parties were incapable of leading revolutionary activity.[37] But for Debray and Guevara, the guerilla who forms the nucleus of the vanguard revolutionary party comes from the cities and transforms the countryside. Debray's insistence on the need for a vanguard party suggests that he might have looked with some skepticism on Fanon's discussion of dissident rebels. And even Guevara made it clear that his maquisards were not the peasants; they needed to be flexible and to adapt to the terrain in which they found themselves, but they were not of that terrain. For Fanon, the maquisard was ultimately a product of fusion with the peasantry. He thought in terms of a symbiosis in which the peasants played an active role, not as those on whom the urban guerillas worked, but as those who worked with the guerillas. Where they were all in accord, was on the need to prevent the division of military and political leadership in the revolutionary movement. Debray pointed to the example of Algeria as one that was to be avoided,[38] a conclusion to which Fanon would certainly have come as he watched the deepening split between the Provisional Government in Tunis and the ALN forces in the interior.

- 3 -

The Bourgeoisie, the Party, and the Nation

If Fanon's treatment of violence and spontaneity merit sharp criticism, which they have received, those who omit to read the pages devoted to the pitfalls of national consciousness with as much attention risk missing the most compelling analysis which Fanon produced. There is an obvious continuity in the discussion of the need for organization as opposed to spontaneity, and in the inability of the national bourgeoisie to provide that necessary organization. It is regrettable that Fanon divided his discussion as he did, allowing those who have concentrated their attention on the earlier chapters to walk away with an erroneous impression and to propagate the view that Fanon was unaware of the most complex issue in the politics of revolution, the need for organization. "In the modern world," Nguyen Nghe wrote,

> the French peasants of 1789 obtained the land by rallying to the bourgeois revolution, the Russian peasants liberated themselves by fighting under the leadership of the Bolshevik party, the Chinese and Vietnamese peasants, by following the working class party in these countries. The Workers Party of Vietnam, for instance, includes 75% peasants in its ranks, the popular Vietnamese Army is made up of 90% peasants, but the revolutionary leadership did not define itself as a peasant one, and the leadership attempts to inculcate militants with an ideology that is not peasant, but working class.

For the revolution which must occur in colonial countries today is not only national, it must be modern. This modern dimension cannot be conceived by the peasantry; it can only be brought
to the country by the bourgeoisie or the working class. There is
a good chance that the bourgeoisie in colonial countries, when
it takes over the national leadership, should then be incapable of
modernising the country. This Fanon saw well.[39]

It was precisely the inability of the bourgeoisie to act in the
national interests, as defined in the Revolution, that Fanon saw
so well. He did not come to the same conclusions as Nguyen
Nghe concerning the role of the working class, but elsewhere
their observations were parallel: in the need for party organization and guidance, in the need to go beyond a national revolution, and of course, in their assessment of the national
bourgeoisie. Fanon saw existing parties as inevitable fronts for
the national bourgeoisie, hence inseparable from them in their
flaws and their weaknesses. Like Nguyen Nghe, he did not think
in terms of the emergence of chauvinistic regimes, save as something to be avoided. The bourgeoisie, from his experience in
Africa, seemed however to be propelling the nation in precisely
that direction. Independent nations bent on implementing their
own revolutions had fallen victims to the rapacity of their bourgeois leadership. It was not an accident that the national bourgeoisie in many of the African countries Fanon knew behaved as
it did. Still, the need for analysis was urgent, if only to point the
way for others. As in so much of his writing, it is the analyst who
is superior. Fanon described national bourgeois behavior with
detachment; that he could not put the patient together again
with guaranteed success was typical. But the diagnosis was
necessary all the same.

What Fanon saw when he observed this class, the bourgeoisie
in Africa, was a false cosmopolitanism; a slavish imitation of its
European counterpart; a total indifference to the needs of the
mass of the population; and worst of all, an economically ineffectual and pretentious minority. Its cosmopolitanism was merely
a function of its alienated and imitative quality. For the bourgeois Fanon encountered, the ideal was not the formation of a
genuine national bourgeoisie, but an instant reproduction of the
European, colonial class that had been displaced. If this was the
motive behind the nationalization moves, as opposed to the
desire to redistribute the productive energies of the nation, then

the fact of nationalization would ultimately be insignificant. The crux of the problem was in the alienation of the bourgeoisie from the rest of the nation. But had it been able to operate effectively as a bourgeoisie, had it been able to do what the European bourgeoisie had done in terms of economic development, its existence might have been justified. Instead, it failed and was left with only the shell of the part—an empty costume that rang hollow.

The failure of the national bourgeoisie was based on its inability to act out the part it had chosen. Having little capital at its disposal, and less in terms of trained cadres and experienced personnel, it was noteworthy for the absence of any productive, innovative work. Primarily concerned with its own betterment, it sought the most expedient methods of improving its situation. Had it been genuinely interested in the national good it would have cast its lot with the revolutionary forces. This is what Fanon meant when he wrote that the national bourgeoisie must betray its classical role and not behave like a national bourgeoisie—he might have added, particularly if it cannot do that well either. As proof of its impotence, Fanon pointed to the reappearance of colonial patterns in trade, in agricultural production, and in the frequently heard petty praise of local artisans and local products. Having stood aside when the national economy was put into motion by foreigners, it continued to implement their plans now that the foreigners had left. Avoiding any serious analysis of national needs, ignored by national parties (or collaborating with them), it was out of touch with the nation. It pursued its own profit mistakenly believing that it was behaving like the bourgeoisie of developed, capitalist countries. It was this dismal picture that convinced Fanon that in underdeveloped countries, unless the national bourgeoisie had the economic and technical means to act, it ought to be replaced. To allow it to exist as it was, exploiting the nation and unaware of the extent to which it was exploited itself, endangered the future of the country. Accustomed to playing an intermediary role during the colonial period, it had been active in trade and commerce within the system of production instituted by the colonizing country; it had never developed the instinct for productive initiative characteristic of the European bourgeoisie at a comparable stage in its national development. The colonial bourgeoisie did not invest in the nation. It was not inclined to take risks if it could profit more safely elsewhere. Hence, this role was also avoided and invariably left to foreign capital.

To disavow the national bourgeoisie for these sins was one thing, but what was to be done? Fanon has been criticized, with justice, for his failure to go beyond this talented, acid-tongued critique. The problems of economic reconstruction within a socialist framework posed innumerable difficulties which he did not begin to discuss, or, some would add, to understand. Nevertheless, he did recommend the organization of such practical innovations as wholesale and retail cooperatives on a democratic basis. Hoping to remove a sector which was often in the hands of the bourgeoisie, Fanon thought in terms of decentralization which would give the masses a direct hand in the organization of this aspect of the economy. There were few other suggestions of direct relevance to the peasantry, which is surprising given Fanon's enormous faith and interest in its revolutionary potential. It has been suggested that others, notably Algeria's first president, Ahmed Ben Bella, were inspired by Fanon's discussions of the Algerian peasantry and went further than Fanon had done, in the elaboration of a program in which the role of the peasants was critical.[40] That Fanon was not despairing about economic development is clear from his discussion, no matter how limited it might be. The men whom Fanon described as the wise men who would replace the bourgeoisie —the intellectuals, civil servants, the elites—were seen as those who would collaborate to provide the necessary planning for the nation. What would characterize these men would be their political commitment. Yet this very train of thought was to lead Fanon to another depressing subject, central to the implementation of all revolutionary changes. When Fanon wrote of political commitment, he was not thinking of individual commitment, but of that guaranteed by a party which was itself guided by an appropriate ideological formation.

Fanon's discussion of the role of the party was written under the shadow of what the party was becoming in FLN-ALN circles, although there were no specific references to the increasing difficulties experienced by the Algerians in this regard. In addition, it would appear that Fanon's conception of the party was molded by what he had seen during his African travels. If anything, all of this added up to what the party ought not to be, as much as a prescription of what, under ideal circumstances, it should be. The ideal party, like the ideal circumstances, was difficult to find. The real party, more readily accessible, was often a model of what Fanon thought ought to be eliminated. Parties that had deteriorated into bureaucratic organizations designed to perpetuate themselves in office and to provide their members with privilege were common; so were parties designed to prohibit politics and what might pass for political thinking. How much of this was an expression of political inexperience?

Fanon's answer was that it was not due to inexperience at all since many of the parties in question had had a pre-independence history and hence were not led by novices. More likely, they were led by men whom Fanon classified as members of the national bourgeoisie, not a group which he believed in, nor a group which he believed held the interests of the nation at heart. Whether there ought to be a single-party or a multi-party system was a secondary question. If the party system was controlled by this national bourgeoisie, it hardly mattered whether one or more parties were tolerated. Yet the question of the single-party system was not ignored. Fanon understood that the single party was one way that the ruling class could protect its interests with minimal interference. He sensed the potential oppressiveness of such an arrangement, as is clear in his argument for the separation of party and state organizations. It is tempting to speculate on what he would have said of those Algerian politicians who maintain that a multi-party system is as dangerous for Algeria as a national assembly, because each increases the sectarian tendencies of the nation.

The kind of party Fanon wrote about in his last testament suffered from the same defects as the class whose interests it represented. It was alienated from the masses. It eschewed decentralization and in so doing was unaware of national priorities. It differed from pre-independence parties only by its use of revolutionary rhetoric, but its willingness to implement a revolutionary program was nil. By common consensus, the national bourgeoisie that made up the bulk of this party and its leadership also selected the principal figure who acted as its leader. Like the party he represented, he spoke in the name of the masses while carefully avoiding them. He might be chosen for his past action during the heroic, revolutionary phase of the nation's history. In this way, he would be a popular figure with whom the nation could identify. But if he was not naive he would understand the nature of his position and his own distance from the masses with whom he allegedly spoke. His demise was parallel to that of the party.

The party, in practice, functioned as an obstacle to communication between the government and the masses. In principle, it ought to have facilitated such communication. Ideally, it would be decentralized and not top-heavy either in appointments or in the concentration of authority. Representative but not isolated, it was to avoid the kind of institutionalization that characterized bureaucratic parties and their cumbersome structures. Fanon explained the deterioration of the party by the inadequacy of ideological training, both before and after independence. He was critical of those people who maintained that it was important to avoid any ideological debate during the liberation struggle in order to prevent division. The idea that national unity could or should be maintained at any cost was, in retrospect, wishful thinking. It was dangerous to put aside issues which determined the future direction of the nation; to believe that postponing their discussion would dissolve opposition was not the case. The weaknesses of the party, and hence, of the nation, did not emerge after independence. They were apparent during the liberation period and it was then that they ought to have been dealt with. If this shell was the party that greeted the nation after independence, little wonder that Fanon could write that independence had not really changed the world for the masses. If parties were nothing more than elaborate information centers maintained with the expensive help of security forces, in what way could one consider them as expressive of the nation's will. Where political life was prohibited, and where decisions were made with feigned efficacy "at the top," how could one tolerate discussion of the people's state? Liquidation, or silencing opposition by other means, was not unnoticed. In the light of such harsh realities, the changing attitude of the people to its government, after independence, did not leave room for surprise. When left to themselves, the masses rumbled in barely audible sounds, Fanon observed, but their anger and resentment were almost palpable.

The image of the party and the government left little room for optimism. But if one recalls Fanon's mood as he completed his travels through Africa, it was very nearly bleak. The rivalry, the tribal interests being revived by colonial powers—or natives working for colonial interests—had depressed him deeply. African unity did not exist. Regionalism was on the increase; religious wars were being fomented, and the narrowest kinds of national interests were being played up with success. To top the list, Fanon was appalled to discover the racism which he found in the North, in the Maghreb, against African blacks. In black Africa, on the other hand, he discovered myths of Arab domination that were not much more encouraging. If this was the progress achieved after independence, what did reaction mean? From the perils of political degeneration, Fanon proceeded to discuss a subject which had been important to him in Paris at the time he wrote his first book. Only now, it was not his own private destiny he was working out, rather, it was a process of unravelling the dynamics of national consciousness. It was not enough to write on party organization, or on the need for ideological training. The abysmal conditions which Fanon saw in Africa led him to return to a theme which was of the essence in the construction of the nation. The national consciousness which Fanon concerned himself with, in all of its manifestations, was also the expression of a national culture. What was this national culture? How could one assure its secure development and at the same time avoid the excesses, a degeneration of national consciousness into a form of chauvinistic pride that precluded the attitudes which Fanon knew to be essential to international solidarity, let alone unity. Fanon was writing on the basis of his African experience. Algerians maintained that he was also writing about Algeria.

-4-

National Culture

Fanon had discussed the question of a national culture in his earlier book, *Black Skin, White Masks.* In many respects, the material added at the end of *The Wretched of the Earth* was an elaboration of those earlier discussions. The essay on the reciprocal bases of national culture and liberation movements was the talk Fanon had presented at the Rome Congress in 1959.[41] On that occasion, he had declared that national struggles were expressions of the national culture. It was a theme which was frequently repeated at the Pan-African Festival held in Algiers ten years later.[42] Fanon's intention had been to emphasize the political nature of the expression which characterized the national culture of a colonial society; and from this assumption, to demonstrate the relationship of liberation struggles to the national culture.

In tracing Fanon's thinking on the subject, a number of phases emerge. For the most part, Fanon's interest lay in negritude and black culture, hence in the African dimension of the subject. Yet, the irony of his involvement in the Algerian liberation struggle, from this point of view, was his relative ignorance of the Arab-Islamic factor in that struggle. There were areas of contact in the experiences of Algerian and African movements. The situation of the colonized was remarkably similar throughout the colonial world, and so were the pattern of reactions which followed. From near assimilation in the colonial culture, the first stage of the colonial period, there followed the rejection of the same foreign culture and a search into the past of the colonized society. Sometimes both phases occurred nearly simultaneously; on other occasions, they occurred simultaneously but among different elements in a colonial society. What followed was more complicated and is in fact very much under discussion today. Fanon wrote about black culture, but it is debatable how much he wrote on the basis of his experience in black Africa, as opposed to his experience as a black man in white European society. What concerned him was the double task of liberating black men and liberating all men from oppression. He resisted what he considered excesses committed in the name of the former. It was in this light that he criticized an unlimited acceptance of negritude; a position he accepted as a temporary necessity but which he eventually abandoned in favor of a more universal stand. That he himself had experienced tremendous pride and happiness in the rediscovery of the black past, the African past, is part of his own biography. But even in his early life, he had struggled with the meaning of negritude as his writings make clear. The central question for him became the liberation, in political and cultural terms, of all colonial peoples. Although he rejected the notion of an international class solidarity of the oppressed struggling against the oppressor when this was dogmatically expressed, he nevertheless agreed that it was the common political struggle against colonialism that must predominate, and that this common effort must not be subverted by chauvinistic excesses. Furthermore, he came to see these nationalist excesses as perverse forms of colonial victories; the victory of a reverse racism that indicated that the colonized were still unfree of the need to combat the colonizer by imitating him.

What Fanon wanted was a nationalist pride that acknowledged the unique historical experience of a people without degenerating into chauvinism. He did not for a moment deny the reality of national sentiment or suggest that peoples could, or ought, to transcend their national identities without having found the means to express them. He insisted that it was only by going through a national phase, a "consciousness of oneself," that men could achieve an international consciousness. "The consciousness of self is not the closing of a door to communication. Philosophic thought teaches us, on the contrary, that it is its guarantee. National consciousness, which is not nationalism, is the only thing that will give us an international

dimension."[43] Still, how could one find a national consciousness, or develop it, and not simultaneously develop a sense of
nationalism in the process? Fanon did not go far enough in this
critique. He sensed the dangers of nationalism, but alternative
forms of communal organization were not discussed.

In the presentation of his arguments on the question of
national culture, Fanon began with a discussion of the relevance of the past in colonized societies. He understood the
need for the return. He understood the role of colonialism in
intensifying this need. And he understood the danger of a
strong reflexive action, to counter the colonial prohibition on
expressions of a national culture. Where was one to draw the
line? There was no question of doubting the legitimacy of
the national claim, or of misunderstanding the desire to
glorify the return to the past.

> The claim to a national culture in the past does not only rehabili-
> tate that nation and serve as a justification for the hope of a future
> national culture. In the sphere of psycho-affective equilibrium it
> is responsible for an important change in the native. Perhaps we
> have not sufficiently demonstrated that colonialism is not simply
> content to impose its rule upon the present and the future of a
> dominated country. Colonialism is not satisfied merely with hold-
> ing a people in its grip and emptying the native's brain of all form
> and content. By a kind of perverted logic, it turns to the past of
> the oppressed people, and distorts, disfigures and destroys it.[44]

It was in response to this disfigurement that the native intellectual, unconsciously taking the methods of the colonizer and
turning them against him, responded by his own evocations of
African culture. Fanon spoke of the racialization of thought, of
the dangers of reverse racism and concentrating on black people
and Africa, of the myth of assuming that there was one black
nation the world over that was identical. The link between black
people was colonial domination where it existed. But beyond
this, differences were manifest and to blur them was to repeat
the distortion of the colonizer. The same line of argument that
Fanon had developed in *Black Skin, White Masks* reappeared. The
African sees himself as the colonizer saw him; undifferentiated,
a representative of blackness, a brother to all other black people.
There were no African peoples, no nations, only the unrelieved
blackness of the natives.

The concept of Negro-ism, for example, was the emotional if not the logical antithesis of that insult which the white man flung at humanity. This rush of Negro-ism against the white man's contempt showed itself in certain spheres to be the one ideal capable of lifting interdictions and anathemas. Because the New Guinean or Kenyan intellectuals found themselves above all up against a general ostracism and delivered to the combined contempt of their overlords, their reaction was to sing praises in admiration of each other. The unconditional affirmation of African culture has succeeded the unconditional affirmation of European culture.[45]

If this had appeared to be a tempting solution some years earlier when Fanon was in Paris and first discovering the consolations of negritude, it no longer appeared to be anything of the sort. Where he had been dismayed by Sartre's advice to restrain the African revivalism on which he had leaned, Fanon was now closer to Sartre's position. He could now write that the "historical necessity in which the men of African culture find themselves to racialise their claims and to speak more of African culture then of national culture will tend to lead them up a blind alley."[46] The only basis on which Africans and black men generally could compare their experience was as blacks in relation to white society. But to go beyond that and to speak of a single culture was a myth. It was to deny the role of history in the predicament of the black masses and in the colonial phenomenon. The supposition that American blacks had the same history, the same interests, and the same problems as Africans was absurd. In relation to white society, there was something to be said. But if these relations in Africa and the United States were altered, what would there be in common? Referring to the Congress held in Paris in 1956 which had brought black writers from Africa and the United States together, Fanon wrote that

little by little the American Negroes realised that the essential problems confronting them were not the same as those that confronted the African Negroes. The Negroes of Chicago only resemble the Nigerians or the Tanganyikans in so far as they were all defined in relation to the whites. But once the first comparisions had been made and subjective feelings were assuaged, the American Negroes realised that the objective problems were fundamentally heterogeneous. The test cases of civil liberty whereby both whites and blacks in America try to drive back racial discrimination have very little in common in their principles with the heroic fight of the Angolan people against the detestable Portuguese colonialism.[47]

Some might argue that even if the "Negroes of Chicago only resemble the Nigerians or the Tanganyikans" in terms of their relationship to white society, that relationship created a common bond and would continue to do so until the society that had forged the bond, would itself be transformed. For the time being, the "test cases" Fanon spoke about differed from the nature of the colonial struggle in Angola, but was it correct to say that underlying reasons for these different forms of struggle were, in themselves, so different? It was, as Fanon stated, only in their inherent characteristics that American blacks and African blacks realized how much they differed from one another. It was only under these circumstances that the "objective" situations of blacks in the United States, in Europe, and in Africa could be observed as distinct.

Fanon's argument against the idea of a common black culture reflected his opposition to the creation of a black self-consciousness as anything more than a phase in the liberation of black men in colonial society. While he had been deeply affected by Senghor's anthology of black and Malagasy poetry in his earlier years, he eventually came to reject Senghor's position as a reactionary one. Negritude was meaningful, but not as a national ideology. There was a time when its attraction was comprehensible and when its irrational appeal was useful. But then, it ought eventually to be transcended and the black man, having recovered his pride and his past, would be free to join other men in a common struggle. It was at this point that one could speak of the "disappearance of the majority of Negroes," as Fanon noted in a reference he made to Senghor.

> At the last school prize-giving in Dakar, the president of the Senegalese Republic, Leopold Senghor, decided to include the study of the idea of Negro-ism in the curriculum. If this decision was due to an anxiety to study historical causes, no one can criticize it. But if on the other hand it was taken in order to create black self-consciousness, it is simply a turning back upon history which has already taken cognizance of the disappearance of the majority of Negroes.[48]

To some people, the assertion that Negroes have disappeared is not as convincing as it was to Fanon. Indeed, it is this assertion that has prompted some American blacks to feel that Fanon was avoiding the issue of blackness which he was perhaps able to do in Algeria, but which it was not possible to avoid elsewhere. It is hardly a question of geography, though. The issue is the national question. In relation to Algeria, Fanon did not hesitate to assert the existence of an Algerian nation, and to argue that national identity must precede any kind of international solidarity. But when he turned to negritude, which he did not see as a form of black nationalism but as a cultural phenomenon, he argued logically—if one accepts his vision of negritude—that it ought to represent but a phase in the self-consciousness of a black colonized society. But what of those who acted as though negritude was not merely a cultural expression, and who built their national consciousness on its expression, such as the Senegalese? According to Fanon, these people were willingly losing themselves in a black mirage. In his terms, to go beyond this phase was not a matter of avoiding confrontation with the phenomenon of blackness, it was to analyze the fact of blackness correctly, not to eternalize it but to put it into place and to return to the matter at hand—the liberation of all men in colonial societies.

When he turned to Algeria and the Arab world in the same context, it was in order to apply his observations on national culture to this part of the world. But the results were not convincing. Fanon observed that the liberation struggle in the Arab world had been marked by a revival of Islam and he wrote about the Arab League as an expression of the same phenomenon. That he did not know that the League had been the inspired creation of the English, was a detail which only served to expose Fanon's innocence of Middle Eastern politics. The irony of the poverty of Fanon's remarks about Algeria and the Arab world lies in the fact that it was in the Algerian national liberation movement that Fanon became so deeply involved. He remained divided between the genuine commitment he had to the Algerian movement on the one hand, and the continuing concern he felt for the predicament of black men and black society. But in the mature period of his life, it was the political commitment to Algeria that took precedence. It is debatable and it will continue to be debated whether or not Fanon's final position on negritude and the politics of black culture was the correct one. For some it may appear to be something quite different.

In the comparison of Algerian and black psychology in a colonial situation there were similarities. The fact of depersonalization, about which Fanon had written very early, was relevant to the situation in the Maghreb. When it came to writing of the Islamic renaissance or the Arab League, as already mentioned, his efforts failed. Fanon recognized that there were serious differences between the Arab states and the African nations, but he did not pursue this. He made occasional references to arabization, but this too was inadequately developed. Though he was initially favorable to the movement for its cultural and political implications, one cannot help but wonder what Fanon would have thought today in viewing the arabization efforts of the Algerian government. For him to have understood the arabization problem would have required a greater familiarity not only with Algerian and Arab culture, but with the complicated relations of that culture and the West. To admit that he did not have either qualification limits him as an observer of the Algerian or Arab cultural renaissance today. If it also serves to redefine his comprehension of Algerian and Islamic society in relation to the nationalist movement, the results can only give us a more realistic picture of Fanon's relation to that movement.

-5-

Fanon's Death and His Influence on the Algerian Revolution

Fanon worked on the final part of *The Wretched of the Earth* in the spring of 1961. His physical condition, which had seriously deteriorated in late 1960, had resulted in his going to the USSR for treatment.[49] From there he returned to Tunis, where he seemed temporarily better. With the worsening of the leukemia, however, Fanon agreed to take the advice given to him by various doctors, including Soviet specialists, to go to the United States for treatment. The details of his trip to the United States, the preparations for the trip, the arrangements made when he arrived in Washington, D.C., have all been subject to considerable speculation. The speculation is in large part the result of an article written by Joseph Alsop in the *Washington Post* of February 21, 1969, which was picked up in the *International Herald Tribune* on the next day, and which has now made the rounds of various journals, and which Alsop seems eager to keep on pushing.[50] Alsop claimed that Fanon had told his CIA case officer that the Soviets had done nothing for him, "except send him to a sanitorium in Uzbekistan and feed him a diet of greasy cabbage and potatoes." According to Alsop, "discouraged, he [Fanon] returned to Tunisia, and in February, 1961, he asked the local CIA representatives for help." Fanon was apparently told that he could get the best treatment in the United States. Was anything expected in return? Alsop writes: "The real quid pro quo, of course, was the opportunity to learn the ins and outs of a most exceptional man, whose genuine importance was already obvious." Fanon did not accept the offer until September. Alsop again writes that when Fanon was brought to Washington, it was by the case officer assigned to him by the CIA. On arrival in Washington, Fanon was lodged at the Dupont Plaza Hotel from October 3 to 10, and subsequently admitted to the National Institutes of Health. The Chief of the Medical Record Department at the Clinical Center notes that one "Ibrahim Fanon, #CC 03-86-00, was admitted to the Clinical Center, National Institutes of Health, Bethesda, Maryland, on October 10, 1961 and expired on December 6, 1961."[51]

The general allegation that Fanon died in the arms of the CIA has never been entirely cleared up. It is possible, given the attitude of the United States government towards the Algerian situation in 1961, that the American Embassy in Tunis did offer help, and that a CIA agent was present to carry out details. But to say this only serves to raise more questions about the interest of the CIA in Fanon. Alsop reports a conversation he had with Dr. David Haywood, the doctor in direct charge of Fanon's case. Haywood is quoted as remembering "the daily, downright brotherly visits of Fanon's CIA case officer, who also had the task of bringing to the hospital Fanon's wife and six-year-old son. Except for doctors and nurses, his wife, his son, and his case officer were, in fact, Fanon's sole companions while his life ebbed away." In the March 3, 1969 issue of *Le Monde*, Fanon's brother Joby claimed that when Fanon went to the USSR he thought he had anemia and not leukemia. It was only after his return from the USSR, according to this account, one year before his death that Dr. Juminer, Fanon's friend and colleague in Tunis, diagnosed leukemia. Fanon eventually died of a double bronchial pneumonia. As for his hospitalization, Joby Fanon writes that "it was facilitated by the Algerian Mission to Washington and by the Department of State." His last point was that Fanon was not isolated in Washington. Not only did he have his wife and son at his side, but other friends visited him, among them Alioune Diop of *Présence Africaine* and Roberto Holden of Angola.

Fanon's body was brought back to Tunisia on the request of

the FLN and buried some miles inside Algerian territory, not far from Ghardimaou. Sources close to Fanon maintain that the present Algerian government refuses to move the body because the area in which it is buried is still dangerous due to the presence of mines. For this reason it also continues to prohibit access to it. The body was accompanied back to Tunis by the CIA case officer, Ollie Iselin, who participated in the funeral ceremonies and had his photograph taken by a *Jeune Afrique* photographer, along with the others present. The picture was reproduced in France and the news was noted in the United States. Iselin was recalled. Alsop, consistent with his general purpose, implied that the case officer was present as a result of his assignment to the case. This was not the only interpretation of the embarrassing incident, however. Among others, Joan and Richard Brace observed differently. In their account of their Algerian experiences they recalled that

> we talked in the lobby of the Majestic for a while, Bouzar (head of Committee for Youth) spoke of the recent death of Frantz Fanon, author of *L'An cinq de la révolution algérienne, Peau noir, masques blancs,* and the book finished on his deathbed, *Les Damnés de la terre.* He mentioned that one of our young State Department members, who turned out to be Ollie Iselin whom we later met, had accompanied the funeral procession. Because Fanon died of leukemia in the United States, the rumor developed that Iselin, who came to Tunis on the plane which carried Fanon's body, had been assigned to accompany it. The Algerians were pleased with this gesture which happened not to be true. Iselin did, however, esteem Fanon and had visited him several times while the former was hospitalized in the United States. So out of personal feelings, not on official duty, Iselin went to the services which were held in Algeria.[52]

In Tunis, Fanon's death attracted a good deal of attention; little of it was devoted to the presence of Ollie Iselin. The staff of *el Moudjahid* expressed its grief. Officials of the GPRA and invited guests attended the funeral, the details of which indicate the importance attributed to the event. It was a sentimental farewell, marked by gestures of solidarity that left no doubt as to the relations that had existed between Fanon and the men with whom he worked. *El Moudjahid* devoted a large part of its December 21 issue to Fanon's funeral, the speeches given on that occasion, and an extremely interesting selection of excerpts from his last book.[53] Introducing *The Wretched of the Earth*, the anonymous author noted that Fanon's responsibilities in the Algerian Revolution and his association with the anti-colonialist movement had made him uniquely able to write of the evolution of the continent. *"Les Damnés de la terre,"* he continued, "is all of us,

> it is we, the colonised, victims of exploitation and racism, struggling for national independence, struggling even harder for the construction of the country after independence. The book does not concern Algeria alone, but all African countries and the countries of the "Third World," whatever their phase of liberation, whatever the path they have chosen. By confronting experience, Fanon wants to construct a theory of decolonization.[54]

The tribute offered in *el Moudjahid* reflected the esteem in which Fanon's colleagues held him. In contrast with the evaluation of a later time, it conveyed the sense of loss which was acutely felt by militants and friends alike. The speeches delivered at the time of his funeral by colleagues in the ALN, and the final farewell offered by the Vice-President of the GPRA, Belkacem Krim, were indications of this mood. *El Moudjahid* also ran a brief biography of Fanon in its December 21 issue. It referred to his consistent efforts on behalf of the Algerian Revolution. It noted that he had been an active member of the Press Commission of the FLN; that he had been a delegate to numerous Pan-African conferences and Chief of Mission in Accra; that he had visited all the capitals of independent African states; and that he had been instrumental in spreading the word about the Algerian Revolution in Africa. The study of Algeria in revolution, *A Dying Colonialism*, was referred to as a condensation of his Algerian experience. His contributions to the two congresses of black writers and artists which he had attended in 1956 and 1959, were described as part of his work as an Algerian and African intellectual, as an intellectual of the third world. Fanon was described as having written from an Algerian perspective, on the basis of his Algerian experience. *The Wretched of the Earth*, which is rarely discussed in any detail in the current analyses of Fanon's work, was described as his major opus; a book addressed beyond Algeria and the Maghreb to all of the people of Africa and the third world.

> Until the last hour, brother Frantz Fanon assumed his role of revolutionary intellectual. His death is an irreparable loss for the Algerian Revolution, for Africa and for the anti-colonialist move-

ment. The staff of *el Moudjahid*, of which he was a part for close to three years, will never forget his penetrating analyses, his energetic interventions, the power of his convictions. It suffers, in a special way, from the emptiness which he leaves among his Algerian brothers.[55]

El Moudjahid then proceeded to give an account of the funeral proceedings. The text, as it appeared in the FLN newspaper, is quoted here in full.[56]

14 h. 30 (2:30 PM)
   Tunis-el Aouina. The special plane carrying Fanon's remains to the Maghreb has just landed. A group of young Algerians transport the coffin to the Salon d'honneur of the airport: a large crowd of Algerian militants is present, while the members of the GPRA present in Tunis gather in front of the coffin covered with the Algerian flag. Women cry; young men, rough fighters do not attempt to control their emotions. Official representatives of friendly countries, by their presence, brought a last homage to the Algerian writer and militant; from the world over, recognized personalities and movements telegraphed.

15 h. (3 PM)
   The coffin is transported to the seat of the GPRA Mission in Tunis.
   In a room filled with Algerian flags, the first wreaths are heaped on the coffin. A heavy silence. A profound emotion reigns in this crowd of brothers and friends who now file through the room. Some sign the open register at the door. Others write a few moving lines: the signature of the Ambassador is next to that of the militant, the sympathy of the Cameroonais is expressed next to the testimony of the Algerian guerilla.
   The wake is organized.

12 December 1961
9 h.
   A brief sober ceremony marks the departure. Vice-President Krim Belkacem utters the words that were awaited, the adieu to our brother Frantz Fanon.

9 h.40
   The ambulance carrying the coffin takes off, followed by about 20 cars to the exit of Tunis; in front of the cortege, workers stop, men and women bow, soldiers and policemen salute. It

is the "climb" to the frontiers. In every gathering, refugees or former Algerian guerillas are there and stand at position, while the convoy passes.

12 h. 20

Ghardimaou. In the courtyard of an ALN country hospital the body is saluted by a detachment. For all of those who have come from Tunis, this is goodby. From now on, the coffin is taken by the ALN; it will be followed by a small group of militants only.

14 h. 30 (2:30 PM)

On the Algerian frontier. Two sections of the ALN do the honors at the entry of the coffin on national soil. The coffin is placed on a stretcher made of branches, and it is lifted to an open space by fifteen djounouds (soldiers).

A remarkable march begins in the forest, while in the crest and the valley, two columns of ALN soldiers assure the protection of the path where the convoy passes. The forest is majestic, the sky is magnificent; the march is carried out in absolute silence and calm while the bearers relieve each other.

In the valley, closer to the North, one hears the cannon thunder. In the sky, two planes pass very high. The war is here, very close, and at the same time, here, there is calm, a cortege of brothers come to accompany the last wish of one of their own.

15 h. 45 (3:45 PM)

In a cemetery of "chouhada." On the very spot of an old engagement, today in liberated territory, the grave is here, carefully prepared. An ALN commander pronounces, in Arabic, the last adieu to brother Frantz Fanon, whom all here knew (three months ago, he had come to spend several days in the ALN to work some more and to talk of Africa). Here is the complete translation:

"The late brother Frantz Fanon was a sincere militant who rose up against colonialism and racism; as early as 1952 he was participating effectively in liberal movements while carrying out his studies in France. From the beginning of the Revolution, he joined the ranks of the National Liberation Front, and was a living model of discipline and respect or principles, during the entire time that he was carrying out the tasks given to him by the Algerian Revolution. . . .

"Before his death, he had expressed the wish that he be buried in Algerian territory, so great was his love for this land, a land for which he sacrified himself. It was our duty to respect his last wish and to carry out his will. The late brother Frantz Fanon finds himself, today, in the midst of his brother martyrs. . . .

"Indeed, you have left us, dear departed brother, but your image, your loyalty, your militantism and your efforts in the realisation of principles—for which hundreds of thousands of Algerian children died—remain for us a living example to which we will continually refer.

"As for us, militants, we will attempt to preserve the principles in which you believed, but we will fight those who will try to destroy them, as we struggle against the cult of personality in order to preserve the Revolution from its enemies and to build a free, independent, democratic and social Algeria, one in which human rights will be respected, as well as those concepts in which you and so many other militants so intensely believed, for which they fought, and for which these martyrs near you now gave their lives. Rest in peace, brother Fanon, your remains will be guarded and defended, if the need arises, by your brothers whose duty it is to liberate all of the homeland, until the day when you will be finally buried in the very heart of Algeria."

16 h. (4 PM)

It is finished. The coffin rests on a bed of lentisk branches: above, branches of cork tree.

In this late afternoon, the sun is setting. Far off in the distance one imagines the plain from which we are separated by the soft crests, blue in the velvety light of winter. Everything exudes beauty and calm. The last wish of Frantz Fanon has been accomplished: he rests among his brothers in Algerian soil.

The speech delivered by the Vice-President of the GPRA, Belkacem Krim, was not different in essence from that offered by the ALN soldier. What was significant was that the Vice-President of the Provisional Government found it desirable to pronounce words on the occasion of the death of this comrade. The tone for Krim's eulogy was set in his opening statement: "In the name of the Provisional Government of the Algerian Republic, in the name of the Algerian People, in the name of all the comrades in arms, and in my own name, I say to you, Adieu."

Krim recalled Fanon's wish to be buried in Algeria and he regretted the fact that he did not live long enough to share in the victory which was so close. But "dead, your memory will stay alive and it will always be evoked among the most noble figures of the Revolution." As his ALN colleague was to do, the Vice-President credited Fanon with joining the Revolution early in its history, and with helping patriots and clandestine militants do their work by protecting them at his own risk. Krim recalled that the exterior delegation of the FLN had appealed to Fanon to come to Tunis to work with it, and he had responded, joining the various publications with which he was subsequently associated. Fanon's work in Africa drew a great deal of attention in this address. Fanon was considered responsible for spreading information about the Algerian Revolution throughout the continent. It was recalled that he had been sent to conferences in Accra, Monrovia, Addis Ababa, Conakry, Tunis, and Leopoldville. Representatives from the countries Fanon had known sent delegates to his funeral and Krim noted that this constituted their testimonial to his mission. As to his writing, the Vice-President spoke of Fanon's impressive literary works. He referred to *The Wretched of the Earth* as a "landmark in the studies of liberation struggles of oppressed people." The conclusion of his brief address was simple and direct. "Frantz Fanon! Your example will always remain alive. Rest in peace! Algeria will not forget you."[57]

Was Belkacem Krim right? Krim himself was found murdered, strangled to death in a Frankfurt hotel room in October 1970. He had been sentenced to death the preceding year in Algeria on charges of "treason and conspiring to assassinate top leaders of the country."[58] Fanon died a natural death at a younger age. What is his status today? What influence did he actually have on the Revolution, and what influence is he credited with at the present time? Influence is, at best, a difficult relationship to document. The case of Frantz Fanon is no exception. Until the history of the Revolution is written by Algerians, in relative freedom, the complete answer will probably not be available. What is left is speculation by foreigners as well as Algerians; speculation that is affected by the political sensitivities which the subject entails, and by the persistence of unresolved political differences in which Fanon had a part.

In an effort to untangle the varied interpretations that are offered, by foreigners and Algerians, it is useful to consider the following sources. First, the foreign commentators whose works have been cited by Algerians, usually to deny their validity. Secondly, the impressions gathered from Algerians who are interested in Fanon and who are not affected by the official pronouncements on the subject. Finally, the official position of the government as expressed since the spring of 1971; a position which appears to be directed at the foreign biographers of Fanon and their remarks about his influence on current leaders of the government.

Informal discussions with students, professionals, and intellectuals leave the impression that Fanon is a familiar figure and that there is a considerable contrast between the view of him held by such people, and the official view propagated by the government. In itself, this does not surprise anyone since the political undertone in the government's position is understood, or at least recognized as such. The relevance of Fanon's political critique, as expressed in *The Wretched of the Earth*, is seen as particularly applicable to Algeria; perhaps more so than the writer was aware of in his own life. Those who are interested find no difficulty in locating Fanon's books. Local bookstores in Algiers, at least, carry the complete works in the original French edition. The city boasts a number of reminders: there is an Avenue Frantz Fanon, and of course, the psychiatric hospital at Blida bears his name. It is not uncommon in these circles, to hear the contrast made between Fanon's popularity in the Ben Bella period, and in the days of Boumedienne. In the earlier period, some writers will point out, Fanon enjoyed an enormous popularity. This is attributed to Ben Bella's sympathy for Fanon, and the more open society that prevailed in that period of Algeria's recent history. One observer, who remains an important figure in the literary life of the capital, recalled that a literary prize bearing Fanon's name had been instituted in the Ben Bella period but it had passed out of existence with the end of the regime. To my knowledge, no one had yet been awarded a Fanon literary prize. In the film industry, which is by all odds an impressive and thriving industry, two young cinematographers, Jacques Charby and Ahmed Rachedi, have been cited as men in whose work the Fanon influence is to be felt.[59] Certainly, insofar as they represent an Algerian angry-young-man generation, they, and some of the younger writers who collaborate on the existing journals and newspaper of the country, recognize the validity of Fanon's political criticisms as applied to their own country. They share his passionate vulnerability to the injustices in society, only unlike Fanon, they are not living in a colonial society. The implications of the contrast are not lost.

To people in this category, primarily young intellectuals, the fact that Fanon was not born an Algerian or a Muslim is irrelevant. If anything, they tend to be secular in their own orientation, and my impression is that their political views approximate his. At the least, these are socialists, if not more committed Marxists with or without organizational links. To such an audience, the position presented informally by the government, which I nonetheless qualify as the official position, is not meaningful. The reasons for this rejection, however, *are* meaningful; not only for the question of Fanon, but for what is reflected in the relationship between this segment of Algerian society and the government.

Since the official position of the Algerian government on Fanon is tied up to what has been written about Fanon, particularly abroad, it is important to reconsider some of these evaluations. The accounts that have roused the greatest reaction have been the two biographies, one by David Caute and the shorter analysis by Renate Zahar. Geismar's biography, which is more uncritically enthusiastic about Fanon, has not yet been translated into French and there seems to be little evidence that it is widely known in Algeria. When it does appear, it is fairly certain that it will meet with more or less the same reception as Zahar and Caute.

In an essay written several years ago, I discussed the question of Fanon's influence in these terms.

It may be ironical that Fanon is enjoying the reputation he has acquired in the West, even if the reasons for it are easy enough to understand. But what influence did he have in Algeria, and how much relevance did his writing have for Algeria and Africa? De Beauvoir points out that no one in Algeria spoke for Fanon, and that this understandably grieved him. But did Fanon speak for anyone? Objectively, of course, Fanon's commitment to the FLN and Algeria is part of the record of the years 1956–1961. He had become Algerian, "par la révolution," and he served in the capacity of editor, political essayist, representative of the Provisional Government, and ambassador at large in Africa. In *Algerian Voices*, Richard and Jean Brace reported that in the winter of 1962 they met a number of Fanon followers. In the Algerian Press

Service, they found the young militant Abdel Kader Ben Toumi who described Fanon's last book as comparable to a "Dostoievskian Populist novel of the nineteenth century," and generally unsatisfactory in its critique of capitalism. On the other hand, Omar Oussedik . . . one of the members of the National Council of the Algerian Revolution (CNRA), formerly in the 'Abbas Ministry, was a Marxist and a devoted reader of Fanon. "It soon became evident that he was fanatically devoted to the ideas of Frantz Fanon, whose *Les Damnés de la terre* was being voraciously read by all Algerians interested in ideological and practical aspects of the Revolution." Another observer noted that many of the theories he expressed in *el Moudjahid* and in his books appeared in the speeches and articles of men such as Ben Yussuf ben Khedda, the last President of the Provisional Government, and former Premier Ahmed Ben Bella. François Bondy, the editor of *Preuves*, who met with Ben Bella prior to his removal, wrote that "Ahmed Ben Bella was perhaps, in his way, the only 'Fanonist leader,'" referring to his espousal of Fanon's faith in the peasants as opposed to the city proletariat. More recently, in a summary of the changes that have taken place since the June 19, 1965 coup, Robert Gauthier described Colonel Boumedienne as a voracious reader of Frantz Fanon, and an apologist for the revolutionary peasantry.[60]

David Caute and Renate Zahar presented similar views, in some instances going considerably further. Caute related that Fanon had influenced both Ben Bella and Boumedienne on "the revolutionary potential of the peasantry."[61] Renate Zahar wrote that at Ghardimaou, Fanon had given courses in political orientation to the cadres of the ALN.[62] She added that Fanon's stay in Ghardimaou with the army of the frontier later permitted Ben Bella and Boumedienne to present themselves as the "heirs of the thought of Fanon and the representatives of socialism and progressivism."[63] It was this claim that was to be cited by el Mili in his official rebuttal and made the object of his counter-argument. In the concluding remarks of her introductory chapter Zahar claimed that "Colonel Boumedienne offered him [Fanon] a last homage," referring to Fanon's burial.[64] These statements are clear enough, but to anyone who has perused the literature on Fanon or had the occasion to listen to men who knew Fanon, there is more to say. Jean Daniel, for instance, currently editor of *Le Nouvel Observateur*, was a man well acquainted with Algeria and its revolutionaries. He claimed that Fanon had had an influ-

ence on the formulations of the Tripoli program that appeared
in the summer of 1962. This is a major claim since the Tripoli
program embodied nothing less than a programmatic definition
of the Algerian Revolution and its objectives. Comprehensive in
its formulations, it came to be regarded as one of the fundamental political building blocks of the Ben Bella regime. Daniel cited
the influence, albeit without offering evidence, of Fanon on Ben
Yahyia, one of the men (along with Harbi) who is credited with
being author of the program.[65] Joby Fanon, on another occasion, recalled conversations that took place in Fanon's Tunis
home, and where the subjects discussed were subsequently to
become part of the Tripoli program.[66] These claims have been
challenged by a number of Algerians, among them Reda Malek
and Mohamed el Mili. The principal themes of the Tripoli program were among the subjects that Fanon was concerned with
in the last period of his life: the relationship of the party and the
state; the need for organization; the primacy of the peasants;
and the need for a general socialist orientation in the nation's
post-war planning. Given the fact that Fanon knew the men who
went to Tripoli personally, and that he had access to the figures
who were to become the members of the Provisional Government prior to 1962 and those who became Algeria's leaders
after independence, it is not unreasonable to suggest that he
participated in discussions which consumed the attention of all
militants at this time.

From this assertion to the more complex allegation that Fanon influenced the people who were in the GPRA or the ALN,
or at Tripoli, is another story. By far the most interesting, it
nevertheless remains difficult at present to offer adequate evidence to substantiate it. We do know that Fanon was politically
close to the men who were elected by the CNRA in August 1961
to head the new government-in-exile. But it would be simplifying matters unrealistically to state that Fanon's sympathies lay
exclusively with the team of Vice-President Belkacem Krim,
President Ben Yussuf ben Khedda, and Foreign Minister Saad
Dahlab. It was during Ben Khedda's term of office that Fanon
went to lecture to the military at Ghardimaou, an event which
doubtless had more to do with Boumedienne than with Ben
Khedda. When one recalls that these two men were often at
odds in this period, Fanon's penchant for the military at this
phase and his stay at Ghardimaou take on particular importance.

Boumedienne is alleged, by some of his colleagues today, to have been a Fanon sympathizer. Jean Daniel is not the only man to remember seeing a portrait of Fanon hanging in his headquarters.[67] Another figure, close to Boumedienne and currently a key man in the regime, Boutefliqa, was also rumored to have been impressed and in awe of Fanon in this period. That Fanon spent a month in Ghardimaou in the company of these and other militants indicates the respect with which he and his ideas were held.

Before turning to the political implications of Fanon's alliances and the subsequent history of the men with whom he chose to ally himself politically, it is useful to consider how the present government views Fanon. Algerian officials who talk and write about Fanon, or who delegate others to do the same, have one thing in common. They consistently avoid any discussion of Fanon's political ideas, either with respect to the FLN or ALN, or since independence. The strong desire to protect the authenticity of the Revolution as an all-Algerian phenomenon is partially responsible for this. Fanon is considered to have been an important militant; one who was particularly useful in making the Revolution intelligible to Europeans. But the suggestion that he had any influence on such major figures as Ben Bella or Boumedienne is immediately contested. In an effort to eliminate this and to render it highly implausible, there is a concerted policy of downgrading Fanon as a theorist of the Revolution. The excessive attention paid to Fanon in the West, as the biographical studies demonstrate, has something to do with this reaction. Here, the Algerians have a point which is not sufficiently appreciated. Fanon may well have had an influence on Algerian politics and even on the present head of state, but to suggest that he was the principal theoretician of the Revolution is not warranted. Any serious reading of the material to have emerged from the revolutionary period confirms the Algerian position on this aspect of the issue.

Once this imbalance is corrected, however, the question of what Fanon represented politically still remains unanswered. While intellectuals are interested in discussing the content of his ideas, or in arguing about his tactics, officials still seem intent on the need to prove that he was not an influential figure, and finally, that he was not even Algerian. The question of influence is dealt with by the oft-repeated phrase, that Fanon's ideas were molded by the Revolution in Algeria, and not vice versa. That he was not a Muslim and not an Algerian is true. But what is the relevance of this? It is surely not to remind readers of the fact that Fanon died before there was an Algerian nation and therefore an Algerian citizenship. Is it to raise the question of whether or not he would have been offered such citizenship in an increasingly tradition-bound nation, a very different kind of republic than the one he willed? In fact, this is at least one of the questions that is raised by this controversy, but it is hardly done in the manner intended. The intention of the official interpreters of Fanon's role in the Algerian Revolution is, as one official put it bluntly, to "de-Fanonize Algeria, and to de-Algerianize Fanon." It is to underline the view that although he helped with "our cause," "he was not one of us." This is meant to finally lay aside the ghost of a too-powerful Fanon, but the implications of this kind of argument reach beyond Fanon. It is this which is ultimately of importance in the official pronouncements, as admirers of Fanon and past militants of the Algerian Revolution realize. To categorize Fanon as a foreigner is not merely to state the obvious; nor is it simply to repeat what is known, i.e. that he belonged to a secular minority. It is to emphasize that the roots of the Revolution lie in the traditional, religious past of the nation. This, in turn, is a subtle way of reminding men that the political orientation represented by men such as Fanon, and he was after all one of a number of Algerians, has been put aside in favor of that which is authentically Algerian. Whether or not the issue is authenticity, or even Algerian identification, is not discussed. The orientation represented by Fanon and the men with whom he allied himself is not distinguished by its being foreign or inauthentic. It is quite simply that the struggle for power has eliminated these men, and their successors—including some of Fanon's former friends and admirers—have chosen another path.

What does it mean to speak of an "official view" on the Fanon question? That there is a remarkable consistency in the discussion of Fanon's place in Algeria by a number of men who happen to be officials of the government is striking. It raises questions about sources of information and about the uniformity of interpretation. But in itself, this might not warrant referring to an official position, although it would strongly suggest that there was one. I use the term in recognition of the fact that it is in the journal of the Ministry of Information that the Fanon question has recently been discussed with authority.[68] And it is the same author of these articles who was, again at the invitation of the Ministry of Information, asked to give a public lecture on the subject. Since, there have been other men who have written on Fanon: on the occasion of the tenth anniversary of his death, *el Moudjahid* published a review of a recent book on Fanon's sociology, and *Algérie-Actualité* published a number of articles of greater scope.[69] In spite of this apparent diversity, there continues to be an impressive similarity in points of view expressed. The book reviewed in *el Moudjahid* was published by the Algerian national publishing house, SNED.[70] Originally presented as a thesis at the Sorbonne in 1969, under the direction of Professor Lucien Goldmann, it was written by Philippe Lucas. According to Kaddour M'hamsadji, whose review consisted of praiseworthy remarks interspersed with lengthy quotes, Lucas' work will not open any difficult questions of a political nature. The same can be said of the abundant material that appeared in *Algérie-Actualité.* For sheer quantity of data pertinent to Fanon's life and works about him, it offered readers an unusual fare. Malek Alloula and Dr. Abdelghani Megherbi were the two authors of the articles on Fanon. The former presented a detailed analysis of Renate Zahar's work, leaving the impression that he regretted its inadequate coverage. Alloula himself, however, concentrated almost exclusively on the philosophical aspect of Zahar's work. Dr. Megherbi, on the other hand, in an article entitled "Frantz Fanon, apostle of non-violence," offered a more eclectic piece. In a paragraph that was meant as a defense of Fanon against those who claim that he forgot the Antilles in his Algerian phase, Megherbi tried to explain what he thought Fanon's conception of commitment involved. For Fanon, it was not biological ties alone that determined a man's commitment. It was "faith in common values based primarily on the dignity and grandeur of men, of all men."[71] While one may question the originality of this observation, it touches on something important in the Algerian treatment of the Fanon case. Megherbi was clearly justifying Fanon's commitment to the Algerian cause— not on the basis of his blood ties—but on the basis of commonly held values. For Megherbi as for Fanon, this was enough. For

official spokesmen on Fanon today, however, it is precisely the
importance of blood ties as opposed to commonly held values
that is emphasized.

As noted above, the official treatment of Fanon can be found
in the three articles published by *al Thaqafa*, and in a talk delivered by the same author, Dr. Mohamed el Mili, writer and Director of Information in the Ministry of Information and Culture.[72]
In el Mili's articles and in his lecture, it is clear that one motive
behind the official response is the desire to answer the allegations made about Fanon by foreign commentators. Another,
which is related, is to clarify Fanon's relationship to the Algerian
Revolution as seen by the present regime. This is accomplished
by first denying the influence of Fanon on any of the important
Algerian leaders; then, by demonstrating that his political writings are themselves a reflection of the influence of Algeria on
Fanon; and finally, by emphasizing the fact that for all of his
devotion, Fanon remained foreign to Algeria's history.

Reporting on the lecture he delivered in March 1971, an *el
Moudjahid* reporter observed that "in the introduction the lec-
turer showed that studies devoted to Fanon have insisted particularly on the influence which he exercised on the Algerian
Revolution. He (el Mili) underlined that some people have even
pretended that responsible Algerian officials profited from
Fanonian thought and presented themselves as his heirs at the
time of the 1962 July crisis."[73] The reference is almost verbatim,
to Renate Zahar. This gross error, according to el Mili, can be
explained by the fact that people know Fanon's last work better
than his earlier books and tend to draw conclusions about him
on the basis of this final product. The relevance of this is somewhat mystifying. Foreign commentators writing about Fanon
have demonstrated again and again that they are familiar with
all of his works. In any event, a close reading of Renate Zahar
reveals that her claims were not based on Fanon's book but on
sources which she did not completely reveal. El Mili's point,
however, is not subtle. One must deny the Zahar allegation and
then proceed to demonstrate that Fanon was the one to be
influenced by events in Algeria, and not vice versa.

In the first of three articles on Fanon and Algeria in *al Thaqafa*,
el Mili revised this view somewhat, acknowledging that Fanon
had had some influence on the Revolution.[74] He took the opportunity of chiding western authors who seemed, according to

him, incapable of resisting the idea that because Fanon was influenced by prominent western thinkers, they should have had a dominant influence in his life. The implication would then be that through him, they influenced Algeria. The contrary was true, for el Mili, whose dominant theme remained that Fanon was a product of Algeria and specifically of the Algerian Revolution. But the process of reducing Fanon to a more convenient status also involved discussing his familiarity with the Algerian environment, Algeria's past. What past could Fanon relate to, in Algeria? asked el Mili. His own Martiniquean past was irrelevant. As for an Algerian past, he had none. Other men who knew Fanon and who share el Mili's view, recall that Fanon seemed astonished to discover that Algerian resistance had been a prominent if unsuccessful feature of Algerian life before 1954. This is taken as evidence of Fanon's innocence, or ignorance. When el Mili was asked whom he considered as the major theoretician of the Algerian Revolution, he answered in a cryptic but significant way. Had Ben Badis been alive at the time (he died in 1940) he would have been the right man; or had Fanon been an Algerian, he would have been the man.[75] The remark made in semi-jest reflected an important point. Fanon's fatal flaw, from this perspective, was that he was neither Algerian nor Muslim.

The factual information is, of course, correct. For el Mili, the fact that Fanon considered himself to be an Algerian is not convincing; he remained a European. It is interesting to contrast this with the view of Fanon held in the United States, where Fanon is regarded as many things, but rarely as the consummate European. Were Fanon's foreign origin, and his not being a Muslim, considered negative factors in his work with the FLN? It hardly seems to be the case. Perhaps the answer is simply that he was useful at the time, and is no longer useful today. El Mili, and others who requested anonymity, speaks with admiration of Fanon's education, of his articulateness, and of his superiority over many of the men he worked with. One official acknowledged that Fanon's connections with the French left were useful. According to this man, Fanon's impressive intellectual stature was also useful in military circles. It was an ideal combination to be able to invite this intellectual, who obviously craved a life of action, to speak before the ALN, before men who were moved to hear their mission spoken of in Fanon's spectacular way.[76]

What of his ignorance of Islam? In his last article in *al Thaqafa*, el Mili admitted that when Fanon first came to Algeria, he knew nothing about Islam. His own atheistic inclinations did not prepare him to consider the role of Islam in Algeria. But, in accord with his general theory of Algeria's powerful influence on Fanon, el Mili finally admits that eventually even Fanon recognized the importance of Islam in Algeria's past.[77] El Mili may have underlined this in order to endorse the present regime's view of the matter, and to return to his favorite topic, that it was Algeria that influenced Fanon. But in the process he contradicted himself. It is ineffective to use the argument that Fanon's foreign birth and his ignorance of Islam made him marginal to Algeria, and at the same time to remind people of his devotion to Algeria and his recognition of the import of Islam in Algeria's cultural life.

The relevance of Fanon's critique in his last work to Algeria today is clearly not mentioned in this material. Nor is there any mention of continuing political problems which haunted Algeria's militants before 1962 and which continue to threaten her today. These are not subjects that are easily discussed, particularly in official publications. For these reasons alone, it is not difficult to understand the preference for Fanon's sociological study of Algeria in revolution, *A Dying Colonialism*. If one choses to emphasize the role of the man as publicist for the cause, and to admire him to the degree that he perpetuated the revolutionary élan, then this book stands out. M'hammed Yazid, who certainly knew Fanon well, and who has had ample opportunity to talk with foreigners about Fanon, concurs in the el Mili view. For Yazid, Fanon was on solid ground when he wrote as a psychiatrist. The suggestion is that he may have known somewhat less in his other polemical works. To those who lived through Algeria in revolution and who retain a commitment to the revolutionary tradition, this book is the statement of an ideal rather than a reality. That it may have corresponded to reality for a brief period of time renders subsequent developments that much more poignant. It is not a reflection on Fanon's work to say so; it is merely an admission of the extraordinary difficulties entailed in making the Revolution as opposed to writing about it.

El Mili has had a number of other theories to offer on the Fanon question. One has to do with his reasons for finally writing *The Wretched of the Earth*; the other is more general and relates to what Fanon's sojourn in Algeria may have meant for him. El Mili contends that Fanon never resolved the color question in his life; and that he chose to live in Algeria because it gave him an opportunity to avoid the question in a seemingly constructive way. What el Mili suggests is that Fanon, who retained a passion for black Africa but did not live in black Africa, immersed himself in the Algerian Revolution and thereby avoided a direct confrontation with the black problem. His commitment was genuine and wholehearted and this permitted him to rationalize his action intellectually.[78] Joby Fanon indicated that Fanon was seriously disturbed by what he had learned of racism in the Maghreb, and without explaining his brother's activity in Algeria in the same way, simply reported that he and Frantz had discussed the issue of racism and that Fanon planned to work on this matter after the Revolution. Joby reported that delegations of black North Africans, especially Tunisians, had come to visit Fanon while he was in Tunis and had complained to him about his lack of interest in their plight. The visit had affected Fanon and it was in connection with this that Joby noted Frantz's plan to return to psychiatric work in this domain after the war's end.[79]

Turning to Fanon's last book, el Mili suggested that what led Fanon to write it was Fanon's bitterness at having been left out of the political inner circle in 1957. El Mili was with Fanon in Madrid at this time, and he recalled that the two men had listened to the news from Cairo about the composition of the National Council of the Algerian Revolution. El Mili maintains that Fanon was hurt by not having been named to the Council and that he took out his frustration in the writing of this angry book.[80] It is curious that another figure prominent in Algeria today, and no less in tune with politics than el Mili, has frankly stated that he believes *The Wretched of the Earth* to be Fanon's most important book. The same official was to add that it might not be a bad idea to take a few leaves out of Fanon's book in discussing Algeria's ills today.

El Mili's contention that Fanon wrote *The Wretched* in order to vent his frustration is quite simply irrelevant. But the fact that Fanon may have been bitter at being left out of the inner ruling elite is possibly true. If anything, it raises more questions than it answers. It is the view of this author that the official position on Fanon in Algeria today is a function of the political changes that have taken place since 1962, aggravated by changes since 1965. Fanon has been put aside along with other Algerians whose political analyses are too acute and apply too well to Algeria today to afford public debate of their views. Two things must be considered: first, the political place which Fanon carved for himself, and his allies or changing alliances; and secondly, the relevance of his critique to Algeria. A combination of both factors helps to explain why, without exaggerating the account of his influence, it is possible to understand the reluctance of the present government to give Fanon any more publicity than necessary.

Fanon had been invited to Tunis in 1956 to work with the external delegation of the FLN. As a result of the reorganization of *el Moudjahid* and the other press organs of the FLN, the Tunisian capital became the headquarters for the FLN press and *el Moudjahid*, its principal organ. El Mili was in charge of the Arabic version of the paper, while Reda Malek held the same position in the French edition. Fanon worked for Reda Malek, and indirectly for M'hammed Yazid. All three men, therefore, knew Fanon well. All three men today insist that Fanon's influence was minimal. At times, their insistence is so persistent that it suggests that the opposite may be true. In the summer of 1956, some months after he had come to Tunis, and hence long enough to have learned something about the issues and personalities involved in the Tunisian capital, the Soummam Valley conference took place. Generally regarded as one of the critical conferences that was to determine future FLN and ALN relations, it witnessed the creation of two important and related structures: the National Council of the Algerian Revolution (CNRA); and the executive body, the Coordinating and Executive Committee (CCE). More significant than the actual structural innovations were the discussions about the relations between the political and military wings of the movement; and specifically, the decision to allow the interior to dominate the exterior factions. These decisions were not implemented consistently, and they contained the seeds of dissension in the ranks of Algerian militants, before and after independence.

Abane Ramdane, the single most important figure in the Soummam Valley meeting, was considered one of the radical militants, and also one of the representatives of the interior who strongly believed in the justice of allowing the interior, given its

heavy responsibilities in the conduct of the struggle, to dominate the exterior. Fanon's friendship with Ramdane has been
denied by el Miĥ. Others, notably G. Pirelli, who knew Fanon,
claimed that he was a great friend and model of Fanon.[81] In the
light of Fanon's anguish over the nature of Ramdane's death, it
is important to be able to determine whether Fanon did or did
not know the man. In any event, the first CCE, the executive
body of the CNRA, included men such as Ramdane, Ben
Khedda, and Dahlab. An earlier reference indicated a similarity
in spirit between themes that appeared in speeches by Ben
Khedda, Dahlab, and Fanon. These were the radical militants
though not the military elements in the FLN circle.

In the spring of 1957, in May, four of the five original CCE
members were forced to leave Algeria and make their way to
Tunis because of the difficult conditions in the interior. Belkacem Krim, Ben Khedda, Dahlab, and Ramdane arrived in Tunis
in this period. On the basis of what is known of Fanon's ideas,
and as one observes his own radicalization as finally expressed
in *The Wretched of the Earth* and in certain features of his articles
in *el Moudjahid*, it appears eminently plausible that Fanon came
to feel politically sympathetic to the positions represented by
this group of men. Eventually, when his alienation from the
GPRA increased and his interest in the ALN became more
prominent, there was to be yet another move in his thinking. If
it were possible to classify the militant radicals in a permanent
way, and to classify the men with whom Fanon worked in a like
manner, it would be that much easier to speak authoritatively of
his political alliances. Algerian history however, in this period of
the Revolution, does not allow such categorization with any
degree of accuracy.

Between the time of its formation and the spring of 1957,
when the CCE members moved to Tunis, the CCE was associated with a number of tactical decisions that affected the
course of the Revolution. One was the use of the strike to mobil-
ize mass support and to demonstrate support of the FLN, the
other was the use of urban terrorism culminating in the Battle
of Algiers. It would be interesting to determine Fanon's position
and opinions on this series of events. His conviction that it was
only through violence that international opinion could be
affected would have led him to endorse urban terrorism. His
Algerian colleagues reproach him, at least in retrospect, for his
excesses in this direction. Fanon was not in Algeria in any case,

when the Battle of Algiers was being fought. If he had anything to say on the subject, it was safely said to friends and militants far away from the scene of battle.

El Mili claims that he and Fanon were in Madrid at the time of the meeting of the CNRA in Cairo,—from August 20 to September 18, 1957. He recalls that the two of them listened to the news coming out of the Egyptian capital and that Fanon could not hide his disappointment on learning of the composition of the new executive. It may be that what disappointed Fanon was not his having been left out but the composition of the second CCE, and what had happened to his colleagues on that occasion. Differences over the size of the CCE and its effectiveness in Algeria, to which Dahlab, Ramdane, and Ben Khedda believed it ought to return, broke out in a serious manner. In Cairo, the CNRA members faced with the proposal of these three men rejected them, "apparently fearing that these three were becoming too powerful. They voted instead for the formation of a large and more functionally specific CCE of nine members. Two of the radical politicians from the previous CCE, Ben Khedda and Dahlab, were eliminated in what one described as 'circumstances full of intrigue' and the other a 'minor coup d'état.' "[82] Quandt quotes Dahlab's observations on the changing character of the new executive as reflecting the "elimination of the politicians by the *militaires* who saw themselves as the real '*combattants*.' "[83] The substitution of the military for the politician, in this instance, revealed the growing importance of the military leaders of the interior. The Soummam decision not to allow the military to dominate the political had been superseded. But these developments did not mark an end to the political struggles of the various factions that had emerged.

In the next two years, further changes were to occur that affected the course of the Revolution, and the course of relations between the interior and the exterior. In September of 1958, the Provisional Government, the GPRA, was formed, thus replacing the second executive. In terms of the FLN's international activities, few deny that this was an important step; internally, however, it did not begin to bring unity into the ranks of the movement. The issues that had been divisive earlier, including the relations between the military and political, remained problematic.

Some time after the formation of the second CCE, a military

coordinating committee known as the COM, Commandant des
Opérations Militaires, was formed. It was originally concentrated in two areas, in Oujda in Morocco, and in Ghardimaou on
the Tunisian side. The creation of the military coordination
committee reflected the inability of the men in Tunis to exercise
complete control over the fighting going on in Algeria. Aside
from power struggles, the reality of the forces in Algeria was
such that those who were on the outside could not hope to
determine all that transpired within French-controlled territory.
It was inevitable that those who did the actual fighting should
demand more control of the political decisions of the Revolution. But even within military circles, there were divisions reflected in the differences between the men inside the country
and those stationed on Algeria's frontiers. Those on the inside
were often ill-equipped and tended to resent what they perceived as the accumulation of material at their expense. Eventually the struggle between the interior military and the frontier
military was resolved in favor of the Etat Major Général, the
single position that grew out of the combination of the east and
west military concentrations. Colonel Boumedienne was in control of the Etat Major. It would be unwise to believe that these
developments occurred without considerable stress. While the
Algerians were fighting the French, they were also engaged in
a variety of internal struggles. The "Colonel's Plot" involved a
challenge by some of the military against the GPRA, and eventually resulted in a shakedown and change in the internal politics
of the Etat Major. It is from this time that the rise to political
power of Boumedienne may be dated.

The unified Etat Major was in operation prior to the fall of
1959. It was in February 1960 that Fanon went to Cairo to
consult with the GPRA about FLN policy in Africa. Of his associates, M'hammed Yazid was now Minister of Information and
Belkacem Krim was the Vice-President. On the basis of what we
know of the importance of the Etat Major in the political-military
decision-making process of the Algerians at this time, one can
assume that when Fanon was assigned to Accra in 1960, and
when he was asked to investigate the opening of a southern front
to strengthen the interior by the movement of arms from Mali
in the south, he embarked on this project with the approval of
the Etat Major. When we learn that it was in this period, in the
last months of his stay in Tunis prior to going to the United

States, in 1961, that Fanon also went to Ghardimaou to lecture to the ALN, this appears to be evidence of a rapprochement between Fanon and the exterior military of the ALN. The period between 1960 and 1962 was marred by serious differences between the GPRA and the ALN. There was increasing evidence that it was the Etat Major that controlled the ALN and not the GPRA. The Provisional Government, in turn, was increasingly involved in the difficult process of negotiations with France. On this subject as well, the differences in outlook between the GPRA and the ALN came to the surface. Fanon was not unsympathetic to those militants who were critical of the GPRA negotiations, and who feared that too much would be conceded by the Algerians in exchange for a cessation of hostilities. The ALN was generally strongly in opposition to the Evian discussions.

In this period, Fanon shared the concern of the military and in spite of the fact that many of the men with whom he had been linked earlier were now in the Provisional Government, he increasingly sided with the critics of the GPRA. Geismar offers the following by way of explanation:

> Because it appeared as though the Algerians in Tunis were more and more concerned about the doling out of power in what they considered an already independent Algeria, Fanon turned toward the nationalist army as another source of revolutionary momentum. He had more faith in the men using the guns than those arranging the peace; warriors, hardened to violence, would be less tolerant of neocolonialist compromises. Fanon was impressed by the toughness and optimism of the general staff headquarters on the Tunisian border. . . . He made three excursions to the general staff encampment in order to lecture on the pitfalls of a successful struggle for national liberation. His greatest concern, by 1961, was that a Moslem bourgeoisie would replace the European settlers without any real restructuring of Algerian society. He had a naive belief that the army would supervise the growth of Third World socialism, remaining immune from the materialistic corruptions of the new bourgeoisie.[84]

It was the ALN that Geismar referred to above writing of the excursions made to the general staff encampment. And it was at Ghardimaou, in particular, that Fanon went to deliver lectures that are well guarded in the Algiers Political Commissariat. One former member of the ALN recalled that these lectures were merely summaries of Fanon's book; an expression that was an attempt to allay any curiosity about their content. But familiarity with *The Wretched of the Earth* suggests many possible subjects, all of them currently controversial.

In 1962, Michel Pablo (also known as Raptis), one of the Trotskyist advisers to Ben Bella who was to be dismissed by the end of 1964, wrote a pamphlet on the Tripoli program and the more general theme of "impressions and problems of the Algerian Revolution."[85] In that pamphlet he devoted one chapter to the ALN, discussing its composition and its functions. He noted that prior to independence, there had already been an organic link between the *wilayas* V, I, and VI, and that these were the *wilayas* that constituted the "essential force of the ex-Etat Major of Colonel Boumedienne." They had the most impressive supply of arms and the most developed political training. It was through these *wilayas* that contact with certain interior *wilayas* was maintained during the war. Acknowledging the hostility between interior and exterior because of the matter of providing arms, Pablo went on to discuss the situation of the army after independence. He expressed unconditional belief in its importance, referring to it as the most structured force existing in the country.

The interest Pablo's analysis represented lies in his association of Fanon with the political training of the army; and, on the basis of his discussion of Boumedienne's position on the politicization of the military, its confirmation of the link between Fanon and Boumedienne. The evidence in Pablo's article is sufficient to endorse the frequent allegations that Boumedienne was indeed a man familiar with and highly sympathetic to Fanonian ideas. It does not inform us of the precise nature of the meeting of minds. But there is enough to suggest that the parties concerned would have much to say on the subject.

Pablo indicated in his essay that the political education of the military took place through the political commissariats, and that the young men who staffed these centers were responsible for the development of the revolutionary doctrine of the military. In terms of their own backgrounds, these ALN officers were frequently ex-students who had left their university work to join with the ALN. In its ranks, they found themselves collaborating with the regular rank and file of the army, the peasants. It was this combination, of intellectuals and peasants, which made the

ALN unique; and which, according to Boumedienne, served to distinguish it from the bourgeois, opportunist, and counter-revolutionary elements that dominated the FLN.[86] In contrasting the political education of the ALN as opposed to the FLN, even during the war, Pablo was convinced of the superiority of the former. There had been "veritable military academies in the East and West (that) possessed political sections that elaborated the doctrine of the Revolution, in the way it is conceived by the army."[87] The concept of a permanent, lasting revolution built on an economic, social, and political program that was as concrete as possible and that was responsible for guiding the revolutionary party and its organized and politically conscious military base, was the way in which Pablo summed up some of the doctrine being perpetuated in the military milieu. He described its objectives as agrarian reform, industrialization, nationalization, and the struggle against illiteracy. In this context, he wrote as follows:

> the political Commissariat of the Etat major, and that of wilaya 5 multiply mimeographed courses on 'capitalism,' 'neo-colonialism,' 'the nefarious role of the national bourgeoisie,' etc., where the ideas and analyses, not simply borrowed from *The Wretched of the Earth* of Fanon, but frankly Marxist, abound and dominate.[88]

In an interview with Colonel Boumedienne, Pablo noted that agrarian reform was the first objective which the national government must accomplish. He endorsed the notion that the Algerian Revolution was a peasant revolution, from the nature of the force that had initiated and virtually sustained it through the entire independence struggle. Among the goals to be obtained for the benefit of the entire society, according to Boumedienne, was the creation of a socialist society free of exploitation. But it was through agrarian reform that a "radical reconversion of society" was to occur. It is clear from Pablo's text that he was much impressed by the charismatic appeal of Boumedienne, though he was candid enough to admit that there were long-range dangers in the omnipotent position of the army. In the Algerian context, however, at the time he wrote, he saw no other organized alternatives whose conceptions of the state were as favorable to the socialist direction in which he himself believed. There is no indication of what Pablo thought of the ideas of Fanon, from his own political vantage point, but his reflections on the possibilities of the ALN appear very similar to those attributed to Fanon as he became closer to the ALN as opposed to the GPRA faction. Whether or not Fanon's view of Boumedienne was similar to that of Pablo is an interesting question but less important than his estimate of what Boumedienne represented politically.

On the basis of Pablo's material, Fanon's presence in Ghardimaou was less isolated an event than it might have appeared earlier. If Fanon was involved in the political training of the commissariat, and if Boumedienne was militant in his own conception of the need to politicize the military and sufficiently in accord with the ideas represented in *The Wretched of the Earth* to include them in the curriculum of the commissariat, then Fanon's role in the important task of politicizing the military would seem beyond dispute.[89] That Boumedienne and Boutefliqa are less anxious to recall this association today may be true. The evidence in the "official position" on the Fanon question certainly points in that direction. Whether or not their motivation is to safeguard the "authenticity" of the Revolution, or merely to avoid discussion of policies to which they have not entirely adhered, is open to question. In any event, Fanon's influence in the Revolution, as opposed to his place in Algeria today, is obviously entangled in the changing political alliances and currents of Algeria. Perhaps, in an effort to tell their version of the story, the men of the Algiers Political Commissariat may one day be moved to talk of this past.

Assuming that Fanon would have remained in Algeria after independence, something which one cannot take for granted given the expulsion of other foreign partisans, what would he have thought? What would his own situation have been? Immediately after independence, critical assessments of the direction of the Revolution abounded. Critics loyal to the Revolution expressed fear about the trends in Algeria's political life; foreign militants warned that the degeneration of the party would prove detrimental to the nation; that militancy was no substitute for politics; and finally, the crisis of the summer of 1962 left few illusions about the unity which revolutionary struggle had brought. Ben Bella, whom certain Algerians maintain was an admirer of Fanon, offered a leadership that was eclectic and highly personal, but also increasingly autocratic. The cult of non-personality that is current in the present regime is designed to underline the difference between the Ben Bella and Boumedienne styles. One may wonder about the difference in internal politics. The party, about which Fanon had lectured and written, struggled with its own factionalism and the role it was to occupy in the decision-making process and the distribution of power in the independent state. The results were not encouraging. Yet, Fanon would doubtless have looked with favor on the experiment of self-management, all the while recognizing the difficulties faced by autogestion at the local level, and in the government. One source, a contemporary of Fanon's, maintains that the organization of councils for self-managed communities was a distinctly Fanonian innovation. Fanon's interest in decentralization and in the primacy of the peasantry would support the claim that he would have endorsed self-management. In other respects, among the Ben Bella projects Fanon might have supported, one can include the African orientation of Ben Bella's foreign policy and his support for national liberation movements. Where he would have stood in the internal conflicts that eventually resulted in the June 19, 1965 coup, is another matter. But the problems that appear from a Fanonian perspective as considerably worse today, or since 1965, than they appeared earlier cannot be blamed entirely on the present regime. The predicament of the FLN was not resolved prior to 1965, and the economic priorities of the present government had supporters earlier. When one looks at the FLN and its situation, however, Fanon's acuteness as a prophet of gloom is vindicated. The emergence of a military clique was not Fanon's idea of the direction of the future. One wonders what he had in mind when he lectured at Ghardimaou. It is doubtful that he would have remained silent at the gradual erosion of political life, or that he would have approved the need for an elaborate security and military network to protect the government from dissidents and perhaps even from its supporters.

If there was anything to which Fanon was committed, it was the notion that the party ought to speak for the masses and that it ought to remain separate from the state apparatus. Today, other than government officials, it is rare to hear anyone speak of the party as relevant to political life; nor is it considered as representative of the masses. As for its relationship to the state apparatus, the party reflects the policy of the government. Efforts at decentralization of the FLN apparatus have been going on for some time, and attention is paid to communal decentralization by the Boumedienne government. But the essence of the question remains untouched. Visits to self-managed farms and conversations with native-born skeptics do not reenforce the view that there is a political revival being encouraged by the government. On the contrary, there is some concern about how the government will sustain the support of the masses and of a largely apolitical youth if it continues to prohibit expressions of political difference. The problem is hardly new, and some Algerian officials are candid in their expressions of concern over it. They are generally less concerned with another subject which Fanon wrote about so persuasively, namely the situation of Algerian women. Irritated with the attention paid to this matter, officials point with anger at those Algerians who choose to write on this difficult matter abroad, and who do nothing to enhance Algeria's image as a revolutionary society.[90] Fanon is occasionally spoken of in this regard, and the reflection has been made in jest, that he quickly came to understand that women's liberation was a fine subject for Algerian militants except when it came to liberating their own sisters or wives.

The arabization program, linked as it is with the tendency to promote conservative support for the government, is another area where Fanon's position appears as currently superseded. Without assuming that all government officials approve the position given Islam by the current regime, it is deemed neither healthy nor wise to publicly denounce it. At the least, this subject alone testifies to the rationale behind the cool attitude toward Fanon and the views he held on this score. If it was not uncommon to hear alarmed outcries from some partisans of Algerian independence on seeing the resurgence of Islam after 1962, it has become progressively less frequent a criticism, at least from within.[91] In November of 1962, Jean Daniel noted in an article in *Jeune Afrique*, that "the Martiniquean atheist Fanon and the Kabyle Christian Amrouche would not feel at ease in hearing M. Tewfik el Madani say: 'We are essentially and above all Muslims,' " or in hearing "Ben Bella proclaim the triple Arab vocation of Algeria."[92] In 1971 it is accepted as a matter of fact that one passes over this question and concentrates instead on the defects of "cosmopolitanism" and those tainted with it. Considering the dimensions of the disease and the possibilities of diagnosing it in important sectors of the governing elite, it is a useful term. "Cosmopolitanism" refers, however, not only to the false sophisticated cosmopolites; it can be conveniently used to categorize those whose ideas are labeled as foreign, the better to damn them.

At the present time it does not appear that the mood of the government is conducive to a public discussion of the issues Fanon wrote about. They are too close and too sensitive. Should this assessment prove wrong, one can only assume that a public airing would prove to be an energizing experience for all concerned. If such a discussion does occur, however, it would doubtless reenforce the validity of Fanon's critical position and its relevance to Algeria today. But it is, in any event, only at such a time that the question of influence can be correctly evaluated and attention paid to the substance of Fanon's thought.

-6-

For Further Study

_____

If Fanon's position in Algeria remains difficult to assess for political reasons, what of his influence outside of the country? In Africa, it is difficult to generalize with any degree of accuracy. After his death, one observer commented that not only would Fanon not have survived in Algeria, he would probably not have lasted long in Africa either.[93] Without giving any explicit reasons for this position, it was apparent from the context of the remark that Fanon was regarded as a foreigner in Algeria and he would have been so regarded in Africa, with the same results. The small group of militant and radical partisans who had contributed their services to the cause of Algerian independence had been ousted after 1962. Whether or not the same combination of political factors would necessarily have come about in Africa and resulted in the expulsion of a man such as Fanon, is not entirely clear. There is no reason for optimism, however. Fanon's anti-colonialism is of course much admired in Africa. B. Juminer writes from Senegal that students are Fanon's ardent admirers.[94] Those who support the orthodox vision of negritude have less generous responses. Given Fanon's criticism of the new bourgeoisie that dominates the newly independent states of the continent, it is difficult to imagine that he would have enjoyed a friendly reception. This much was evident in his own reflections on Africa as they appeared in _The Wretched of the Earth_. Among opposition elements throughout the continent, however, Fanon's analysis of colonialism and the need for armed struggle are doubtless welcome.

In the pages that follow the application of Fanon's ideas to two different areas is sketched out for further study. One is the case of the black liberation movement in the United States, and the second is that of the Palestinian Resistance organizations in the Middle East. Although it will be obvious to those who know something of either subject, it is worth repeating that what follows is nothing more than a sketch for lengthier consideration. Moreover, even the classifications suggested here—the designation of the Palestinian Resistance, or the black liberation movement—require some definition. It is important in the American case to consider Fanon's influence in the country as a whole, among radicals, among black radicals, and in less directly politicized circles. In the Palestinian case, the influence of Fanon is less explicit, and probably more limited. Why it is, for instance, that *Black Skin, White Masks* is the only Fanon book not to be translated into Arabic is important. It tells us something of the nature of the identification with Fanon's world, and in the process it is revealing of the Arab experiences. It is not the psychology of the colonized that interested Fanon's publishers in the Middle East but his analysis of the political dynamics of imperialism and the situation of the third world. The American situation is different. Fanon's first and last books are of equal importance in the American black community. *Black Skin, White Masks* coincided with the resurgence of a black identity, first culturally and then politically. *The Wretched of the Earth* was perceived as relevant because of its analysis of colonization and its endorsement of violence. In any event, both books reflect two different though related moments in Fanon's development; the same may be said of the significance of the impact of these two books on its readers.

If Fanon's posthumous progress in Africa is worth studying, even more so is the serious question of his influence on black revolutionaries in the United States. Here, his influence in a popular as well as an organizational sense has been apparent as well as explicitly acknowledged for some time. Fanon himself wrote briefly on the black situation in America in *Black Skin, White Masks* and in *The Wretched of the Earth*. But his references were brief and they were primarily designed to underline the contrast between the situation he found in France, for black men, as opposed to what he believed existed in the United States.[95] In *The Wretched of the Earth,* Fanon touched on the

differences that existed between American blacks and Africans.[96] In 1956, at the first Congress of the African Cultural
Society held in Paris, he observed that "the Negroes who live in
the United States and in Central or Latin America in fact experience the need to attach themselves to a cultural matrix. Their
problem is not fundamentally different from that of the Africans.
The whites of America did not mete out to them any different
treatment from that of the whites that ruled over the Africans."
Referring to the Paris Congress in a later note, Fanon indicated
that "the American Negroes of their own accord considered
their problems from the same standpoint as those of their African brothers." But this sense of common history and destiny was
gradually replaced by an awareness of the differences that had
marked the individual communities.[97] Once he had become
aware of this difference Fanon emphasized it in clear terms. Did
he speak or believe that he spoke for American blacks, or did his
own position reflect his determination to undermine the concept of a universal negritude with which he found himself in
deep conflict. Fanon's answer was to emphasize the importance
of history.

> Negro and African-Negro culture broke up into different entities
> because the men who wished to incarnate these cultures realised
> that every culture is first and foremost national, and that the
> problems which kept Richard Wright or Langston Hughes on the
> alert were fundamentally different from those which might con-
> front Leopold Senghor or Jomo Kenyatta.[98]

Fanon's initial appeal in American black circles was not based
on his considerations of national culture, nor on his discussion
of negritude. Yet he has been cited as the intellectual guide in
the awakening that has characterized the black community and
that has involved a reconsideration of the question of black
culture. Fanon's role in this can be attributed to his powerful
exposé of the psychology of colonization and the process of total
psychic alienation common to the colonized and the oppressed,
whom he increasingly identified with one another. Out of this
has come the endorsement for self-affirmation, for rejection of
masks and the false identity they imply. It is this which made
Black Skin, White Masks so important a book in the American
milieu, although it is certainly not the only one to explore the
situation. Fanon was interested in American black literature, and

in France during his *Présence Africaine* period, he was in touch with Africans, Americans, and West Indians. In a more recent day, he would certainly have known of the work of Eldridge Cleaver, whose *Soul on Ice* reflects a consciousness in search of itself that has striking similarities with Fanon's work.[99]

To proceed from a recognition of the definition of alienation in Fanon's terms, to the realization that such a condition defined oppressors and oppressed in the same way as it did colonizer and colonized, had obvious implications. The notion that American blacks are a colonized people has replaced the concentration on the existential predicament of the colonized. Paralleling Fanon's development, a subjective condition has been transcended not only in an effort to understand its roots, but finally in an effort to alter the external conditions responsible for it. If *Black Rage,* a book which investigated the social dimensions of black psychology, was close to one phase of Fanon's thought, the emphasis is now clearly on another.[100] It is the political diagnosis that has become the central preoccupation. Horace Sutton, writing in the summer of 1971, claimed that

> to read Fanon now is to find the source of many of the bold moves of the black Left, among them violence itself, the call for reparations for offences to oppressed peoples, and the summons to effect the rebirth of a native culture and with it a singular identity.[101]

The final assessment of the influence of Fanon on black consciousness in the United States will require a far more comprehensive subject than his penetration of political thinking. But in the more limited domain, in the experience of the Black Panthers for instance, Fanon's influence has frequently been cited. Cleaver, for one, has written and spoken of Fanon on several occasions. In his review of *The Wretched of the Earth* in 1967, in *Ramparts,* he referred to it as a "classic study of the psychology of the oppressed peoples, . . . now known among the militants of the black liberation movement in America as 'the Bible.' "[102] Interviewed by Lee Lockwood in Algiers, Cleaver claimed that "the most important thing is that he [Fanon] describes the consciousness and the situation of a colonized people." But for Cleaver, Fanon had done considerably more. He had legitimized violence, he had raised people to a level of consciousness where "they're willing to fight for their freedom."[103] That Fanon was a formative influence in the actual organization of the Panther Party was acknowledged by Cleaver in a conversation recorded in *Front,* in which he cited Fanon along with Malcolm X as the two central figures critical to the formation of the party.[104] Bobby Seale has said as much in his oft-quoted description of how he took Fanon to Huey Newton having read *The Wretched of the Earth* himself no less than six times.[105]

To what extent Fanon has been read and used as a source for black activists remains a matter of some debate. To some more skeptical thinkers, it is doubtful that there has been as much serious study of Fanon as is claimed, and the distinction between carrying Fanon's books and reading them, or integrating them into party action, is a useful one to make. Moreover, there are some preliminary questions which the application of Fanon to the United States makes it imperative to consider. Is the analogy between blacks in the United States and Algerians in Algeria a valid one to make? Is it possible to reconcile the militant black nationalism, with its exclusivist overtones, that has emerged in some black circles, with the internationalist, humanist emphasis that was increasingly evident in Fanon's writing? To some blacks it appears that Fanon's internationalism was nothing more than an evasive tactic reflecting his inability to deal with the fact of blackness. Is the contrast between the recognition of the meaning of blackness in American society as opposed to what it was for Fanon in North Africa, something which can be reduced to such terms? Whatever the differences may be, Fanon's politics, so closely intertwined with his life, have become as much the subject of discussion and controversy as his written works. At the time of writing, it appears that Fanon's popularity is on the wane. The moment has passed when the pride and the inspiration he inspired led to a wave of admiration more general than critical. For this reason, it may now be possible to reconsider Fanon, and the appreciation of him in black circles, in a more dispassionate way.

The influence of Fanon on the Black Power movement, or more particularly, on some of its leaders, is perhaps the most dramatic instance of Fanon's influence outside of Algeria. It is not the only one, however. Generally speaking, partisans of liberation struggles in the third world have responded to Fanon with the recognition appropriate to his work. Whether as an inspiration or a guide, he has been accepted by those who believe in the necessity of armed struggle. His conception of violence has been abstracted and enthusiastically endorsed, and his writing on the psychology of colonization has been taken up as a reflection of the revolutionary impact of struggle on the family, the position of women in traditional societies, and the innermost reaches of man's feelings towards himself. In the Middle East, Fanon's name has been associated with those of Giap, Mao, and Che, as one of the revolutionary leaders acclaimed by militant elements in the Palestine Resistance movement. It has been estimated that no less than six editions of *The Wretched of the Earth* have appeared in Arabic; and with the exception of Fanon's first book, his other works have also been translated.[106] Comparisons between Palestinians and Algerians are not novel, and Fanon's popularity may be explained, at the outset, by this connection. But his most avid readers, who are at times also his most severe critics, do not consider Fanon as a guide to Algerian experience, but as an analyst of imperialism. They point to his discussion of the lumpenproletariat as one which may have application in the Arab world. If those involved in the Palestinian movement have been the discoverers of Fanon, it would seem that they have not limited his potential application to the Palestinian situation.

In the Resistance movement, itself a complex and politically varied movement, Fanon has had an uneven history. Direct evidence of his influence is difficult to find; but frequent references to his work have reenforced the impression that he has contributed to the thinking of some individuals and groups. It has been said that Fanon was used in the training sessions of the Baath Party (The Arab Baath Socialist Party), a party that was in opposition in Syria and Jordan in the late 1950's. At the time, before the creation of the UAR, in which action the Syrian Baath played a role, Fanon was a popular reference. More recently, the same thing was discovered to be the case in Fatah training centers, where it was reported that Fanon's works were studied along with those of Mao, Giap, Debray, Guevara, and Castro. "From Fanon, the description of the psychology of the colonized and the necessity of the recourse to violence, were used. . . ."[107] This emphasis is borne out by the nature of the selections chosen by Fatah to be published in small, abridged versions of original works. The popular appraisal of Fanon's relevance to the Middle Eastern situation was reflected in a paper submitted to the Arab-American University Graduate Convention that was held in the winter of 1969. On that occasion, the author upheld the view that Fanon's analysis applies to the Palestinian people. Elaborating on this theme, he wrote:

> Only through armed struggle and violence will they [the Palestinians] be able to liberate their land and regain their national identity.
>   Through armed struggle and violence, the Palestinian people can rid themselves of all the remnants of dispersion and isolation. Violence serves as a cure for the diseases they faced; the despair, the inaction, and isolation. . . . By adopting armed struggle and violence, al Fatah has been able to create the spirit that Fanon spoke of.[108]

The highly romanticized notion that violence serves as a cure for the diseases listed has been challenged from within the Resistance movement itself, by those left-wing elements who reject both the eulogy of violence and, in fact, the popularity of Fanon. To some Marxist-Leninists in the resistance movement, Fanon is an example of the pitfalls of spontaneity and the dangers of the lack of party organization. That these are precisely the weaknesses about which Fanon wrote is beside the point. The criticism would appear to be directed at the more facile exponents of Fanon and Fanonism, than at the man himself.

An openly negative assessment of Fanon's importance in the ideological formation comes from one of the intellectual leaders of the Palestinian movement. He minimizes the role that Fanon has played and frankly claims that he belongs to those "who have written about resistance from the galleries but who are not part of the leadership of the movement. How much awareness of this small group of the relevance of Fanon's ideas to our revolution has affected first the thinking of the leaders, and second their action, is a question that needs investigation but that is—in my view—very marginal."[109] Yusuf Sayigh's disclaimer is important but it does not eliminate the question entirely. In some areas, among Palestinian women or those who support them in the larger framework of an Arab revolutionary movement, the relevance of the Algerian situation as described by Fanon in *A Dying Colonialism* remains a model.[110] What they aspire to is the right to participate in political action, and in the long run to share, equally with men, in the creation of their people's history. The current phase of the Palestinian situation suggests that Fanon along with other guides will undergo a process of reevaluation.[111]

There are other aspects of Fanon's legacy that remain open for further study and those suggested here will probably open the door to more questions. Before he died in 1961, Fanon was planning to resume psychiatric work in Tunis. In the past, that is after he had moved to Tunis and become directly involved with the FLN, he had continued to work at the same time in various psychiatric clinics. There is no reason to assume that he would have ended that double labor after 1961. Whether or not he would have survived in the difficult political climate of Algeria after independence is more problematic. On the basis of experience of other foreigners with comparable political ideas, he would probably have had a difficult time of it in the heady Algerian atmosphere. But then Ben Bella's foreign coterie survived for a time and managed to introduce some serious ideas and institutional innovations before leaving. Fanon would surely have attempted as much although he too might soon have found himself attracted to the opposition groups that were forming even then. If he had written nothing more, it is probable that he would have had the opportunity to compare his own thoughts as expressed in *The Wretched of the Earth* with the demands of independence.

The conception of neutralism was at best an illusion of a possible, coveted isolation from the stresses of the cold war. But the economic imperatives of development, the choice of industrializing or restructuring the nation's agricultural life, were political decisions that had to be made with the national as well as the international stakes in mind. These were not the strongest pages in Fanon's work, yet they represented problems that increasingly concerned him. He understood the predicament of small nations, the need to attack underdevelopment and imperialism globally.[112] But how would he have acted had he been empowered to do so, in Algeria? His attitude towards Europe expressed an ambivalence which was not compatible with the needs which Europe would have to provide. He argued that Algeria and other such nations ought not to imitate Europe. "So, comrades," he wrote, "let us not pay tribute to Europe by creating states, institutions and societies which draw their inspiration from here."[113] But the stamp that Europe had left on Algeria was deeper than even Fanon had realized. Was the issue a false one? Was it essential to break with this past, and was it historically possible? Did returning to authentic roots imply denying what had also become part of the national history, albeit one imposed forcibly from the outside? Was there a confusion here, in Fanon's words, of an existential problem with a political and economic one?

In the post-independence period, Algeria turned to a wide range of states for aid, though she resumed the extraordinary close ties of trade with France that had marked pre-independence history. Fanon might have opposed this choice, and the evidence of his dissatisfaction with the Evian agreements suggests that he understood what was involved. Without speculating on what he might have suggested, it is fair to say that on the basis of *The Wretched of the Earth,* his forte was not a programmatic approach to the problems of underdevelopment or the persistence of economic imperialism. Yet his ability to diagnose the universal characteristics of colonizer and colonized, his unique talent for translating these characteristics into meaningful human terms, allowed him to write from a vantage point few others have approached. He dreamt of a new man and it is a dream that continues to haunt those dissatisfied with existing men. He passionately wished for a world that would free the wretched of the earth, but he was prepared to resist methods that would sacrifice men for future generations. He understood that his own conception of neutralism must somehow be more than a guarantee of permanent poverty. "There is no question of a return to Nature," he wrote. "It is simply a very concrete question of not dragging men towards mutilation, of not imposing upon the brain rhythms which very quickly obliterate it and wreck it. The pretext of catching up must not be used to push man around, to tear him away from himself or from his privacy, to break and kill him."[114] The expression was characteristic of the man, of both the psychiatrist and the revolutionary. Fanon had not abandoned his loyalty to either role and both merged for the same end, for the liberation of man. Colonialism had torn men away from themselves; it had broken the colonized and it had warped the colonizer. The end of colonialism was to witness the birth of the new man. Militant and uncompromising as he was in his beliefs, Fanon was not beyond recognizing that the new dawn was filled with threats that were as capable of breaking and killing men as those of an earlier day. That he did not live to see the aftermath of Algerian independence did not deprive him from understanding as much. And it may have been with this apprehension in mind that he concluded his last testament as he was to conclude his life, with words of unwavering hope. "For Europe, for ourselves and for humanity, we must turn over a new leaf, we must work out new concepts, and try to set afoot a new man." The work remains to be done.

Notes

All references to Fanon's works in the Notes and text are to the American editions of his books. Full information on the original French and American editions are given in the Bibliography.

PART I. IN THE BEGINNING: THE SEARCH FOR ROOTS, 1925–1952

Chapter 1. Biographical Notes to 1952

1. Albert Memmi, *The Colonizer and the Colonized*, trans. H. Greenfeld (New York: Orion Press, 1965), originally published under the title *Portrait du colonisé précédé du portrait du colonisateur* (Paris: Editions Buchet/Chastel, Corrêa, 1957).
2. David Lowenthal, "Race and Color in the West Indies," *Daedalus*, Spring 1967, p. 588.
3. *Ibid.*, p. 597.
4. "West Indians and Africans," *Toward the African Revolution* (New York: Grove Press, Evergreen Books, n.d.), p. 26.
5. Aimé Césaire, "M. Césaire déclare à L'Express," *L'Express*, No. 1037 (May 24–30, 1971), p. 21.
6. Albert Belville, "Perspectives d'avenir des Antilles et de la Guyane," *Partisans*, No. 10 (May–June 1963), pp. 72–86; also see the introductory comments by Marcel Manville on p. 71. The second part of this study appeared in the July–August issue in 1963, pp. 101–121.
7. Jean Lacouture, "Comment peut-on être antillais," *Le Monde*, August 27–September 2, 1970, p. 6.
8. *Toward the African Revolution*, p. 169, etc. The article was reprinted from the January 5, 1960 issue of *el Moudjahid*.
9. "Le processus de libération nationale est engagé," *Révolution Africaine*, No. 383 (June 25–July 1, 1971); dossier No. 30.
10. Peter Geismar, *Fanon* (New York: Dial Press, 1971). Geismar's biography is one of the four studies published on Fanon, along with those of Zahar, Caute, and Bouvier. The Philippe Lucas study, recently published in Algiers by SNED, should be added here although I have not had a chance to consult it. Geismar, more than any other of these authors, however, was interested in writing a biography rather than an analysis of Fanon's work. Nevertheless, he chose to say relatively little on personal matters that had an impact on Fanon and his politics. It is a regrettable omission.
11. The material that follows is taken from interviews with Marcel Manville held in Paris on June 2, 1970, and with Joby Fanon, in Paris, on January 2 and 4, 1971. Except where information is attributed to Manville, it comes from two lengthy conversations with Joby Fanon.

12. *Black Skin, White Masks* (New York: Grove Press, 1967), p. 163, n. 25.
13. In addition to the interviews with Fanon, I met with Professor François Tosquelles on January 4, 1971. As will become apparent in a reading of the text, Tosquelles was a central figure in Fanon's psychiatric training. I am grateful to Professor and Mrs. Tosquelles for the warm reception they accorded me on a cold winter day, and for the nature of our lengthy exchange on Fanon and things Fanonian. All subsequent references to Tosquelles' views on Fanon, except where otherwise indicated, are taken from this interview.
14. Geismar, *Fanon*, p. 11
15. *Ibid.*, pp. 3–4.
16. *Thus Spake Zarathustra*, in *The Portable Nietzsche* (New York: Viking Press, 1954), p. 139.
17. *Black Skin, White Masks*, pp. 102–103.
18. "M. Césaire déclare à *l'Express.*" This is an exposition of Césaire's views in 1971 and, retrospectively, in 1946.
19. Interview with Marcel Manville, June 2, 1970; a conversation on the same subject took place between Manville and Geismar, as quoted in Geismar, *Fanon*, p. 43.
20. Bouvier, *Fanon*, p. 31.
21. A somewhat different account of what transpired is given in Geismar's text, *Fanon*, pp. 47–48, but the essentials of the case are identical.
22. There are some differences on the date of the marriage. According to David Caute, *Fanon* (New York: Viking Press, 1970), p. 99, it occurred in 1953; Tosquelles in our interview recalled, but with some hesitation, that it was in 1953; Geismar, on the other hand (*Fanon*, p. 52), states that it occurred in 1952; Zahar, in *L'Oeuvre de Frantz Fanon* (Paris: François Maspéro, 1970), p. 7, gives October 1952 as the date.
23. The title of Fanon's medical thesis was, "Troubles mentaux et syndromes psychiatriques dans l'hérédo-dégénération spino-cérébelleuse. Un cas de maladie de Friedrich avec délire de possession." Faculté de Médecine, Lyons, 1951–1952.
24. Albert Memmi, "Fanon," *New York Times Book Review*, March 14, 1971, p. 5.
25. Editorial, "The West Indian Nation in Exile," *West Indian Nation in Exile*, 1967, n.p. The conference cited was held at Sir George Williams University in Montreal, and was sponsored by the Caribbean Conference Committee. The citations given are to be found on pp. 2–3 of the editorial statement; no pagination in text.
26. Simone de Beauvoir, *La Force des choses*, Vol. 2 (Paris: Gallimard, 1963), p. 429.
27. Geismar writes that it was in 1946–1947, in Martinique, that Fanon read, "Nietzsche, Karl Jaspers, Kierkegaard, and Hegel. He was particularly impressed with the new works of Jean-Paul Sartre; he began to think about a career in drama" (*Fanon*, p. 43). Zahar suggests that it was after his move to Lyons that he was in touch with the ideas of Jean Lacroix, Merleau-Ponty, Kierkegaard, Nietzsche, Hegel, Marx, Lenin, Husserl, Heidegger, and Sartre. She also notes that in this period he wrote some unpublished plays (*L'Oeuvre de Fanon*, p. 6).

Chapter 2. Conscience and Consciousness: The Relevance of Hegel and Sartre

28. Wilfrid Desan, *The Marxism of Jean-Paul Sartre* (New York: Doubleday & Co., Anchor Books, 1966), p. 27.
29. Mohammed C. Sahli, *Décoloniser l'histoire* (Paris: François Maspéro, 1965); Abdallah Laroui, *L'Idéologie arabe contemporaine* (Paris: Maspéro, 1967); Anouar Abdel-Malek, *Anthologie de la littérature arabe contemporaine* (Paris: Editions du Seuil,

1965); see the "Introduction à la pensée arabe contemporaine." These are not the only writers who use this interpretation of decolonization, but they are among the most eloquent and the most incisive of the contemporary commentators on the subject.

30. The material that follows is largely summarized and paraphrased from the passage on Lordship and Bondage in the J. B. Baillie translation of Hegel, *The Phenomenology of Mind* (New York: Harper & Row, Publishers, Torchbooks, 1967).

31. *Ibid.*, p. 233.

32. *Black Skin, White Masks*, pp. 218–219, n. 6.

33. *Ibid.*, pp. 220–221, n. 8.

34. Hegel, *Phenomenology of Mind*, pp. 236–237.

35. Fanon, *Peau noire, masques blancs* (Paris: Editions du Seuil, 1965), p. 213.

36. See, for instance, the article "Méconnaissance de Fanon" in *Partisans*, June–July–August 1965, pp. 91–92. The editors noted that this article, which was critical of Jeanson, had been sent to them from Algiers, where excerpts had appeared in *Jeunesse FLN*.

37. Josie Fanon, "A propos de Frantz Fanon, Sartre et la racisme et les arabes," *el Moudjahid*, June 10, 1967, p. 6.

38. *Black Skin, White Masks*, p. 138.

39. Jean-Paul Sartre, *Being and Nothingness*, trans. H. Barnes, special abridged ed. (New York: Citadel Press, 1969), pp. 340–341.

40. *Black Skin, White Masks*, pp. 115–116; especially pp. 181–183. "Certain pages of *Anti-Semite and Jew* are the finest that I have ever read. The finest, because the problem discussed in them grips us in our guts" (p. 181). This is followed by a footnote reference to a passage in Sartre's text which emphasized the inauthenticity of the choice offered to the Jew by anti-Semites and condescending liberals. The Sartre passage ends with the following line: "In this situation there is not one of us who is not totally guilty and even criminal; the Jewish blood that the Nazis shed falls on all our heads."

41. Jean-Paul Sartre, *Anti-Semite and Jew*, trans. G. J. Becker (New York: Schocken Books, 1965), pp. 134–135. The original appeared in 1946 under the title *Réflexions sur la question juive* (Paris: Paul Morihien).

42. Irene L. Gendzier, "Reflections on Fanon and the Jewish Question," *New Outlook*, Vol. 12, No. 1 (January 1969), pp. 13–20.

43. *Black Skin, White Masks*, see Chaps. 5 and 6, "The Fact of Blackness" and "The Negro and Psychopathology."

44. Sartre, *Anti-Semite and Jew*, p. 90.

45. *Ibid.*, p. 152.

Chapter 3. *Présence Africaine* and Negritude

46. *Anthologie de la nouvelle poésie nègre et malgache de langue française*, ed. Léopold Sédar-Senghor, preceded by *Orphée noir* by Jean-Paul Sartre (Paris: Presses Universitaires de France, 1948).

47. Lilyan Kesteloot, *Les Ecrivains noirs de langue française: naissance d'une littérature*, Editions de l'Institut de sociologie de l'Université Libre de Bruxelles, 1965.

48. *Orphée noir*, p. xi.

49. *Ibid.*, p. xii.

50. *Ibid.*, p. xli.

51. "La Négritude en question," *Jeune Afrique*, No. 532 (March 16, 1971), p. 65.

52. Kesteloot, *Ecrivains noirs*, p. 26.

53. *Ibid.*, p. 20. Another estimate of the importance of *La Revue du monde noir* is given in Jacques Louis Hymans, "French Influences on Leopold Senghor's Theory of Negritude, 1928–1948," *Race*, Vol. 7, No. 4 (April 1966), p. 366–367.

54. Kesteloot, *Ecrivains noirs*, p. 110.

55. *Ibid.*, p. 111.

56. *Ibid.*, p. 113.

57. Alioune Diop, "Niam N'goura ou les raisons d'être de *Présence Africaine*," *Présence Africaine* (Paris-Daker), No. 1 (October–November 1947), p. 7.

58. Jean-Paul Sartre, "Présence noire," *Présence Africaine*, p. 29.

59. See the article by Maurice Watteau, "Situations raciales et condition de l'homme dans l'oeuvre de J.-P. Sartre," *Présence Africaine*, No. 2 (January 1948), pp. 209–229 (Part 1); for continuation see *ibid.*, No. 3 (March–April 1948), pp. 405–417.

60. Senghor's article entitled "Subir ou choisir" appeared in a special issue, Nos. 8–9, of *Présence Africaine* edited by Th. Monod, pp. 437–443. No date is given. The article by Maghemout Diop, "L'Unique Issue: l'indépendance totale," appeared in the special issue called *Les Etudiants noirs parlent, Présence Africaine*, No. 14 (1952), pp. 145–184.

61. *Toward the African Revolution*, see the article "West Indians and Africans," pp. 17–28.

62. *The Wretched of the Earth*, see the section entitled "On National Culture," pp. 165–199, and especially pp. 188–189.

63. Interview with Mrs. A. Diop at *Présence Africaine*, June 1, 1970.

64. Interview with Reda Malek, May 26, 1970.

65. This information comes from a letter written by Joby Fanon to *Le Monde*, dated March 3, 1969, which answered the accusation by J. Alsop that Frantz Fanon had died in Washington, D.C., in the arms of the CIA. In Joby's letter, the presence of Diop and Holden, and Josie Fanon and her son are mentioned. The allegations of a CIA presence at Fanon's death will be discussed in a later section of this book.

Chapter 4. *Black Skin, White Masks: A Synthesis*

66. Geismar, *Fanon*, p. 50.

67. *Black Skin*, p. 86.

68. *Ibid.*, p. 89, n. 9.

69. *Ibid.*, p. 12.

70. See the excellent anthology compiled by Albert Memmi, *Anthologie des écrivains maghrébins d'expression française* (Paris: Présence Africaine, 1964). David C. Gordon, in *North Africa's French Legacy, 1954–1962*, handles the same problem within a political context. His book was published by Harvard Middle Eastern Monographs in 1964.

71. The cases of Kateb Yacine and Malek Haddad are illustrative of the Algerian dilemma, but these are by no means the only authors to be affected by this situation. Any discussion with contemporary writers in Algeria reveals this to be one of the most sensitive and difficult problems facing the modern state. The intensity with which arabization is pursued, even though it is motivated by political considerations as well, cannot be understood except by an appreciation of what the language problem means. Literacy is extremely limited, and those who have had schooling, until recently, were French-speaking and French-reading as a result. The trend is to change this pattern and to reintroduce Arabic as the language of Algeria. In the interval, however, a genera-

tion of writers and intellectuals who have contributed to the nationalist movement, and who are unreservedly patriotic, nevertheless find themselves unable
to address their fellow compatriots in their own language. This elite is still
French-speaking. The intensity of the problem is different in Morocco and in
Tunisia, largely because French administration in those territories did not
discourage the learning of Arabic to the same extent as it did in Algeria.

72. *Black Skin*, p. 146.
73. *Ibid.*, p. 98.
74. Albert Memmi, *Agar* (Paris: Editions Buchet/Chastel, Corrêa, 1955). See the preface
to the 1963 edition.
75. For another example of the same theme, see the brief discussion of Bertène Juminer's work in Lilyan Kesteloot, *Anthologie négro-africaine* (Belgium: Marabout
University, 1967), pp. 410–412.
76. Mayotte Capecia, *Je suis martiniquaise* (Paris: Editions Corrêa, 1948).
77. *Ibid.*, p. 59.
78. *Black Skin*, pp. 80–81.
79. *Ibid.*, pp. 105–106.
80. *Ibid.*, p. 109.
81. Sartre, *Anti-Semite and Jew*, pp. 53–54.
82. *Black Skin*, pp. 161–181, and throughout sections of the chapter on "The Negro and
Psychopathology"; Joel Kovel, *White Racism: A Psychohistory* (New York: Pantheon Books, 1970); and Winthrop D. Jordan, *White over Black* (Baltimore:
Penguin Books, 1969).
83. Sartre, *Anti-Semite and Jew*, pp. 48–49.
84. "A Note on an Early Ingredient of Racial Prejudice in Western Europe," by G. R.
Dunstan, with a psychiatrist's comment by R. F. Hobson, in *Race*, Vol. 6, No.
4 (April 1965), p. 377.
85. Kovel, *White Racism*, p. 67.
86. *Ibid.*, p. 68.
87. *Black Skin*, p. 177.
88. Roger Bastide, "Dusky Venus, Black Apollo," *Race*, Vol. 3, No. 1 (November 1961),
p. 15.
89. *Ibid.*, p. 18.
90. *Black Skin*, p. 192.
91. *Ibid.*, p. 192.
92. *Ibid.*, p. 197.
93. *Ibid.*, p. 123.
94. *Toward the African Revolution*, p. 27.
95. *Black Skin*, p. 135.
96. *Ibid.*, p. 133–134.
97. *Ibid.*, p. 135.
98. O. Mannoni, *Prospero and Caliban*, trans. P. Powesland (New York: Frederick A.
Praeger, 1964); originally published in Paris under the title *Psychologie de la
colonisation* by Editions du Seuil, 1950.
99. *Ibid.*, p. 170.
100. *Ibid.*, p. 85.
101. *Ibid.*, p. 86.
102. For a discussion by Fanon of the Mannoni thesis, see "The So-Called Dependency
Complex of Colonized Peoples," Chap. 4 in *Black Skin*.

PART II. TOWARD A PSYCHOLOGY OF COLONIAL RELATIONSHIPS, 1953–1959

Chapter 1. A View of Psychiatry and the Nature of Therapy

1. Geismar, *Fanon*, p. 59; Zahar, *L'Oeuvre de Fanon*, p. 7.

2. See, for example, "R. D. Laing and Anti-psychiatry: A Symposium," in *R. D. Laing and Anti-psychiatry, Salmagundi*, No. 16 (Spring 1971), p. 144.

3. See, for instance, Michel Foucault, *Madness and Civilization: A History of Insanity in the Age of Reason*, trans. Richard Howard (New York: Pantheon Books, 1965); the writings of Thomas S. Szasz, especially "Politics and Mental Health," *American Journal of Psychiatry*, Vol. 65 (1958), p. 509; Seymour Halleck, "Therapy Is the Handmaiden of the Status Quo," *Psychology Today*, Vol. 4, No. 11 (April 1971), pp. 30–34, 98–101; David Cooper, *Psychiatry and Anti-psychiatry* (New York: Ballantine Books, 1967); *R. D. Laing and Anti-psychiatry* (see note 2 above), and especially the article by Morton Schatzman, "Madness and Morals," pp. 159–184; Erving Goffman, *Stigma* (Harmondsworth, Middlesex: Penguin Books, n.d.; originally published by Prentice-Hall, New York, 1963); Herbert Marcuse, "Aggressiveness in Advanced Industrial Society," in *Negations: Essays in Critical Theory*, trans. J. Shapiro (Boston: Beacon Press, 1968), pp. 250–254.

4. Geismar, *Fanon*, p. 53.

5. In the summary of the proceedings of the *Congrès des médecins aliénistes et neurologistes de France et des pays de langue française*, 51st session, Pau, July 20–26, 1953, see both the joint article by Tosquelles and Fanon, "Indications de la thérapeutique de Bini dans le cadre des thérapeutiques institutionnelles," pp. 545–552; and "Discussion du rapport de psychiatrie," pp. 101–103.

6. "Indications de la thérapeutique de Bini dans le cadre des thérapeutiques institutionnelles," p. 549.

7. "Quelques Problèmes sur les services généraux et l'organisation hospitalière thérapeutique," by Drs. Tosquelles, Gentis, Bidault, Paillot, and Enkin (of Saint Alban), in the proceedings of the *Congrès des médecins aliénistes et neurologistes de France et des pays de langue française*, 54th session, Bordeaux, August 30–September 4, 1956, pp. 1079–1084.

8. For a discussion of reforms and innovations in psychiatric hospital treatment that bears comparison with the Tosquelles and later Fanon (Blida-Joinville) experiments see the following: the discussion by Erik H. Erikson of the Austen Riggs Center, "Identity and Uprootedness in our Time," in *Insight and Responsibility* (New York: W. W. Norton & Co., 1964), pp. 98–99; David Cooper, *Psychiatry and Anti-psychiatry*, see the chapter on Villa 21; Erving Goffman, *Asylums* (New York: Doubleday & Co., Anchor Books, 1961); for a discussion of Kingsley Hall and a brief discussion of communities set up by the Philadelphia Association under the direction of R. D. Laing, see, respectively, the article by Morton Schatzman cited earlier, "Madness and Morals," in *R. D. Laing and Anti-Psychiatry* (note 2 above), and in the same text, " 'Anti-Psychiatry': An Interview with Dr. Joseph Berke," pp. 185–192. Tosquelles' experiments are developed in his book, *Le Travail thérapeutique à l'hôpital psychiatrique* (Paris: Editions du Scarabée, 1967). See also *Structure et rééducation thérapeutique* (Paris: Editions universitaires, 1970).

9. Tosquelles et al., "Quelques problèmes sur les services généraux et l'organisation hospitalière thérapeutique," p. 1081.

10. "Indications de la thérapeutique de Bini dans le cadre des thérapeutiques institutionnelles," p. 552.

11. Tosquelles, Gentis, Paillot, Bidault, and Enkin, "A quoi peut servir la cour de quartier," pp. 1082–1084.

12. *Ibid.*, p. 1084.

13. Included in the *Congrès des médecins aliénistes et neurologistes de France*, 51st session, 1953, pp. 363–368.

14. *Ibid.*, p. 364.

15. *Ibid.*, p. 363.

16. *Ibid.*, p. 364.

17. *Ibid.*, p. 365.

18. *Ibid.*, p. 368.

19. Fanon, M. Despinoy and W. Zenner (of Saint Alban), "Notes sur les techniques de cures de sommeil avec conditionnement et contrôle électro-encéphalographique," *Congrès des médecins aliénistes et neurologistes de France*, 51st session, 1953, pp. 617–620.

20. Included in the proceedings of the 1953 Congress at Pau, pp. 539–544.

21. *Ibid.*, p. 540.

Chapter 2. Blida-Joinville and the Experiment That Failed

22. Another paper offered at the 1953 Congress at Pau, written by Drs. Despinoy, Fanon, and Zenner, all from Saint Alban, was "Notes sur les techniques de cures de sommeil avec conditionnement et contrôle électro-encéphalographique."

23. Zahar, *L'Oeuvre de Fanon*, p. 7.

24. Geismar, *Fanon*, p. 60.

25. In the fall of 1970 *el Moudjahid* carried three articles containing interviews with doctors from the Mustapha hospital in Algiers. The subject discussed was the hospital crisis, that is, the inadequate facilities in existing hospitals. Psychiatric care was discussed as well. See "L'Hôpital Mustapha: des problèmes . . . mais quelles solutions," Nos. 1–3, in *el Moudjahid*, November 22–23 (p. 4); November 24 (p. 4); November 25 (p. 4). A history and discussion of the current situation at the Psychiatric Hospital at Blida appeared in *el Moudjahid* on December 29 and 30, 1971 ("1 médecin pour 400 malades").

26. *L'Information psychiatrique*, 4th ser., No. 1 (January 1955), pp. 11–18.

27. See the reference to Porot in *The Wretched of the Earth*, pp. 241–244.

28. *L'Information psychiatrique*, 4th ser., No. 1 (January 1955), p. 12.

29. "L'Hospitalisation de jour en psychiatrie, valeurs et limites: 1. Introduction générale; considérations doctrinales en collaboration avec le Dr Geromini," *La Tunisie médicale*, Vol. 38, No. 10 (1959).

30. *L'Information psychiatrique*, 4th ser., No. 9 (October–November 1954), pp. 349–361.

31. This article, according to Geismar, *Fanon*, was "extracted from a longer medical thesis done by Azoulay under Fanon's guidance, *Contributions à l'étude de la socialthérapie dans un service d'aliénés musulmans*, submitted to the Faculté de médecine, University of Algiers, 1954" (p. 84, n.).

32. The material cited here was obtained from interviews and observations made at the Frantz Fanon Psychiatric Hospital in Blida, on December 29, 1970, and in the course of subsequent discussions held in Algiers in the following week. I am grateful to M'hammed Yazid, who was at that time Algerian Ambassador to the United Nations, for his help in arranging the visit to the hospital; and to M. Longo of Blida, for his generosity in time and spirit, in answering the many questions that came up, and for showing me around the quarters of the hospital; and to others, who were welcoming and patient with their foreign guest.

33. Geismar, *Fanon*, p. 64; in "La Socialthérapie dans un service d'hommes musulmans," p. 349, Fanon and Azoulay write that at the time of their arrival, "our four colleagues were responsible for the medical surveillance for more than 600 patients each."

34. In the *New York Times Book Review*, March 14, 1971, p. 5, Memmi claimed as follows: "Furthermore, neither in Algeria nor in Tunisia did he understand the language, so he, like the other foreign doctors, had to hold consultation with his patients through an interpreter. He knew better than anyone what constituted a psychiatric scandal. He came to admit that his hospital reforms were relatively futile because he did not sufficiently take into account the mentality and mores of his patients." One must assume that Memmi was not aware of Fanon's feelings on the question since there was no difference of opinion or attitude between the two men on this matter.

35. "La socialthérapie dans un service d'hommes musulmans," p. 349.

36. *Ibid.*, p. 351.

37. Geismar, *Fanon*, p. 88.

38. "La socialthérapie dans un service d'hommes musulmans," p. 351.

39. *Ibid.*, p. 355.

40. *Ibid.*

41. *Ibid.*, pp. 355–356.

42. *Ibid.*, p. 356.

43. *Ibid.*, p. 358.

44. *Ibid.*

45. According to Geismar, *Fanon*, p. 69, Fanon had a few European allies in the hospital at Blida, Dr. Lacaton and three interns, Sanchez, Geromini, and Azoulay.

46. "Conduites d'aveu en Afrique du Nord," by Fanon and Lacaton, *Congrès des médecins aliénistes et neurologistes de France et des pays de langue française*, 53rd session, Nice, September 5–11, 1955, pp. 657–660.

47. *Ibid.*, p. 659.

48. "L'Attitude du musulman devant la folie," Drs. Frantz Fanon and François Sanchez, *Revue pratique de psychologie de la vie sociale et d'hygiène mentale*, No. 1 (1956), pp. 24–27.

49. *Ibid.*, p. 24.

50. *Ibid.*, pp. 26–27.

Chapter 3. Politics and Medicine: From Algeria to Tunisia

51. Mouloud Feraoun, *Journal 1955–1962* (Paris: Editions du Seuil, 1962), p. 45.

52. Geismar, *Fanon*, pp. 93–94.

53. Bouvier, *Fanon*, p. 49.

54. *A Dying Colonialism*, trans. H. Chevalier (New York: Grove Press, 1st Evergreen ed., 1967), p. 174.

55. *Ibid.*, p. 139, n. 7.

56. See the chapter "Medicine and Colonialism," *ibid.*, pp. 121–145.

57. The article, "The North African Syndrome," is reproduced in the first part of *Toward the African Revolution*.

58. The place and treatment of Algerian workers in France has been the subject of extensive discussion in France and Algeria, particularly since the winter of 1970–1971. There is little doubt that the oil negotiations which eventually broke down between France and Algeria, and which resulted in the decision by President Boumedienne to nationalize 51% of the oil holdings of the country, has increased the tensions between the two governments and peoples. The prospect of French retaliation against Algeria, by the dismissal of the Algerian workers currently in France, has put the migrant worker in a vulnerable position. An excellent account of the more general predicament of the foreign

migrant workers in France appeared in "La peur des 'Autres,' " *L'Express*, No. 1037 (May 24–30, 1971), pp. 28–31. In Algeria the press has been waging a campaign to make people aware of the situation. See "Le racisme contre l'émigration algérienne en France," by Wahid ben Azzouz, in *Révolution Africaine*, Nos. 365–366 (February 19–25, February 26–March 4, 1971). *El Moudjahid* has had a series of articles on the same subject, among them, "La Réinsertion: un problème national," May 30–31; "L'Offensive de haine contre les Algériens émigrés en France," June 1.

59. *Toward the African Revolution*, p. 11. This is a subject about which Drs. Fanon, Azoulay, and Sanchez wrote several years later. The unpublished joint study referred to is entitled "Introduction aux troubles de la sexualité chez les nord africains," 1954–1955.

60. *Toward the African Revolution*, p. 12.

61. *Ibid.*, pp. 9–10.

62. *The Wretched of the Earth*, pp. 238–251. There is an important error in the Constance Farrington translation of *The Wretched of the Earth* (New York: Grove Press, 1966), 1st Evergreen ed., 2nd printing. On p. 238, at the beginning of the section on criminality and the Algerians, the text, in translation, reads: "Criminal impulses found in North Africans which have their origin in the National War of Liberation." The original, in the 1961 Maspéro edition of *Les Damnés de la terre*, reads: "De l'impulsivité criminelle du Nord-Africain à la guerre de Libération nationale" (p. 224). Translated, this should read: "From the criminal impulsivity of the North African to the War of National Liberation." The implications of the incorrect translation are the very opposite of what Fanon wished to say.

63. *Ibid.*, p. 242.

64. *Ibid.*, p. 244.

65. Excerpts taken from "Letter to the Resident Minister (1956)," *Toward the African Revolution*, pp. 52–54.

66. From a letter to the author by Bertène Juminer, November 16, 1971.

67. Geismar, *Fanon*, p. 132, writes: "Although he had no taste for pseudonyms, Fanon worked at Manouba under the name of Dr. Fares. He followed normal FLN procedure in the matter."

68. This was substantiated in conversations with Reda Malek in Paris on May 26, 1970. Malek recalled that Fanon was not liked at the Tunisian clinic, Manouba, principally because he upset things when he arrived and angered the director of the hospital. The same director is still at the hospital, or was at the time of the interview. This sentiment is endorsed in the account given by Geismar, *Fanon*, in the chapter "The Oxygen of Revolution," which deals with Fanon's medical work in Tunisia.

One of the more interesting stories of Fanon's difficulties at Manouba concerns the accusations leveled against him by the director of the clinic, Ben Soltan. Geismar writes that Ben Soltan was anxious to get rid of Fanon and since he could not do it for professional reasons, Fanon's work being generally highly respected, he manufactured political reasons. "In 1959, the director accused Fanon of being an undercover agent spying on both the Tunisians and Algerians for the state of Israel. He was to be ousted from the hospital as a Zionist and a threat to Tunisia's internal security. . . . The dossier against Fanon maintained that he was part of a Jewish clique in the hospital that was continually having secret meetings" (p. 139). Manville noted that Fanon had had many Jewish colleagues, both in Paris and in North Africa. With reference to the accusations, however, the Tunisian Minister of Health dismissed them, against the will of Ben Soltan.

69. "L'Hospitalisation de jour en psychiatrie, valeurs et limites." Fanon wrote the general introduction and the two doctors collaborated on the doctrinal section. The material that follows in the text is taken from these two parts of the article.

70. *The Wretched of the Earth*, p. 206. For the entire section on "Colonial War and Mental Disorders," see pp. 203–251.

71. Dr. Paul Adams, "The Social Psychiatry of Frantz Fanon," *American Journal of Psychiatry*, Vol. 127, No. 6 (December 1970), p. 112.

72. *The Wretched of the Earth*, p. 205.

73. *Ibid.*, p. 215.

74. *Ibid.*, p. 220.

75. *Ibid.*, p. 221. For a recent example of a situation which bears some similarity, see the article "Belfast Children Found Deeply Disturbed by Violence," *New York Times*, March 14, 1971, p. 3, which discusses the work of a Scottish psychiatrist, Dr. Morris Fraser, in the context of the struggle taking place in Northern Ireland. For other testimony by children 10–14 years of age, see G. Pirelli and P. Kessel, *Le Peuple algérien et la guerre, lettres et témoignages d'Algériens, 1959–1962* (Paris: François Maspéro, 1962), pp. 109–111.

Chapter 4. From Psychological Observation to Political Action

76. Albert Memmi, *The Colonizer and the Colonized* (New York: Orion Press, 1965). Memmi discussed Fanon in his book *Dominated Man* (Boston: Beacon Press, 1968); see the chapter "Frantz Fanon and the Notion of 'Deficiency.'"

77. *Ibid.*, p. 85.

78. *A Dying Colonialism*, p. 47.

79. *Ibid.*

80. See the article "Frantz Fanon et la révolution algérienne," *el Moudjahid*, March 20, 1971, p. 3; and "Fanon et la pensée occidentale," Mohammed Amghar, *el Moudjahid culturel*, June 2, 1971.

81. Bouvier, *Fanon*, p. 49.

PART III. THE MILITANT, 1956–1961

Chapter 1. The Travail of Independence

1. Germaine Tillion, *France and Algeria, Complementary Enemies* (New York: Alfred A. Knopf, 1961), p. 133.

2. *Ibid.*, p. 135.

3. See Edward Behr, *The Algerian Problem* (Harmondsworth, Middlesex: Penguin Books, 1961), p. 51.

4. P. Kessel et G. Pirelli, *Le Peuple algérien et la guerre. Lettres et témoignages d'Algériens, 1954–1962* (Paris: François Maspéro, 1962), p. 33.

5. William B. Quandt, *Revolution and Political Leadership: Algeria, 1954–1968* (Cambridge, Mass.: MIT Press, 1969).

6. Quoted in "Sept ans de lutte," *el Moudjahid*, Vol. 3, No. 91 (March 19, 1962), p. 713. The wartime issues of *el Moudjahid* cited here are part of the special Yugoslav edition printed in three volumes in 1962. They are incomplete, in that several issues were not found at the time of publication. This author was told that the complete set of *el Moudjahid* remains in a few private hands and has not been available to the public at large or even to the Bibliothèque nationale in Algiers. In the present text, the *el Moudjahid* articles will be identified by the volumes of this series (Yugoslavia, 1962).

7. "Nos positions," *el Moujahid*, Vol. 3, No. 9 (March 9), p. 682. Extract from the November 1, 1954 tract.

8. "Sept ans de lutte," *el Moujahid*, Vol. 3, No. 91 (March 19, 1962), p. 713.

9. As quoted in C. S. Maier and D. S. White, eds., *The Thirteenth of May: The Advent of de Gaulle's Republic* (New York: Oxford University Press, 1968), p. 74.

10. *Ibid.*, p. 79.

11. *Ibid.*, p. 98.

12. Tillion, *France and Algeria*, Chap. 2.

13. Maier and White, *The Thirteenth of May*, p. 102, See also the article by Jacques Soustelle, "The Wealth of the Sahara," in *Foreign Affairs*, July 1959.

14. See the account by Paul Henissart, *Wolves in the City* (New York: Simon & Schuster, 1970).

15. I refer to the Editions de Minuit editions, Henri Alleg, *La Question* (Paris, 1958); Georges Arnaud and Jacques Vergès, *Pour Djamila Bouhired* (1957); Pierre Vidal-al-Naquet, *L'Affaire Audin* (1958); *La Gangrène*, (1959).

16. Henissart, *Wolves in the City*, p. 46.

17. "Déclaration générale," *el Moudjahid*, Vol. 3, No. 91 (March 19, 1962), p. 706.

18. *Ibid.*, p. 717.

Chapter 2. A Committed Press: *el Moudjahid*.

19. From an interview with Dr. Mohamed el Mili, Director of Information in the Ministry of Culture and Information, August 12, 1971.

20. As cited in David C. Gordon, *The Passing of French Algeria* (New York: Oxford University Press, 1966), p. 122, n. 34.

21. "Frantz Fanon, notre frère," *el Moudjahid*, Vol. 3, No. 88 (December 21, 1961), p. 647.

22. Geismar, *Fanon*, pp. 93–94.

23. Mohamed Lebjaoui, *Vérités sur la révolution algérienne* (Paris: Gallimard, 1970), pp. 239–240. See Bouvier, *Fanon*, p. 49, for mention of Mandouze and his relation with Fanon.

24. Lebjaoui, *Vérités*, p. 239.

25. Bouvier, *Fanon*, pp. 63–64.

26. "Un exemple toujours vivant," *el Moudjahid*, Vol. 3, No. 88 (December 21, 1961), p. 648.

27. *Peau noire, masques blancs* (Paris: Editions du Seuil, 1965), p. 213.

28. I have not seen any articles written by Fanon for *Résistance algérienne*, or references to such articles in any detailed fashion. It would be a useful task for those in possession of the necessary information to analyze that periodical in the same way that *el Moudjahid* was reviewed, in order to discover Fanon's contributions.

29. Interview with Dr. el Mili, August 12, 1971.

30. "La famille algérienne dans la révolution," *el Moudjahid*, Vol. 2, Nos. 53–54 (November 1959), pp. 543–545.

31. "Accra: L'Afrique affirme son unité et definit sa stratégie," *el Moudjahid*, Vol. 11, No. 34 (December 24, 1958), pp. 114–115.

32. "Culture nationale et guerre de libération," *el Moudjahid*, Vol. 2, No. 39 (April 10, 1959), pp. 220–222.

33. Interview with Dr. Mohamed el Mili, August 12, 1971.

34. Interview with M'hammed Yazid, September 11, 1970.

35. *Toward the African Revolution*, pp. 64–72.

36. *Ibid.*, pp. 73–75.

37. *Ibid.*, pp. 70–71.

38. This sentiment emerged in numerous conversations in Algiers, with officials of the Party as well as government. It is apparent in an indirect way in the material

el Moudjahid published on the role of the French left. It is analyzed later in this section.

39. See, for instance, *Toward the African Revolution*, pp. 158–162.

40. *Ibid.*, pp. 106–112; 120–126. In *The Wretched of the Earth*, see the first two sections, "Concerning Violence" and "Violence in the International Context."

41. *Toward the African Revolution*, pp. 144–149.

42. See, for example, *el Moudjahid*, Vol. 1, No. 16 (January 15, 1958), p. 286 ("JFK and Mansfield"); Vol. 3, No. 73 (November 24, 1960), pp. 316–318 ("Les 3 visages de M. John Kennedy").

43. *Toward the African Revolution*, pp. 108–109.

44. *Ibid.*, p. 110.

Chapter 3. The French Left and Algeria

45. The three articles written by Fanon on this subject have been combined in the section entitled, "French Intellectuals and Democrats and the Algerian Revolution," in *Toward the African Revolution*, pp. 76–90.

46. *Ibid.*, p. 76.

47. *Ibid.*, p. 78.

48. *Ibid.*, pp. 87–88.

49. *Ibid.*, p. 83.

50. *Ibid.*, p. 88.

51. "L'Algérie n'est pas la France," *Les Temps Modernes*, No. 119, November 1955, pp. 577–579.

52. *Ibid.*, p. 615.

53. See the editorial, "Pouvoirs 'spéciaux,' " *ibid.*, No. 123, March–April 1956, pp. 1345–1353.

54. Jean-Paul Sartre, "Le colonialisme est un systeme," *ibid.*, p. 1371.

55. *Ibid.*, p. 1386.

56. *La Question* (Paris: Editions de Minuit, 1958), p. 111.

57. "A propos du Manifeste des 121," *Les Temps Modernes*, Nos. 175–176, October–November 1960, pp. 671–672.

58. "De la violence," *Les Temps Modernes*, No. 181, May 1961, pp. 27–70.

59. "A propos de la génération algérienne," *Partisans*, No. 1, September–October 1961, p. 147.

60. See the response of Ahmed Taleb, for example, "Conférence sur Camus," *Discours du Ministre de l'Education Nationale*, Vol. 2, 1967–1968, Algiers, pp. 29–64; and by the same author, the letter dated Fresnes, June 10, 1959, in *Lettres de prison, 1957–1961*, pp. 59–60.

61. As quoted in Conor Cruise O'Brien, *Camus* (London: Collins, Fontana), p. 75.

62. *Ibid.*, p. 85.

63. Bouvier, in *Fanon*, pp. 67–68, discusses some of the reactions to Fanon's articles, "Les réactions sont très violentes. Dans 'France-Observateur', organe, avec 'L'Express', des démocrates et progressistes français, G. Martinet ne mâche pas ses mots." Bouvier cites articles by Martinet in *France Observateur*, January 2 and 9, 1958, and notes that a substantial correspondence followed the exchange. The brief article in *el Moudjahid* that dealt with the reaction to the articles on the French left was "Après la réponse de France-Observateur,' " *el Moudjahid*, Vol. 1, No. 16 (January 15, 1958).

64. See for instance, "Des universitaires français prennent position sur le problème algérien," *el Moudjahid*, Vol. 1, No. 21 (April 1, 1958), pp. 395–400.

65. "Les déserteurs," *el Moudjahid*, Vol. 3, No. 64 (May 12, 1960), p. 84.

66. *Ibid.*, p. 85.

67. "Le réveil de l'intelligence française," *el Moudjahid*, Vol. 3, No. 79 (September 25, 1960), p. 231.

68. "Ou en est la gauche française," *el Moudjahid*, Vol. 3, No. 73 (November 24, 1960), pp. 309–310.

69. *el Moudjahid*, Vol. 3, No. 87 (November 22, 1961), pp. 625–626.

70. "Le parti communiste français face à la révolution algérienne," *el Moudjahid*, Vol. 1, No. 21 (April 1, 1958), p. 401.

71. *Toward the African Revolution*, p. 82.

72. "Culture nationale et guerre de libération," *el Moudjahid*, Vol. 2, No. 39 (April 10, 1959), p. 222.

73. "La politique internationale des blocs et la guerre d'Algérie," *el Moudjahid*, Vol. 1, No. 20 (March 15, 1958), p. 380.

74. *Ibid.*

Chapter 4. The Minority Question

75. Ya'akov Firestone, "The Doctrine of Integration with France Among the Europeans of Algeria, 1955–1960," *Comparative Political Studies*, July 1971, p. 181. On the situation of the Europeans, see the excellent work by Pierre Nora, *Les Français d'Algérie* (Paris: Julliard, 1961).

76. The position of Dr. Mohamed el Mili, expressed in the interview of August 12, 1971, was that Fanon did not know Ramdane at all. G. Pirelli, who knew Fanon and had close experience with the Revolution, claims that Ramdane was a friend and model for Fanon, *Fanon*, Estratto da 'I Protagonisti', Vol. 14 (Milan: Compagnia Edizioni Internazionali Milano), p. 394.

77. For a discussion of this as seen in 1955, see Colette and Francis Jeanson, *L'Algérie hors la loi* (Paris: Editions du Seuil, 1955), Part 4, Ch. 4, "La Faucille et le croissant"; and for contrast, the description of Algeria in *The Algerian Revolution*, published by the Organization for Afro-Asian Solidarity, Cairo, n. d., p. 3.

78. See the section, "The Colonizer Who Refuses," in Part 1, "Portrait of the Colonizer," in the 1965 edition by the Orion Press, New York. Also see Nora, *ibid.*, Chap. 5 on this issue.

79. Fanon's discussion of this question appears in *A Dying Colonialism*, Chap. 5, "Algeria's European Minority."

80. *Ibid.*, p. 152.

81. "Extraits de la plate-forme," *el Moudjahid*, Vol. 1, special issue, No. 4, *Editions Résistance algérienne*, pp. 70–71.

82. *Ibid.*, p. 70.

83. *Ibid.*

84. *Ibid.*, p. 63.

85. "Les minorités en Algérie," *el Moudjahid*, Vol. 2, No. 50 (September 14, 1959), p. 451.

86. *Ibid.*, p. 452.

87. *Ibid.*, p. 453.

88. "Le FLN et la question de la minorité européenne," *el Moudjahid*, Vol. 3, No. 77 (January 29, 1961), p. 396.

89. *Ibid.*

90. Reprinted as Document No. 61-9-E in "Perspectives for a Settlement in Algeria," issued by the Algerian Office, New York City, 1961.

91. "Le FLN et la question de la minorité europeene," *el Moudjahid*, p. 399.

92. "Les Accords franco-algériens," *el Moudjahid*, Vol. 3, No. 90 (March 9, 1962), p. 689.

93. *Ibid.*

94. *A Dying Colonialism*, pp. 153–157.

95. *Ibid.*, pp. 156–157.
96. *Ibid.*, p. 157.
97. *Ibid.*, p. 157.
98. Michael R. Marrus, *The Politics of Assimilation* (Oxford: Clarendon Press, 1971), p. 234.
99. For a discussion of Algerian Jews see Michel Ansky, *Les Juifs d'Algérie: du décret Crémieux à la libération* (Paris: u.p., 1950); André Chouraqui, *Between East and West: a History of the Jews of North Africa*, trans. M. B. Bernet (Philadelphia: Jewish Publication Society, 1968); a sympathetic account is given in the article by André Serfati, "Juif Algérien," *Partisans*, February 3, 1962, pp. 68–77; an attempt to analyze the Jewish response to the Algerian problem was presented by Marcel Liebman, "Les juifs devant le problème algérien," *Les Temps Modernes*, No. 180 (April 1961), pp. 1328–1342; the American Jewish Committee issued a statement on "French Jewry Today—the Impact of North African Immigration," in October 1966, that was the logical continuation of its earlier study, "The Jews in North Africa: Current Situation," October 1963. In addition to the Algerian sources cited in the text see Lebjaoui, *op. cit.* Ch. 8.
100. "Les minorités en Algérie," *el Moudjahid*, Vol. 2, No. 50, p. 452.
101. "Appel de la fédération de France du FLN," *el Moudjahid*, Vol. 2, No. 59 (February 5, 1960), p. 644–645.
102. Liebman, "Les juifs devant le problème algérien," p. 1337.
103. A.R. Abdel-Kader, *Le conflit judéo-arabe* (Paris: François Maspéro, 1962), p. 373.
104. The official handbook, *Algérie: Quelques données économiques et sociales repertoire des organismes officials*, cites the number of Jews in Algeria as three to four thousand (p. 11), (Algiers: SNED, 1964).

Chapter 5. The Maghreb and Africa

105. G. Pirelli, *Fanon*, p. 394.
106. "Un exemple toujours vivant," p. 649.
107. *Toward the African Revolution*, p. 94.
108. "Pétrole maghrébin et visées impérialistes," *el Moudjahid*, Vol. 1, No. 28 (August 22, 1958), pp. 557–560; "Les capitaux et les investissements dans le maghreb arabe," *el Moudjahid*, Vol. 1, No. 29 (September 17, 1958), pp. 591–592.
109. See pp. 113–143 in *Toward the African Revolution* for Fanon's *el Moudjahid* articles on African politics exemplified by Houphouet-Boigny, for instance, and those who cooperated with France.
110. *Ibid.*, pp. 192–193.
111. *Ibid.*, p. 197.
112. "Le Congo et l'Algérie," *el Moudjahid*, Vol. 3, No. 68 (August 5, 1960), p. 166.
113. *Toward the African Revolution*, p. 156.
114. *Ibid.*, p. 187.
115. *Ibid.*, pp. 185–186.
116. "Revolutionary Theories," *Monthly Review*, Vol. 21, No. 1 (May 1969), pp. 30–31.
117. *Toward the African Revolution*, p. 179.
118. *Ibid.*, p. 188.
119. *Ibid.*, p. 187.

Part IV. The Summing Up: *The Wretched of the Earth*

Chapter 1. The Question of Violence

1. Belkacem Krim in his eulogy at Fanon's burial suggested this connection; see "Un Exemple toujours vivant," *el Moudjahid*, Vol. 3, No. 88 (December 21, 1961), p. 649.

2. Geismar, *Fanon*, p. 143.

3. Juminer letter to author dated November 16, 1961.

4. Simone de Beauvoir, *La Force des choses*, Vol. 2 (Paris: Gallimard, 1963), p. 425.

5. *Ibid.*, pp. 429–30.

6. The contrast between the view presented by Dr. Mohamed el Mili in the August 12, 1971 interview, to the effect that Fanon did not know Abane Ramdane, and the statement by G. Pirelli, which suggests the opposite, is less mysterious than it might first appear to be. The implications of a friendship would make Fanon's remarks about his, Ramdane's, death that much more pointed, and it would place his own political situation in a different perspective, as I have pointed out later in the text. Between the expression of el Mili and that of Pirelli, I have no hesitation in accepting the latter if only because the political interests at stake in el Mili's remarks appear to have much to do with his statement. This is generally characteristic of what I refer to as the "official position" heard in Algeria today on the role of Fanon in the revolutionary period and hierarchy.

    Pirelli writes as follows: "È degli inizi di quest'anno un grave episodio: l'uccisione, per mane di alcuni esponenti dell'FLN, di uno dei maggiore esponenti rivoluzionari, Abane Ramdane. Fanon, che aveva in lui un grande amico e maestro, deve rendersi corresponsabile, per disciplina rivoluzionaria, della compilazione di una falsa versione della morte di Ramdane, publicata in 'El Moudjahid'." Pirelli, *Fanon*, p. 394.

7. *The Wretched of the Earth*, p. 33. In the same section, Fanon had written: "In the colonies the economic substructure is also a superstructure. The cause is the consequence; you are rich because you are white, you are white because you are rich. This is why Marxist analysis should always be slightly stretched every time we have to do with the colonial problem. Everything up to and including the very nature of precapitalist society, so well explained by Marx, must here be thought out again" (p. 32–33).

8. *Ibid.*, pp. 73–74.

9. Hannah Arendt, *On Violence* (New York: Harcourt, Brace & World, 1969), p. 71.

10. Interview with Marcel Manville, June 2, 1970; Reda Malek, May 26, 1970.

11. *The Wretched of the Earth*, p. 51.

12. Zahar, *L'Oeuvre de Fanon*, p. 92.

13. See the discussion in Caute, *Fanon*, p. 86, and Sorel, *Reflections on Violence*, trans. T. E. Hulme (London: Collier-Macmillan Ltd., Collier Books, 1950).

14. Zahar, *L'Oeuvre de Fanon*, p. 86.

Chapter 2. Peasants, Parties, and Spontaneity

15. Nguyen Nghe, "Frantz Fanon et les problèmes de l'indépendance," *La Pensée*, No. 107 (February 1963), pp. 23–36.

16. *Ibid.*, p. 27.

17. Worsley, "Revolutionary Theories," p. 45.

18. *The Wretched of the Earth*, p. 88. The following material is drawn from the section "Spontaneity: Its Strength and Weakness," pp. 85–117.

19. *Ibid.*, p. 88.
20. Nguyen Nghe, "Frantz Fanon et les problèmes de l'indépendance," p. 29.
21. *The Wretched of the Earth*, p. 108.
22. *Ibid.*, p. 114.
23. *Ibid.*
24. *Ibid.*, p. 115.
25. Nguyen Nghe, "Frantz Fanon et les problèmes de l'indépendance," p. 30.
26. *Ibid.*, p. 32.
27. Zahar, *L'Oeuvre de Fanon*, pp. 100–101.
28. *Ibid.*, p. 103.
29. *Ibid.*, p. 105.
30. "Coexistence pacifique et 'tiers monde,' " pamphlet published by *Révolution socialiste* (Algiers, August 1970), p. 15.
31. M. Pablo, "Où va la révolution algérienne," *IVe internationale*, March 1963, p. 27.
32. "La révolution algérienne à l'heure des options décisives," *IVe Internationale*, July 1962, p. 3.
33. Robin Buss, *Wary Partners: The Soviet Union and Arab Socialism*, Adelphi Papers, No. 73, The Institute for Strategic Studies, December 1970, p. 22.
34. As cited in "Les Principes de base du parti communiste chinois," *Partisans*, No. 16 (June–July–August 1964), p. 32.
35. E. Che Guevara, *La Guerre de Guérilla*, trans. G. Chaliand and J. Minces (Paris: François Maspéro, 1967).
36. Régis Debray, *Revolution in the Revolution?* trans. B. Ortiz (New York: Grove Press, 1967).
37. François Maspéro, in an interview on May 27, 1970, mentioned the fact that Guevara had planned to write a book on Fanon before he was killed.
38. Debray, *Revolution*, p. 110.

Chapter 3. The Bourgeoisie, the Party, and the Nation

39. Nguyen Nghe, "Frantz Fanon et les problèmes de l'indépendance," p. 31.
40. François Bondy, in "The Black Rousseau," *New York Review of Books*, March 31, 1966, wrote that "Ahmed Ben Bella was perhaps, in his way, the only 'Fanonist' leader. Nearly two years ago he told David Rousset and myself that only peasants, not city workers, should be trusted as revolutionaries, and that the Party should be independent enough to control the State. This is pure Fanonism. . . ." David Gordon, in *The Passing of French Algeria* (New York: Oxford University Press, 1966), p. 128, n. 40, quotes a speech of Ben Bella given in Blida on December 26, 1963, in which Ben Bella referred to Fanon's "testament spirituel et politique" and the "doctrine qui garantit la révolution algérienne."

Chapter 4. National Culture

41. It is published in *Présence Africaine*, Nos. 24–25 (February–May 1959), as "Fondement réciproque de la culture nationale et des luttes de libération," pp. 82–89. It was subsequently reprinted as the second essay in the section "On National Culture," in *The Wretched of the Earth*.
42. See *La Culture africaine*, le symposium d'alger, July–August 1969, SNED; the articles by René Depestre, "Les fondements socio-culturels de notre identité," and by Joseph Ki-Zerbo, "Positions et propositions pour une néo-culture africaine."

43. *The Wretched of the Earth*, p. 198.

44. *Ibid.*, p. 170.

45. *Ibid.*, p. 171–172.

46. *Ibid.*, p. 173.

47. *Ibid.*, p. 174.

48. *Ibid.*, p. 189, n. 1.

Chapter 5. Fanon's Death and His Influence on the Algerian Revolution

49. Geismar, *Fanon*, p. 178.

50. See for instance, Alsop's letter to the editor of the *New Statesman* published on January 30, 1970, p. 150.

51. Letter to the author from the Department of Health, Education, and Welfare, Public Health Service, National Institutes of Health, Bethesda, Maryland, January 29, 1971.

52. Richard and Joan Brace, *Algerian Voices* (Princeton, N.J.: D. Van Nostrand Co., 1965), p. 130.

53. The material chosen for citation in *el Moudjahid* was taken from the section on the party and the masses in *The Wretched of the Earth*.

54. "Les damnés de la terre," *el Moudjahid*, Vol. 3, No. 88 (December 21, 1961), p. 649.

55. *Ibid.*, p. 647.

56. *Ibid.*, pp. 647–648.

57. *Ibid.*, p. 649.

58. "Algerian Exile Found Murdered," *New York Times*, October 21, 1970, p. 8.

59. William Walling, "Algerian Cinema to Give Them New Faces," *Africa Report*, June 1971, p. 29.

60. Irene Gendzier, "Frantz Fanon: In Search of Justice," *Middle East Journal*, Autumn 1966, pp. 541–542.

61. Caute, *Fanon*, p. 55.

62. Zahar, *L'Oeuvre de Fanon*, p. 13.

63. *Ibid.*, p. 14.

64. *Ibid.*, p. 15.

65. Interview with Jean Daniel, May 26, 1970.

66. Interview with Joby Fanon, January 4, 1971.

67. Several Algerians, who wish to remain anonymous, have claimed that they recall this.

68. Dr. Mohamed el Mili is the author of three articles dealing with Fanon and Algeria. The first, entitled, "Fanon and Western Thought," appeared in the March 1971 issue of *al Thaqafa*, pp. 10–25; the second, "The Algerian Revolution and Fanon" appeared in the May 1971 issue of the same periodical, pp. 40–54; and the third, "The Algerian Roots of Fanon's Thought," was also published in *al Thaqafa*, November 1971, pp. 22–45.

69. "L'Oeuvre de Fanon aujourd'hui," *Algérie-Actualité*, December 5–11, 1971, contains a number of articles and bibliographical studies of Fanon. Malek Alloula's article, "L'Oeuvre de Fanon aujourd'hui," and that by Dr. Abdelghani Megherbi, "Frantz Fanon apôtre de la non-violence," are the two main pieces.

70. Kaddour M'hamsadji, "Sociologie de Frantz Fanon," *el Moudjahid*, January 14, 1972.

71. Megherbi, "Frantz Fanon apôtre de la non-violence," p. 19.

72. "Frantz Fanon et la révolution algérienne," *el Moudjahid*, March 20, 1971, p. 3. This is a review of the talk given at the Mouggar auditorium by el Mili.

73. *Ibid.*

74. The first article in the series (cited above in note 68), was reviewed in brief and published in *el Moudjahid Culturel* by Mohammed Amghar under the title "Athaqafa, Fanon et la pensée occidentale," p. 5.

75. Interview with Dr. el Mili, August 12, 1971.

76. From an interview with an official who knew Fanon during the war period and recalled seeing him in action lecturing to the military. Anonymity requested.

77. This appears in el Mili's last article, "The Algerian Roots of Fanon's Thought," p. 43.

78. Interview with Dr. el Mili, August 12, 1971.

79. Interview with Joby Fanon, January 2, 1971.

80. Interview with Dr. el Mili, August 12, 1971.

81. Pirelli, *Fanon*, p. 394. In the book published by Pierre Bouvier on Fanon, the author cites an article by Josie Fanon in which she describes the people whom Fanon protected at Blida. She mentions members of the CCE, military officials of the region, and others. Bouvier adds, "Parmi les dirigeants, Abane Ramdane, Ben Khedda" (p. 54).

82. William Quandt, *Revolution and Political Leadership: Algeria, 1954–1968* (Cambridge, Mass.: MIT Press, 1969), p. 130.

83. *Ibid.*, p. 131.

84. Geismar, *Fanon*, p. 179.

85. "Le programme de Tripoli," published by the Communist Party International, French section of the 4th International; supplement to "L'Internationale," No. 129, and to "Quatrième Internationale," October 1962; see especially the section entitled "L'ALN. 'Fer de lance' de la révolution."

86. *Ibid.*, p. 39.

87. *Ibid.*

88. *Ibid.*, p. 40.

89. There is another brief reference to this association of Fanon with the *État Major* in the Jeanson postface quoted earlier. Jeanson wrote of Fanon on his way to Tunis, "en transit pour Tunis, où il allait rejoindre l'état major politico-militaire de la Révolution algérienne." "Reconnaissance de Fanon," *Peau noire, masques blancs,* p. 213. This is in the 1965 Seuil edition.

90. Fanon's writing on Algerian women and the Revolution in *A Dying Colonialism* is a highly optimistic portrait of what occurred in the Algerian family. While the changes described may have occurred at the time of the Revolution, the changes in Algerian society in regard to this subject were not lasting. This remains a sensitive and complex subject which nevertheless ought to be studied. The book which may be considered a first and dynamic step in this direction is that by Fadela M'rabet, *La Femme algérienne*, followed by *Les Algériennes*, published in one book by François Maspéro, Paris, 1969.

91. See the pamphlet "L'Algérie qui se cherche," by Daniel Guerin (Paris: Présence Africaine, 1964), pp. 76–77, for a discussion of the revival of Islam in the state.

92. "L'Algérie, les Français et l'arabisme," *Jeune Afrique*, No. 109 (November 19–25, 1962), p. 8.

Chapter 6. For Further Study

93. Bondy, "The Black Rousseau," *op. cit.*

94. Letter to the author, November 16, 1971.

95. *Black Skin, White Masks*, p. 221.

96. *The Wretched of the Earth*, p. 174.

97. *Ibid.*

98. *Ibid.*, pp. 174–175.

99. For a reference to Cleaver and Fanon, see Maxwell Geismar's introduction to *Soul on Ice* (New York: McGraw-Hill Book Co., 1970).

100. William H. Grier and Price Cobbs, *Black Rage* (New York: Bantam Books, 1969).

101. Horace Sutton, "Fanon," *Saturday Review of Literature*, July 17, 1971, pp. 16–19, 59–61. The quote is from p. 16.

102. As cited in Eldridge Cleaver, *Post-Prison Writings and Speeches* (New York: Vintage Books, 1969), p. 18.

103. *Conversation with Eldridge Cleaver* (New York: Dell Pub. Co., Delta Books, 1970), pp. 90–91.

104. Ania Francos, "Une Interview inédite d'Eldridge Cleaver, Ministre de l'Information en exil du Black Panther Party: la sale histoire des Etats-Unis," *Front*, No. 1 (Paris, September 1969), p. 31.

105. Sutton, "Fanon," p. 59; also, Gene Marine, *The Black Panthers* (New York: New American Library, Signet Books, 1969), pp. 31–32.

106. Letter to the author by David C. Gordon, February 12, 1971.

107. G. Chaliand, *La Résistance palestinenne* (Paris: Editions de Seuil, 1970), p. 11.

108. "The Palestinian Revolution: 'al-Fateh': Origins and Strategies," by H. I. Hussaini, pp. 14–15.

109. Letter to the author from Yusuf A. Sayigh, March 4, 1971.

110. *Free Palestine*, Vol. 2, No. 3 (July 1970).

111. It may be of interest, though not directly relevant to the uses made of Fanon by some of the Palestinian Resistance, that in 1967, on June 10, *el Moudjahid* ran an article written by Josie Fanon expressing her distaste for Sartre's position during the June War. She urged that his preface to *The Wretched of the Earth* be removed from forthcoming editions of Fanon's work. The article was an occasion for an attack on the position of the left in France, with reference to the Algerian Revolution and the June War. ("A propos de Frantz Fanon, Sartre, le racisme et les arabes.")

112. "Sur un premier bilan du fanonisme," Robert Paris, *Partisans*, No. 8 (January–February 1963). This is a review article of Enrico Coletti Pischel's "Fanonismo e'questione coloniale, Problema del socialismo."

113. *The Wretched of the Earth*, p. 255.

114. *Ibid.*, p. 254.

115. Nguyen Nghe, "Frantz Fanon et les problèmes de l'indépendance," p. 34.

Bibliography

The material that follows includes Fanon's works and a brief listing of the books published about him. Articles and other relevant references may be found in the Notes.

I. WORKS BY FANON

A. Unpublished material

"Conférence sur les catégories de l'humanisme moderne" [Lecture on the categories of modern humanism], unedited text of a conference held at Blida, 1955. This is cited by Renate Zahar only. I have not seen references to it, but it may be in the library of the hospital at Blida. Use of the library was restricted on those occasions when I was in Blida, although in principle it is open with permission of the director.

"Introduction aux troubles de la sexualité chez les nords africains" [Introduction to sexual problems among North Africans], written in collaboration with Drs. Azoulay and F. Sanchez, 1954–1955.

Several plays were written by Fanon in the period 1949–1950:

    Les Mains parallèles [Parallel Hands]
    L'Oeil se noie [The Drowning Eye]
    La Conspiration [Conspiracy]

B. Published articles and papers dealing with psychiatric work

Most of the items here were written as collaborative efforts. They are listed according to the periodicals in which they appeared. Additional material, by way of notes, may be found in the hospital library at Blida, according to local doctors.

Les Annales médico-psychologiques, Vol. 2 (June 1953), 51st session, Pau, 1953.

    "A propos d'un cas de syndrome de Cotard avec balancement psychosomatique" [Concerning a case of the Cotard syndrome with psychosomatic fluctuation], with Dr. Despinoy.

Congrès des médecins aliénistes et neurologistes de France et des pays de langue française [Congress of institutional psychiatrists and neurologists of France and French-speaking countries], 51st session, Pau, July 20–26, 1953.

    "Sur quelques cas traités par la méthode de Bini" [On several cases treated according to the Bini method], with Dr. F. Tosquelles.

"Indications de thérapeutique de Bini dans le cadre des thérapeutiques institutionnelles" [Notes on Bini therapy in the context of institutional therapy], with Dr. F. Tosquelles.

"Sur un essai de réadaption chez une malade avec épilepsie morphéique et troubles de caractère graves" [On an attempt at readaptation in the case of a patient suffering from narcolepsy and serious character disorders], with Dr. F. Tosquelles.

"Notes sur les techniques de cures de sommeil avec conditionnement et contrôle électro-encéphalographique" [Notes on the methods of sleep therapy with conditioning and electro-encephalographic control], with Drs. Despinoy and Zenner.

————, 53rd session, Nice, September 5–11, 1955.

"Conduites d'aveux en Afrique du Nord" [Confessional behavior in North Africa], with Dr. Lacaton.

————, 54th session, Bordeaux, August 30–September 4, 1956.

"Le TAT chez la femme musulmane, sociologie de la perception et de l'imagination" [The TAT in Muslim women; the sociology of perception and the imagination], with Dr. Geromini.

Revue pratique de psychologie de la vie sociale et d'hygiène mentale, No. 1 (1956).

"L'Attitude du musulman maghrébin devant la folie" [The attitude of the Maghreb Muslim towards madness], with Dr. F. Sanchez.

La Tunisie médicale, Vol. 36, No. 9 (1958).

"A propos d'un cas de spasme de torsion" [Concerning a case of torsion spasm], with Dr. L. Levy.

————, Vol. 37 (1959).

"Premiers Essais de méprobamate injectable dans les états hypocondriaques" [First attempts with injectable meprobamate in hypochondriac states], with Dr. L. Levy.

————, Vol. 38, No. 10 (1959).

"L'Hospitalisation de jour en psychiatrie, valeurs et limites: 1. Introduction générale; considérations doctrinales" [Day hospitalization in psychiatry, values and limitations: 1. General introduction; theoretical considerations], with Dr. Geromini.

Conscience maghrébine, No. 3 (1955).

"Réflexions sur l'ethnopsychiatrie" [Reflections on ethnopsychiatry].

L'Information psychiatrique, 4th ser., No. 9 (1954).

"La Socialthérapie dans un service d'hommes musulmans. Difficultés méthodologiques" [Sociotherapy in a ward of Muslim men. Methodological difficulties], with Dr. Azoulay. Publication of L'Hôpital psychiatrique de Blida-Joinville.

————, 4th ser., No. 1 (1955).

"Aspects actuels de l'assistance mentale en Algérie" [Current aspects of mental health aid in Algeria], with Drs. D'Equequer, Lacaton, Micucci, and Ramée. Publication of L'Hôpital psychiatrique de Blida-Joinville.

Maroc Médical, January 1957.

"Le Phénomène de l'agitation en milieu psychiatrique. Considérations générales—signification psychopathologique" [The phenomenon of agitation in a psychiatric environment. General reflections—psychopathological meaning].

C. Books

Original French editions are cited first, followed by the American translations used in this text.

Peau noire, masques blancs. Paris: Editions du Seuil, 1952.

Black Skin, White Masks. Translated by Charles L. Markmann. New York: Grove Press, 1st Evergreen ed., 1967.

L'An V de la révolution algérienne. Paris: François Maspéro, 1959. The 1966 edition carried the title *Sociologie d'une révolution.*

A Dying Colonialism. Translated by Haakon Chevalier. New York: Grove Press, 1st Evergreen ed., 1967.

Pour la révolution africaine. Paris: François Maspéro, 1964.

Toward the African Revolution. Translated by Haakon Chevalier. New York: Grove Press, Evergreen Books, 1968.

Les Damnés de la terre. Paris: François Maspéro, 1961. Copyright 1963 held by Présence Africaine publishing house, although it was originally published by Maspéro in 1961.

The Wretched of the Earth. Translated by Constance Farrington. New York: Grove Press, Evergreen Books, 1966.

II. STUDIES ABOUT FANON

Bouvier, Pierre. *Fanon.* Paris: Editions universitaires, 1971.

Caute, David. *Fanon.* London: Collins, Fontana, 1970.

Geismar, Peter. *Fanon.* New York: Dial Press, 1971.

Zahar, Renate. *L'Oeuvre de Frantz Fanon.* Translated by R. Dangeville. Paris: François Maspéro, 1970.

Lucas, Philippe. *Sociologie de Frantz Fanon.* Algiers: SNED (Société nationale d'édition et de diffusion), 1971.

Index

Irene L. Gendzier is an associate professor of history at Boston University.